SPIRITUAL HEALING
MIRACLE OR MIRAGE?

by
ALAN YOUNG

DeVorss & Company
P.O. Box 550
Marina del Rey, California 90294-0550

ISBN: 0-87516-460-9

Library of Congress Card Catalog Number:
81-82932

Cover design from an original oil painting by Joy Young

1st Printing	1981
2nd Printing	1982
Expanded Edition	1986
4th Printing	1989
Dutch Language Edition	1986
French/Canadian Edition	1989

Printed in the United States of America

To all those who are serving

in any way to relieve the

suffering of humanity.

Acknowledgments

I acknowledge with many thanks the following who have helped to make this book possible:

Gayle Burnham for dedicated transcription.
Lorna Catford for gifted editing.
Carolyn Conger for encouragement and helpful comments.
Brugh Joy for his teaching and helpful comments.
My wife, Joy Young, for her loving support and the use of her beautiful oil painting for the cover.

I also wish to express my gratitude to those who have kindly permitted me to include in this book their own experiences of healing. Although their names and other identifying features have been changed or omitted, the details are so personal that I consider it to be a privilege to be allowed to share them in this way.

Contents

Note: Bible quotations are from The Revised Standard Version.

SPIRITUAL HEALING:
MIRACLE OR MIRAGE?

Introduction

Spiritual Healing has been accomplished by men and women throughout the ages, and there are many spiritual healers of both sexes in current times. The sex of the healer has absolutely no bearing on the subject, nor does it make any difference if the person seeking help is a man or a woman.

However, in order to avoid the constant repetition of *he* or *she* and *his* or *hers,* I have used either the masculine gender, or *they* or *their,* to designate both sexes. I trust that the former usage will cause no offense to feminine readers— certainly none is intended. As to the latter method, some people have said that it is grammatically incorrect. At one time it was, but now Webster assures me that it is correct if the singular antecedent is indefinite, and it is in this context that I have used it.

Many of the ideas presented in this book are my own. There are no absolutes in these thoughts and no intention of creating dogmatic statements that cannot be questioned. Other ideas are from various writers, healers and thinkers, and wherever possible their source has been indicated and permission to quote obtained. Events which are reported as facts have been verified to the best of my ability. I hope that the information and experiences compiled here will be interesting and challenging reading for those who are curious about the subject of Spiritual Healing and for those who desire to contribute to their own healing.

I will be very interested to hear from any reader who cares to share his or her experience in applying the principles described in this book, either as a healer or as one who has been healed. Also of value would be any healing experiences which are different and might add to our understanding of the whole subject.

Alan Young.

Preface to the Expanded Edition

Since this book was first published the author has worked with hundreds more individuals with various problems and has learned much from this experience. As a result it has become apparent that the book needed to be expanded to include the new information.

The major additions are in chapters 3, 4, and 5 which deal with inner causes of disease and how to discover and work with them. These chapters now include new material on the effect of Past Lives, and on the Possession or Attachment by discarnate entities which have caused problems in this life.

LOVE ONE ANOTHER

AS I HAVE LOVED

YOU

(John 15:12)

CHAPTER 1

MIRACLE OR MIRAGE?

Is Spiritual Healing a Miracle or a Mirage? I suggest that it is neither; it is Natural and Real, as the following pages will attempt to illustrate.

Natural, because the Creator of this Universe, which includes humanity, built into each human body a natural healing mechanism which will heal any disease or dysfunction if it is allowed to do so.

Real, because over the last two thousand years, and long before that, there have been thousands of recorded cases of permanent healings by this unseen power. Also there are many people walking around today in perfect health who can testify to their being healed without physical or mental treatment in any way; only the Divine Power of the Creator was involved, with or without the aid of another human being acting as a channel for that power.

I can testify, from my own experience in working with other people, of instant healing of broken bones that had failed to heal for months; tumors and cysts that exploded or dissolved; a diabetic's dramatic drop in blood sugar after 25

1

years of the disease; lifetime depressions changed to happiness; and many other changes for which there were no orthodox medical explanations. Some of these cases have been included in this book.

It is true that the healing often seems like a miracle because it does not conform to the thinking of the great majority, nor to the commonly accepted "laws of nature." Especially does it confound the orthodox practice of scientific Western medicine, which must frequently fall back on the non-committal designation of "Spontaneous Remission," meaning "We have to admit a healing has occurred, but we did not expect it and do not know how it happened."

Unfortunately the healing may sometimes seem like a mirage because it is only temporary. After the first exhilarating realization: "I have been healed!" and the disappearance of symptoms, these same symptoms, or others that are equally serious or worse, appear. People then say that the cure was an illusion; it was only hysteria or imagination. This may be true in some cases, however in others the real reason for the return of the disease is that the *cause* of the problem was not discovered and eliminated; only the symptoms were healed, and since the cause remained the disease reappeared. (More on this aspect of healing will be found in Chapters 3, 4 and 5.)

Premature death, disease, sickness, and physical and mental disability, have been part of humanity's experience throughout recorded history. At the same time there have always been those who dedicated their lives to healing and to the relief of suffering by any means that seemed to work. Some used physical methods such as cutting and bleeding, or oral remedies such as herbs and chemicals, while others relied on appeals to the God, or Gods, of their belief.

The earliest healers were the Witch Doctors. They are still found among primitive tribes untouched by civilization when discovered by explorers. The first Witch Doctors were the oldest men in the tribes. It was assumed that if they had survived the many hazards of life, including natural disasters, diseases and wild animal attacks for longer than anyone else, they must be the wisest tribe members; certainly they had the most experience. Later a self selection process gradually developed; one person in the tribe would come forward with special psychic gifts and understanding, and as long as he could produce results, including healing, that others could not, he was respected.

As with all talents or gifts, there are individuals who use them for selfish or evil purposes; thus we find some Witch Doctors indulging in Black Magic, and using their powers to injure or kill other people. However, the great majority would not do this, but were and are, basically good, helpful servants of their tribe.

It is not clear exactly when the American Indian Medicine Men first appeared on the scene, but they were very much a factor in the healing of disease for at least two thousand years before the White Man arrived on these shores, and they are still important among traditional Indians. They definitely used Spiritual Healing, believing in one God, The Great Spirit, and in the power of prayer to bring them His guidance as they needed it. They also paid close attention to visions and dreams, interpreting them as messages from The Great Spirit. They were holy men, and not exclusively healers. They also had psychic gifts of precognition, telepathy and inner vision. The word "Medicine" in Indian culture does not mean drugs or herbs, but refers to any powers beyond the normal and natural.

Shortly after reaching puberty they usually became aware, by means of a vision obtained after several days of fasting and isolation, that they were to become a Medicine Man; then, as they demonstrated their powers to other members of the tribe they gained respect and support.

Thousands of years before the White Man discovered Hawaii the Polynesian residents of those islands had learned the secret of Spiritual Healing, and even of the raising of the dead. Certain individuals, known as Kahunas, or Keepers of the Secret, were trained for this service. They were so successful that the white missionaries, who were unable to heal the sick as effectively as the Kahunas, accused them of practicing Black Magic. Since the Kahunas also coupled their healing skills with some non-christian rituals, and in certain cases used their knowledge to kill their enemies, or those who had displeased them, they were outlawed as soon as the White Man gained enough control. However, they continued to practice in secret and were seldom arrested because no Hawaiian policeman or judge would dare to offend a Kahuna.

While much of their knowledge has been lost, there are still some who practice the art in secret. The Kahunas recognized the difference between the conscious and the subconscious mind, and the power of the latter, long before Freud introduced this concept to the Western world. They also believed in a 'High Self' which could be called upon for healing, and which acted as the liaison between the Supreme Creative Intelligence and the conscious self. If we set aside their different rituals and names, there really is no variance between their basic healing system and that of the modern spiritual healer.*

For thousands of years Spiritual Healing was part of the service in temples of worship in Egypt, Greece and the Orient, and priests were the healers. Some were even looked up to as minor gods themselves. Simultaneously, others in China were using acupuncture, increasing the flow of the energy of life (Chi) by removing blockages.

Three thousand years ago, the Egyptian, Imhotep, became so famous as a healer that after his death he was worshipped as the Egyptian God of medicine. About the same time, Asclepius was achieving great fame throughout Greece as a healer who could on occasion even bring life back to the

---

*I am indebted to Max Freedom Long's book *The Secret Science Behind Miracles*[1] for much of this information on Kahunas.

dead. After his own death he was regarded as a healing God and temples were built throughout Greece and named after him. In these temples sick people were allowed to sleep in order to invite a healing dream, which was then interpreted for them by a priest. These experiences were often followed by recorded healings, many of which were sheer miracles by our standards. The priests believed that each patient bore within himself the elements of the cure that he needed, and that their function was only to help the patient discover these. Now, thousands of years later holistic healing centers are springing up in this country with the same belief.

Two thousand five hundred years ago, kings were often considered to have the gift of healing, and healing their subjects was one of their responsibilities. The Old Testament is replete with records of Spiritual Healing, such as when Elijah healed the widow's son "whose illness was so severe that there was no breath left in him", (1 Kings 17:17-23) or when Elisha restored life to the child of the Shumanite woman, (2 Kings 4:18-37) or when Elisha healed the commander of the Syrian army of leprosy, telling him to wash in the river Jordan seven times (2 Kings 5:1-14).

Two thousand years ago, Jesus, who was probably the greatest spiritual healer of all times, in only three years of teaching, healing and living, revolutionized the world. Ever since then people have argued and fought about exactly who Jesus was, with beliefs ranging all the way from God Himself incarnate in a human body to simply a wise and good man. Regardless of one's particular belief on this point, few will dispute that he was in fact a truly great spiritual healer. There is much we can learn about this subject by studying his actions and words.

Jesus stated that the purpose of his ministry was to bring to the world the good news that the kingdom of heaven was at hand, and in reality was inside each individual; that the forgiveness and love of God were theirs for the asking; and that if they first sought the kingdom of heaven all their needs would be met. However, it is apparent from the New

Testament that Jesus did more than spread the good news. He spent a great deal of those three years in healing the sick, and occasionally restoring the dead to life. It appears that he did this in order to demonstrate the love of God for all of His children and the power of God over all of life, and to show living proof of the words that he taught. Jesus' medium was healing, his message was unconditional love; his healing demonstrated and exemplified that love in a beautiful way.

The words and actions that Jesus used with some of these healings are discussed in the next chapter. However, for the moment, let us consider his amazing promise to all of us:

> He who believes in me will also do the works that I do, and greater works than these will he do, because I go to the Father. Whatever you ask in my name, I will do it. (John 14:12-13)

The first to accept this promise at its face value were the twelve apostles who made healing an integral part of their teaching ministry wherever they went. One dramatic case was when Peter spoke to the beggar who had been lame from birth, saying, "I have no silver and gold but I give you what I have; in the name of Jesus Christ of Nazareth, walk". Immediately the man's feet and ankles were made strong and he walked and leaped (Acts 3:2-8). More generally it was reported that "the people also gathered from the towns around Jerusalem, bringing the sick and those afflicted with unclean spirits and they were all healed" (Acts 5:16). Not only the apostles, but also the great convert and evangelist Paul, healed many people.

This ability of Christians to heal the sick continued for the first three or four hundred years after the founding of the Christian church. Many healings were reported by St. Justin Martyr (100-165 A.D.) and by St. Jerome (340-420 A.D.) and by others reporting between these two historians. Gradually however, the church became corrupted by man's self importance and drive for material power. Consequently the source of the healing power was forgotten or ignored and the ability to heal declined proportionately.

Despite the virtual disappearance of Spiritual Healing practices in the churches a few individuals (some of them honored as saints by the Roman Catholic church) continued to believe in and practice Spiritual Healing. Saint Francis of Assisi, Martin Luther and John Wesley were three such people. In special healing shrines such as Lourdes in France and Fatima in Portugal, many recorded "miracle" cures have taken place.

During this same period the Eastern religions produced many individual healers who performed what the general public called "miracles". They too have their healing shrines at many places, especially in India and Japan.

The American Indians have long believed in healing by the Great Spirit. Some of their rituals may seem somewhat strange to the uninitiated, but their healing is definitely based on spiritual laws. Their dedication and beliefs are summarized in a rather beautiful way by Brad Steiger in his book *Medicine Power*[2] as follows:

1. The vision quest, with its emphasis on self-denial and spiritual discipline being extended to a lifelong pursuit of wisdom of body and soul.

2. A reliance on one's personal visions and dreams to provide one's direction on the path of life.

3. A search for personal songs to enable one to attune oneself to the primal sound, the cosmic vibration of the Great Spirit.

4. A belief in a total partnership with the world of spirits and the ability to make personal contact with grandfathers and grandmothers who have changed planes of existence.

5. The possession of a non-linear time sense.

6. A receptivity to the evidence that the essence of the Great Spirit may be found in everything.

7. A reverence and a passion for the Earth Mother, the awareness of one's place in the web of life, and one's responsibility toward all plant and animal life.

8. A total commitment to one's beliefs that pervades every aspect of one's life and enables one truly to walk in balance.

In the middle of the nineteenth century there developed a new understanding of the scientific truths behind the teachings of Jesus, and of the connection between the mind and the body in instances of disease. Phineas Quimby, a successful spiritual healer from 1846–66, is generally considered to be the re-discoverer of these old concepts, and the first to attempt to describe Spiritual Healing in scientific terms. He maintained that we create what we believe. That is, our apparent reality is a manifestation of our belief system. He also asserted that the only way to eradicate disease must be through the mind which originated it.

Out of this beginning evolved several new denominations. Christian Science was founded by Mary Baker Eddy, one of Quimby's patients and students. Unity was founded by Myrtle and Charles Fillmore. Charles was healed of an incurable disease by the power of his own thought alone, after twenty-five years as a chronic invalid, and eventually lived to be 94! Religious Science was established by Ernest Holmes, and has much in common with the above two denominations. Many thousands of Spiritual Healings have been reported by all three of them.

In the last few decades there seems to have been a revival of the use of the healing power by famous public healers as well as by members of individual churches. Well known healers such as the late Kathryn Kuhlman and Harry Edwards have successfully helped to heal many persons who are alive today. Healings have been performed in modern churches such as St. Stephen's Episcopal Church in Philadelphia, Mount Washington Methodist Church in Baltimore, and many churches that are less well known. I am also aware of many spiritual healers who work independently of churches and without publicity.

In many countries Spiritual Healing is still outlawed by the authorities, who classify it as Black Magic or fraudulent charlatanism. However, in Great Britain it is widely recognized and accepted, and there are over 5000 healers accredited by the National Federation of Spiritual Healers. This permits them official access to over 1500 hospitals. Most British doctors will co-operate with these healers if their patients request them to do so. There are many spiritual healing centers throughout Great Britain for both contact and absent healing. These include the Harry Edwards Spiritual Healing Sanctuary at Burrows Lea, Shere, Surrey; the White Eagle Lodge at Liss in Hampshire; and the Spiritualist Association of Great Britain at 33 Belgrave Square in London.

The Need for Spiritual Healing

Despite advances in modern medical research the need for healing of all kinds is as great as it ever was. Although many diseases such as small pox, infantile paralysis and the Plague, have been practically eliminated, and some like pneumonia, have been reduced from 'probably fatal' to 'temporarily serious', others such as cancer, heart disease and multiple sclerosis have appeared with increased potency or frequency. It has been estimated that today over fifty million people in the United States suffer from arthritis in one form or another.

Every day doctors classify their patients' illnesses as *terminal* because they have no hope of a recovery. The medical profession freely admits that in spite of the billions of dollars spent on research, there is a long list of diseases for which there is no known successful treatment. I heard of one doctor who said that every day he was becoming more aware of the limitations of orthodox medicine. In fact it was a delight for him when a patient walked in with something that he could actually cure. Even then he knew that it was the body that healed itself; he only assisted. John Diamond, M.D. put it this way. "It is hard to be proud of the usual medical treatment today. We do so little really deep down to help the individual. And most doctors are painfully aware of this, and are depressed about it."[3]

According to *Time Magazine* it is estimated that in the

United States alone there are 20 to 35 million blind, deaf or otherwise physically handicapped persons, including eight million school age children. Joseph Chilton Pearce, in his book, *The Magical Child,*[4] says that there is "an epidemic increase in infantile autism in all the technological countries of the world. Childhood schizophrenia is also on the rise, as are silent crib deaths, brain damage, hyperactivity dysfunction and mental retardation".

The tremendous need for Spiritual Healing is also indicated by the mail of Harry Edwards, the famous English healer who died in December, 1976. He received over half a million letters a year requesting Spiritual Healing!

Concurrently with this great need there is a growing concern over the dangers inherent in orthodox medicine. Although medical discoveries in the last hundred years have brought much relief from suffering and death, modern medicine still involves many risks.

The use of surgery has increased with many wonderful results. However, obviously any time that you cut into the human body there is a risk of human error and unforeseen side effects and reactions such as formation of blood clots, excessive hemorrhaging, heart failure or infection.

Doctors are well aware of these dangers, and many will use surgery as little as possible, relying on a spiritual approach, and a deep faith in the body's ability to heal itself. Others, however, because of a legitimate fear of malpractice suits, will try every possible test and appropriate drug or surgical procedure so that no one can accuse them of overlooking anything. Thus the general public is partly responsible for being exposed to these greater risks.

There is also a hazard from the expanded use of drugs, which are all toxic to one degree or another—even aspirin. A physician has literally thousands of different drugs to choose from, all of which can be prescribed in various amounts. Every human body is different, and no doctor can ever be sure of a patient's reaction to any specific drug or combination of drugs. An adverse reaction could be quite mild or it could result in death. In spite of this, nearly all

American doctors prescribe at least one drug for the great majority of their patients' complaints. Here too the public is partly to blame because most people insist on receiving some kind of medication, believing that without this the doctor has not fulfilled his function.

Then, too, the financial and material cost of disease and dysfunction has reached fantastic proportions, and continues to sky-rocket. It is estimated that the U.S. Public now spends over three hundred billion dollars annually on medical expenses, and this total continues to climb every year at a tremendous rate. No one has yet been able to figure out how to stop this. For prescription drugs alone we spend over five billion dollars each year, plus another two billion for non-prescription drugs such as aspirin. In addition, of course, there is the financial loss in wages and productive work while incapacitated, and the immeasurable cost of the physical and mental suffering incurred by those who are sick and by their families.

Holistic Healing

In the last few years it has become more widely recognized that the origin of disease is not material and therefore it can seldom be permanently cured by materialistic methods. Nor is the origin usually external to the body, but rather is it more often the result of deep mental and emotional forces, that have been active for a long time, which finally manifest themselves as disease.

In other situations the beginning of the disease may originate from some external cause but the natural healing ability of the body is unable to cope with it. It is theorized that this is due to some mental, emotional or spiritual conflict which has weakened that person's immune system. It has thus allowed the bacteria, virus or unhealthy cells to multiply instead of being destroyed.

It is interesting to note that psychics who can see and interpret auras (the colorful forcefields that surround and radiate from all living bodies, even plants) report that they can see the onset of a disease three to six months in advance of its physical manifestation. They are able to foretell disease by observing changes in the color and intensity of the aura.

Therefore, only as the cause is uncovered and eradicated can the disease be permanently healed. This realization has given rise to a lot of talk about Holistic Healing, and Holistic Healing Centers have been started in many places. Holistic in this sense means healing of the whole person. The whole person includes body, mind, emotions and spirit, which are inter-related, inter-dependent and united. Disease in one of these areas tends to affect the other three.

What Does the Word "God" Mean?

Perhaps at this point I should define what I mean by the word "God", since I will be using it throughout this book, and some people, particularly of the younger generation, take offense by the use of this word, due to past associations or experiences in their lives.

I do *not* mean an old man with a white beard sitting on a white cloud, watching everything that we do and ready to execute wrathful judgment whenever, in His opinion, we stray from the straight and narrow path. I *do* mean the "Something" that is greater than ourselves; is the Creator of this Universe and everything in it, including you and me; is the very essence of Unconditional Love, Divine Intelligence, Infinite Power, Unbelievable Peace, Perfection, Beauty, Truth, Joy and Energy; is the One Source of all that is real; in fact is All There Is. This Divine Force is everywhere in the Universe; it is at the very center of each one of us. It is Pure Consciousness. If we wish to do so, we can contact that God within and receive guidance, protection, assistance and healing.

I hope that if you are uncomfortable with the word "God" for one reason or another you will, whenever you see that word, substitute one of the other terms or one of your own choosing.

Notes for Chapter 1

1. Max Freedom Long. *The Secret Science Behind Miracles.* DeVorss & Company, Marina Del Rey, California. 1948

2. Brad Steiger. *Medicine Power* p. 71 Doubleday & Company, Inc. Garden City, New York. 1974

3. John Diamond, M.D. *Lectures on a Spiritual Basis for Holistic Healing.* Institute of Behavioral Kinesiology, P.O. Drawer 37, Valley Cottage, New York, 10989.

4. Joseph Chilton Pearce. *Magical Child* p. 14 E.P. Dutton, New York. 1977

GOD DOES NOT HEAL

GOD DOES NOT MAKE US ILL

ALL WE HAVE TO DO

IS TO

ALLOW THE PERFECTION THAT IS

CHAPTER 2

WHAT IS
SPIRITUAL HEALING?

SPIRITUAL HEALING OCCURS when, by the application of Spiritual Laws, the Power of God manifests itself in a living being who is suffering from some disease, injury or malformation, and a change for the better takes place, which is greater or faster than the normal medical belief system would expect. It is frequently a complete return to normal health and physical form.

The healing may happen in a special place such as Lourdes where many "miracles" have occurred, thus increasing and supporting the faith of the individual. It may happen in a church or chapel, or simply at home or in the process of daily living. Contact between the one in need and God may be direct, resulting from prayer or attunement with the Divine. It may be with the help of some individual who offers himself as an instrument for the healing power of God and channels it to the specific person who has asked for such help.

Techniques Used by Spiritual Healers

Spiritual healers use various techniques which are mental aids for the healer and the one desiring to be healed. The methods themselves have no healing power; they are simply procedures which assist the healer in attuning to the Divine power, thus enabling the body to heal itself. In those cases where the healer's hands are used there is also a psychological assurance to the sick person that something is being done. This is particularly true when that person feels the healing energy that is coming through the healer's hands as warmth, tingling or pressure. This makes it easier for some people to believe that a healing will result. Jesus touched the sick person in a number of cases, probably for the same reason. Sometimes if there is a blockage to the flow of the energy within the subject's body the sense may be one of temporary pain.

Some of the techniques in use today are:

1. The healer prays to God for the sick person.

2. The healer endeavours to raise his consciousness to the Divine, and then mentally to merge his essence with the essence of the sick one, affirming the unity and perfection of all three. A healing is not requested or pictured but it frequently occurs.

3. The healer centers his thoughts and energy into the very center of his being near his heart, and then mentally projects unconditional love-energy to the one in need, leaving the latter to use it in any way that his Higher Self chooses.

4. The healer visualizes a ray of white light and love going from his heart center to the person he has been asked to help. He pictures it like a laser beam which is not dissipated even when it is projected for thousands of miles. (Note: a real laser beam projected from the earth to the moon spreads out less than two miles).

The above methods are used in what is generally called non-contact Healing. Whether the one in need is thousands of miles away, or sitting in the same room, there is no attempt at any overt action by the healer. When the sick person is not even in the same room this method is also called Absent Healing. Many consider this to be the highest form of Spiritual Healing because no physical contact is involved, neither by hand, eye nor voice, and frequently the one seeking help is unknown to the healer. Since there is no space or time in the spirit world, Absent Healing can be just as fast and effective as those methods involving the physical presence of both parties.

If the ability to channel healing power in this way is adequately developed it saves a great deal of time and thus enables the healer to help many more people. It also saves a lot of travel expense, and permits the healer to reach people who are too sick to travel, or too far away to make a visit economically feasible. Some Absent Healers find it helpful to hold a letter from, or a photograph of, the one in need in their hands at the time they channel the healing power to that person. The one disadvantage of Absent Healing is that it seems less likely to uncover the cause of the disease, and therefore the cure is not as likely to be permanent (see Chapter 3).

In contrast to all of this is Contact healing where both the healer and the sick person are present in the same place, and the healer's hands are involved in some way. Usually this is by the "laying-on-of-hands" which is a very old method used by the Chinese, Egyptians and Greeks long before it was referred to in the New Testament as a method used by the Christians. It has been used by some priests, ministers and church elders ever since.

However, there are variations in the way that the hands are used. Three of the most common are:

1. The healer places his hands on the head or the shoulders of the sick person, or on the part of his body which is known to be diseased or in pain. The healer then prays for healing and mentally pictures the healing energy of God passing through his hands to the one in need.

2. The healer is sensitive to the energy emanating from

different parts of the sick person's body, and from experience knows where the energy is abnormal, thus indicating a disease, a malfunction, or a blockage in that part of the body. The healer then places his hands over that particular area directing the healing power to that place.

3. The healer places his hands briefly over each part of the body while the sick person is lying down in a relaxed, receptive state. The sequence in which each part of the body is covered by the hands varies between healers. I believe there are three reasons for covering the whole body. The first is to ensure that healing energy is transferred to every one of the 49 energy centers of the physical body. These have been known for thousands of years to the Hindus who call them Chakras. This is a Sanskrit word meaning 'wheel', because to clairvoyants the centers look very much like a spinning wheel. Psychics who can see or feel the movement of energy have confirmed that there are vortexes of energy radiating from these same points. Much of this has also been scientifically supported by Kirlian photography.*

The energy of life pours into these centers, giving life and health to the physical body. The energy also radiates outwards from each center, contributing to the welfare of all within the body's environment. This two-way flow is necessary if stagnation and disease are to be avoided. Without the flow in both directions we would become like the Dead Sea in the Middle East, which has no outward flow, and has become so loaded with salt that nothing can live in it. When the healer passes his hands over the whole body, the life force energy which is channelled through him can then activate or recharge any of these energy centers which have become blocked or sluggish. (See diagram on page 264.)

For an equally long time the Chinese have known about over sixteen hundred points in the body where the insertion

---

*Note: This is a fairly recent discovery whereby the energy radiating from plants, animals and humans can be recorded in color on photographic film. Variations in human emotions will show up as changes in the shape and color of the radiation.

of fine acupuncture needles will restore health by removing blockages in the flow of the energy of life which they call 'Chi'. Modern electronic instruments have detected these same points as having especially low skin resistance to electromagnetic energy. If the healer gradually covers the whole body with his hands he will automatically send energy to every acupuncture point. The energy of life being channelled through his hands, which energy is believed to be electromagnetic, will then activate any point that is blocked. This happens even if neither the healer nor the sick person knows which points are blocked.

The third reason for this procedure is that the one who is receiving the healing power can often feel it in the form of heat or tingling like an electric current in various parts of his body. Psychologically this is very reassuring that healing is actually taking place.

In all three of the above methods the healer may place his hands so that they are lightly touching the body, or he may keep them a few inches away, depending on his beliefs and what he feels is right for him.

Most agree that there is a colored radiation of energy around the physical body. This is known as an aura, and it can be seen by some people. When a person is ill their aura will change from bright colors such as gold, blue, green, white, etc., to dull greys or browns. Some touch the physical body because they believe that the aura itself does not become diseased, but it merely mirrors the condition of the physical body. When the latter is healed the colors of the aura will become brighter and change from greys and browns to the other colors. Others do not touch because they believe that the aura does become diseased or malfunctioning, and that this in turn affects the physical body in the same way. Therefore, by holding the hands a few inches away from the body they will heal the aura. This will then result in a healing of the physical body.

Still others maintain that there is an Etheric body surrounding both the physical body and the aura. This is a complete body made of the ethers and it always retains its original state of perfection. They too will keep their hands a few inches away in order to channel the power through the etheric body to the physical, bringing the latter into alignment with the former.

Another difference that observers may notice is that some healers use both hands, whereas some use the left hand only and some the right, whichever seems best for them.

There is one other use of the hands for healing which is more direct. In the Philippines healers perform what they call 'Psychic Surgery'. This seems to involve the healer's hands separating the atoms of the flesh, or the cells of the body, without cutting them; then entering the body to remove diseased tissue; then immediately closing the separation without serious loss of blood or subsequent infection. This has become quite controversial. No doubt some fraudulent practitioners have entered the picture; however, those with uncontaminated reputations readily admit that the power to do this is not theirs and they give all the credit to God. The best of these healers also explain that the only reason they materialize blood and tissue is to satisfy the doubts of the sick people. Without this material evidence that 'surgery' has been performed many will not believe that a healing has occurred, even though it has. This disbelief can re-create the disease.

Further variations which may apply to any of the above techniques are:

a. The use of audible words such as prayers, affirmations or descriptions of what the healer believes is happening or what he psychically observes during the healing.

b. Background music. Some believe there is healing energy in the very vibrations of suitable music; others find that it adds to the relaxation and therefore to the receptivity of the patient.

c. Complete silence throughout the process.

The specific methods or techniques used are of minor importance compared to the faith that the healer has in the power and goodness of God, and that all things are possible. Actually, if one believes that God, or a Supreme Intelligence, or a Divine Energy, created human beings, including that marvelously complicated and organized vehicle for the soul known as the human body and the fantastic mind and spirit that inhabits that vehicle, then it is not so hard to believe that the same Supreme Intelligence can heal any disease or malfunction of that body or mind. Mentally visualizing and affirming the perfection in which the whole person was created, *and now is,* contributes much towards effecting the healing.

It is on this point that Spiritual Healers diverge in their thinking, even though both approaches seem to be equally successful. Some hold the thought that all of God's creation, including every human being, is perfect and remains so; that disease is an illusion created by humanity (Joel Goldsmith called it Hypnotism),[1] that simply does not exist in reality. They therefore concentrate on thoughts of God, the perfection of His creation, and the unity of God, the patient and themselves, with no attempt actually to heal the patient. If this higher consciousness is attained and the one in need is receptive, a healing will frequently follow.

Others hold that although God's creation is perfect and good, and His is the only power, the sick person has placed a mental block between himself and that realization. This can be unblocked by the healer acting as a channel for the power of God, which can be directed by prayer to the problem that is carried in the consciousness of the one in need. With the blockage removed a healing will usually occur.

In either case the healer knows that the sick person is a child of God, and therefore loved by God with all the devotion of a father. He also remembers that the Kingdom of God, or a Divine Center, is within the other, just as surely as it is within the healer, and that the ultimate authority over both is God.

Another ingredient that nearly all spiritual healers have in common is their desire that God's will be done, whatever that might be. Naturally the spiritual healer wants the sick person to be well, otherwise he would not be trying to serve humanity as a healer. However, if he is asking for specific results in accordance with his own will, then he may be healing for his own satisfaction or ego reinforcement. This would be contrary to Spiritual Law and probably make his efforts ineffectual. The desire to heal must always be secondary to the sincere wish or prayer that whatever transpires will be that which God sees as best for the other person's own soul evolution, even if it is the death of their physical body.

The healer must also have complete faith in the method that he is using. It is helpful but not essential that the sick person likewise believes in it. It *is* essential, however, that he be receptive to the healing energies, or at least to whatever is happening. If he is not, then it is highly unlikely that any healing will occur.

The main function of the healer is to be the contact or liaison between the one in need and the spirit world, first to inform the spirits of the need, secondly to request help, and finally to act as a channel for the healing power. Some believe that there is also a transformation involved here; in some way the body and mind of the healer transforms the spirit power into a physical power that dissolves or builds tissue.

I say 'spirit world' rather than God, because it has been shown to me that the so-called 'healer' is merely the next to last link in a lengthy chain of beings uniting God (the first link) and the one in need (the final link). In this chain there are spirit doctors and healing angels (see Chapter 7), spirit teachers, master teachers and even higher beings linking us with the Divine Source, or All There Is. All are dedicated to helping and serving those below them in the hierarchy of the total universe.

Once the contact has been made, the healing process will usually continue without further effort or knowledge on the part of the healer. An interesting confirmation of this was experienced in the healing of a clairvoyant. While I was channelling the healing power to him, he saw a Spirit Guide who told him that for the next ten days, just before going to sleep at night, he was to contact me mentally; also that it was not necessary for me to know when he was doing this, nor for me to contact him mentally or intercede for him. We interpreted this to mean that, having been responsible for the initial contact, I could be used as a continuing contact between him and the Spirit world without any conscious involvement on my part. He followed these instructions and his healing, which had been instantaneous, remained complete.

Healing Procedures Used by Jesus

In view of the different techniques being used by modern day spiritual healers, it is interesting to note that Jesus also used a variety of methods. Presumably the one he used at any particular time depended on the circumstances, and particularly on the needs and the state of consciousness of the sick person. For example:

1. He laid his hands upon the sick person. (Luke 13:11-13)

2. He touched the part of the body that needed healing. (Matthew 9:29 & 20:33-34; Mark 7:32-37)

3. He spat on a blind man's eyes and then twice laid his hands on him. (Mark 8:22-26)

4. He told the sick person to do something. For example he told ten lepers to show themselves to the priests. (Luke 17:14)

5. He combined physical action by him and instructions for action by the sick person. For example: Jesus spat on the ground, made clay with the spittle, anointed the man's eyes, then told him to wash in the pool of Siloam. (John 9:1-7)

6. People touched him or his garments and were healed. (Mark 5:24-34 & 6:56; Matthew 14:36)

7. He used words alone. He told the man who was paralyzed, "Your sins are forgiven, rise take up your bed and go home." (Matthew 9:2 & 6) He said to the man by the pool

at Bethesda who had been ill for 38 years: "Rise, take up your pallet and walk". (John 5: 8)

8. He used absent healing, the sick one being elsewhere. (Matthew 8:5-13 & 15:28; John 4:46-53)

An analysis of all of Jesus' recorded healings of individuals shows that; He *touched* the person in ten cases, usually when they were dead, blind, deaf or had leprosy. This was possibly to give aid to the person's faith (or the faith of the relatives in the case of the dead). Twelve cases did not involve touching. *Touching His garment* is mentioned in two cases—here the sick people chose their own means to reinforce their faith. *The faith* of the sick one is mentioned seven times. The faith of a friend or relative was mentioned in nine reports. In seven cases faith is not referred to, but no doubt it was a factor.

Jesus made it very clear, however, that in all cases the healing power came from God and was not his own. "The Father who dwells in me does His works". (John 14:10)

The Power Is Not the Healers'

All genuine spiritual healers readily acknowledge that the healing power is not their own, and that they merely act as a channel for the power of God, or the Divine Creator of the Universe. The late Kathryn Kuhlman was probably the most famous spiritual healer in the U.S.A., if not in the world, during the last thirty years. Numerous healings occurred during all of her special healing services, and many of them were permanent. They started almost as soon as she finished the opening prayer, while people remained in their seats. However, she constantly emphasized that she herself could do nothing except love everyone. It was the love and power of God and His Holy Spirit that healed people; and everyone should give Him the glory. In fact it is reported that she had a constant fear that if she let the praise and adulation of the crowds go to her head and swell her ego, she would lose the ability to be a channel for the power. Evidently she was successful in remaining humble, because the healing power continued to pour through her until her death in 1976.

There is only one *source* of energy and that is God. There is also only one *energy,* but we experience it in different forms such as heat, electricity, gravity, healing, disease and so on. We cannot create energy nor can we destroy it, but we can use the power of our thoughts to change the form in which it is manifested in our lives. We may use this one energy for good or evil, for health or disease, as we choose with our minds. This energy is life itself, and, wonder of wonders, at its source it is further discovered to be *unconditional love.* This unconditional, infinite love is the main key to all Spiritual Healing of body, mind, emotions and spirit, and to life, happiness and peace of mind.

Perhaps at this point I should define what I understand to be the meaning of this unconditional love. It is a pure love which is non-sexual, non-possessive, and without the slightest desire to control the other person. It is a deep caring for others; expecting nothing in return; a desire only that others follow their own individual paths and expressions, completely free in every way. It is trust in the Divine plan for each of us as individuals and for the relationships amongst us. It is also trust that other people instinctively know what is right for them and that they will learn and grow from any mistakes they may make. There is no wish to impose one's own ideas and beliefs upon others, however right they may seem for oneself; the fact that they may not be right for the other is acknowledged. Unconditional Love is free of any involvement in meeting one's own needs; it is not based on a sense of obligation or duty towards others. It is not motivated by a sense of guilt because of some past action or omission in connection with others. It does not arise out of past experience with others nor depend on future expectations—it is strictly in the present moment and yet timeless. It may require, at times, a willingness to surrender desires which obstruct a true expression of that love.

Unconditional Love must include oneself as the object, as well as other people; not in a selfish, self-centered manner but with the same desire for unobstructed growth along one's own distinctive path, as one would have for others' growth.

It includes the willingness to receive the love of others and of God. While it is true that it is difficult to love someone else if you do not love yourself, it is also true that there is seldom a sense of fulfillment without loving others. Thus it is an unbroken circle with no starting or ending point. At the very center is the Divine Creator of us all.

The scriptures tell us that one of the main purposes of life is to serve our fellow man, for in that way we serve our Creator. Yet it is apparent that many people who serve others with great devotion and energy become ill themselves. Exploring why this should be I have found that they nearly always have failed to love themselves. Underneath their self-sacrificing service for others there is a resentment and unhappiness at their denial of their own needs, and this makes them ill. However since they are just as much a part of God as the ones they are trying to help they are equally important to God, and if God is to be served they need to care for and love themselves with as much devotion and energy as they give to others.

It is an incredible fact, and indeed a great blessing to the Universe and to Mankind, that "God is Love". (John 4:8) Jesus came to demonstrate to the world just how great that love is by his teaching—"Love one another as I have loved you": (John 15:12); by his actions—when the rich young man was unwilling to give up his wealth and follow Jesus, Jesus loved him and let him go: (Mark 10:21-22); by his example —while the nails were being driven into his hands he said, "Forgive them Father for they know not what they do" (Luke 23:34); and, finally, by his willingness to die for us— "Greater love has no man than this, that a man lay down his life for his friends". (John 15:13) Jesus also emphasized the fact that the Kingdom of God is within us (John 17:21), which means that God is also within us, and therefore that Infinite Love is within us. If we can accept that as reality then we have unlimited love to share with the sick, and it is this which will make them well.

Jesus was completely at one with God and with that energy and love. He demonstrated this not only by healing the sick and the physically handicapped, but also by returning the dead to life, feeding thousands from a few loaves and fishes, calming a storm, and walking on water. It is this same power to which the spiritual healer opens himself, to the best of his ability. The clearer he is as a channel, and the more he is in tune with the infinite, the more successful he will be as a spiritual healer. Incidentally, over the past two thousand years, and in different parts of the world, a few individuals have demonstrated that not only does man have the power to heal but he also has the power to restore life, to control nature, to defy gravity and to materialize objects.

Just how phenomenal this power is was demonstrated by the famous Brazilian healer, Arigo.[2] Not only did the power channelled through him heal people almost instantaneously, but he also often operated on the physical body with an unsterilized kitchen knife, without sterilizing the patient's skin. No case of infection ever resulted from these abnormal practices. He often cut deep into the body and stopped all bleeding with only a word of prayer. He always operated without any anesthetic, but caused absolutely no pain or fear in the patient. An incredible performance repeated many times each day and explicable in no other terms but Spiritual Power. (See Chapter 7 for more information on this remarkable man.)

Another key to Spiritual Healing is the realization that we are all one with God; that there is an indivisible unity of all Creation, including God, Jesus, angels, spirits, men and women, boys and girls, animals, birds, trees, flowers, mountains and oceans. We are united by the fact that God placed part of Himself within each one—like an artist who places part of himself in his paintings or sculptures. The reality of this analogy has been discovered by a potter friend of mine who has learned to sense with his hand the energy vibration emanating from his finished works. He finds that the greatest energy radiates from the very place on the work of art at which it "came together" in his mind during its creation.

This concept of the unity of all is easier to understand now that science has discovered the technique of *Holography* by which three dimensional photographic film can be produced. This can then be cut up into an infinite number of small pieces while retaining the *total* picture (rather than a fragment) in each piece. In a similar manner God and His Universe are one indivisible whole, and yet appear complete in billions of separate manifestations such as human beings.

What Happens in a Spiritual Healing?

The incredibly intricate design of the human body, with its marvelous brain which has greater potential than thousands of the most advanced computers, and its powers of motion, manipulation, reproduction and adaptability to its environment, also contains a beautiful built-in healing mechanism designed to maintain health and life.

For example, if you cut your finger you probably wash it under running water, place a bandage on it and forget it. A few days later you remove the bandage and find that the wound has healed. You have taken for granted a great deal of activity which took place automatically after the injury. Your blood pressure was lowered to minimize the bleeding. The clotting ability of the blood was accelerated in that area. The spleen reservoir released extra blood into the circulation, and with it were millions of leucocytes which destroyed any foreign bacteria which had invaded the body because of the open wound. If the need was great enough, your bone marrow rapidly increased the production of these invaluable germ fighters, but ceased to do so directly after the need had been met.

Lymph and plasma were transported to the wound to keep it moist. The platelets in your blood created a substance which closed off the capillaries and lymphatic ducts to prevent further invasion of harmful bacteria. Your blood then formed a substance which covered the surface of the wound temporarily, while underneath new tissue and skin were being formed. At the same time the severed ends of capillaries and nerves gradually rejoined, and muscle fibers grew and met and became one again.

All of this cleansing, healing and rebuilding process occurred without any conscious intervention by your brain or mind (other than the awareness that an injury had occurred and healing was necessary), so there must have been some other separate intelligence at work. The mind can support and strengthen this activity by positive, affirmative thinking, or it can interfere and obstruct the process by negative thinking, but nevertheless an intelligence is at work unconsciously. We will see later that this intelligence resides in the very cells of the body.

It is also well known that the body has a built in immunization system. We all develop cancerous cells one or more times during our lives, but when this happens in the healthy body, the immunization defense immediately springs into action. Antibodies and other positive organisms increase, attacking and destroying the diseased cells, in order to allow new ones to grow and take their place. This ability of the body to protect itself against attack has developed over millions of years.

This immunization system has also been used by modern medicine to eradicate great killers and torturers of the past, such as yellow fever, the Plague and small pox. Minute quantities of the disease-creating bacteria, which have first been destroyed but which are still recognized by the immune system as that particular kind of foreign matter, are introduced into the body. This results in an increase of the appropriate kind of anti-bodies, and consequently in the strengthening of the immune system's ability to attack that specific type of bacteria if it should ever be introduced into the body in a live state.

It is this same immunization system which makes it so difficult to transplant organs from one body to another; the system is designed to reject anything abnormal or foreign, including someone else's heart or kidney. It is therefore necessary to give the patient special drugs that suppress his immune system so that it will not reject the foreign organ. Unfortunately this also means that while the drug is being taken the immune system is unable to fight off any other disease. There have been cases reported of transplanted organs containing undetected cancerous cells which then multiplied at a rapid rate while the defense mechanism was inoperative. It is then necessary to stop administering the drug and thus allow the immune system to be reactivated. It then destroys the cancerous cells, but at the same time rejects the transplanted organ.

Thus when an immunization system is in normal working order it is incredibly powerful and can easily eliminate even a substantial amount of rapidly multiplying cancer cells.

As well as immunization and healing abilities our bodies contain many life support systems that are constantly at work, keeping our bodies healthy and strong and sustaining life. These include:

Vascular system: circulates blood, taking oxygen and other nutrients to all parts of the body.

Respiratory system: intakes oxygen and exhales carbon dioxide.

Lymphatic system: circulates lymph (of which there is twice as much as there is blood), which collects and removes waste products.

Digestive system: intakes food and beverages, extracts and converts the ingredients that the body needs, and eliminates the rest.

Acupuncture Meridians: circulates the energy of life to all parts of the body every 24 hours. These meridians have been measured and traced electronically and by radio activity, confirming what the Chinese have known for thousands of years.

Chakras (The energy centers previously described): Absorb and radiate the energy of the Universe at various points in the body. They are believed to be closely tied to the acupuncture meridians but it is not yet known exactly how.

It seems that the healing and immunization mechanisms, and the life supporting systems all operate automatically with great power and precision in a person who is physically, mentally, emotionally and spiritually, in balance and in tune with the Universe. However, it is believed that they can be weakened, suppressed or blocked by the power of the human mind or emotions in a number of different ways. (This will be explored in Chapter 3.) If a blockage or weakening does occur in one or more of these systems, discomfort, pain, disease or even death may follow. It is also believed that when the Spiritual Healing power is channelled to a sick person, it reactivates or stimulates the weakened healing or immune system of the body, or it unblocks the life support system that has become obstructed. Then the body heals itself using its own God given powers.

It also seems likely that the energy and life force that surrounds us, which we constantly absorb to replenish the energy that we expend, can be prevented from flowing freely into a person by negative forces (attitudes, thoughts or actions) and this results in sickness. However, our physical body wants to be well; it is our mind and our emotions that divert it from this normal condition. Spiritual Healing opens up the channels again and the life force flows in without impediment.

Of course, the phenomenon of the body healing itself is true of all types of healing. When a doctor performs surgery he may remove a portion of the body, or sew two parts of the body together but the body itself has to do the healing. Drugs may stimulate, depress, or destroy, but the actual healing is accomplished by the body. Acupuncture, relaxation, visualization, exercise and massage all heal by unblocking the natural healing mechanism of the body.

Further confirmation of this self-healing power is found in the records of Edgar Cayce, the famous American clairvoyant who died in 1945 after giving thousands of "readings" for sick people over a period of forty-three years.[3] He was not a Spiritual Healer in the usual meaning of that term, but his unique ability, while in a trance, to tune in psychically to the other person, present or not, enabled him to diagnose the exact cause of an illness which had baffled doctors, and to tune in to universal sources of knowledge for the cure. While still in a trance, he prescribed many unusual remedies that he received from these sources. When the remedies were followed exactly the sick person nearly always became well. The point that interests us here is that he always maintained that his prescribed remedies were not designed to cure the disease but were meant to restore the balance and co-ordination of the forces within the physical body. When this restoration occurred healing followed.

Physicists Help to Explain

Einstein stated that matter and energy are two different forms of the same thing; that matter is energy reduced to the point of visibility; and that each can be changed into the other. Physicists have now proved the truth of these statements and have shown scientifically that what appears to the naked eye as solid matter actually consists of atomic particles in rapid motion at different rates of vibration. Each atom is composed of a positively charged nucleus surrounded by one or more negatively charged electrons, all moving at high speed in what is proportionately a vast amount of space. The nucleus consists of energy, light (a form of energy), and life itself.

Further examination of the nucleus and electrons by techniques developed by modern physicists shows that these constituents of the atom are made up of sub-atomic particles which sometimes appear as substance and sometimes appear as waves, depending on how the observer looks at them. In fact, physicists tell us that they are not *things;* they are only interconnections between things, which are themselves interconnections between other things, and so on *ad infinitum.* In other words, everything in the Universe is interconnected and thus inter-related—we are all one, as the mystics have been preaching for centuries.

Physicist Fritjof Capra, the well known lecturer and author of *The Tao of Physics*[4], said in a lecture:

In the universe there are no isolated building blocks—only a complicated web of relations between the various parts of the unified whole. These relationships always include the human observer and his consciousness in an essential way. The observer is not only necessary to observe the properties of the particles, but he is essential to even bring about these properties—all these properties are an expression of the particles' interaction with the human observer; so there is no split between mind and matter.

If we expand this to the physical level that we see with our own eyes we realize that we are all inter-connected with each other, and that the relationships among us, and between us and God, are the only things that are real. Also in terms of physics we might say that the reality of our bodies consists of the relationships among the sub-atomic particles that make up our apparent bodies. The relationship can be harmonious and healthy or in a state of conflict or disease, depending on the minds of the observers, and that means you and me!

Thus the human body is composed of trillions of atoms, all in constant motion, which are held together by an unseen force that physicists call "electro-magnetism". Teilhard de Chardin calls this force "love". In his book, *The Phenomenon of Man,* [5] he states that the basic attraction which brings particles together to form bodies of increasing complexity— the atom, the molecule, the cell, the multicellular organisms, the individual human, and eventually all of humanity is LOVE. At each level of increasing consciousness a synthesis occurs and a wholeness emerges. When we bear all this in mind, it is easier to understand how these atomic particles can be disarranged into a form of disease, and to see that most often the cause for this misalignment is a lack of love received or expressed by the patient, or a suppression of love by feelings of anger, hostility or resentment. Conversely, we also begin to see that healing results from the infusion of Love which rearranges the human body into the form of perfect health in which it was created and held together by Love.

Water seeks its own level automatically. An unsupported object will always drop towards the earth. God does not have to intervene in these instances. He created the law of gravity in the first place and it continues to work by itself. Likewise, He made us perfect and whole in the beginning, and subject to a spiritual law which automatically and naturally returns us to that state of perfection and wholeness whenever we remove the obstruction and distortion of our own thinking and desires and open ourselves completely to God's will. One way to do this is by thinking about the unity of God and man, the beauty of nature and the many synonyms for God—Love, Truth and so on, so that we leave no room for negative thoughts. If we consciously try to resist or deny them, their power will only increase. The spiritual healer, by acting as a channel for God's power, assists in the process of removing blockages and negativity, and in returning the body and mind to its original state of perfection.

Because the body consists of energy and atoms in constant motion, it is continually being rebuilt, renewed, and reformed in accordance with the thought patterns that surround it. The thoughts that influence the body include those of the owner of the body and of people in his environment, as well as the beliefs of the world in which he lives. The health and vitality of the body depends to a large extent upon the quality of those thoughts.

You might pause here for a moment to consider the kind of body that you are building for your future use. Will it be healthy, harmonious, energetic and pleasant to look upon, or will it be diseased, dissonant, tired and ugly? It is all up to you and your thoughts.

In one of his readings channelled from the universal sources Edgar Cayce said:[6]

> Each atomic force of a physical body is made up of its units of positive and negative forces, that brings it into a material plane. These are of the ether, or atomic forces, being electrical in nature as they enter into a material basis, or become matter in

its ability to take on or throw off. So as a group may raise the atomic vibrations that make for those positive forces as bring divine forces in action into a material plane, those that are destructive are broken down by the raising of that vibration! That's material, see? This is done through Creative Forces, which are God in manifestation.

We still have much to learn about vibrations, but physicists tell us that the physical body and other physical objects are vibrating at a low frequency rate. Sound is a higher vibration; light is still higher. It is believed that the healing power used by those in the Spirit World as servants of God, is even higher. This higher vibration is able to act on the lower vibration of the physical and etheric body of the one who is sick, recharging the vitality of the latter and healing the former by changing their vibrational rates and patterns to the original state in which they were created.

Perhaps even more remarkable is the discovery that each of the cells in our body has an intelligence of its own.

In her book *The Healing Secrets of the Ages*[7] Catherine Ponder states:

> Brain thinking cells are found throughout your being and body. This intelligence is waiting to be recognized and released for its healing mission. Thus your whole body is really mental and thinks as you want it to.

The late Harry Edwards, the famous English healer, says in *The Healing Intelligence*[8] that:

> Every one of the billions of cells in the body is a complete living organism. . . . It possesses a 'brain' which is the nucleus; it has purpose and therefore consciousness, an intelligence.

It is theorized that the cells become diseased because their intelligence has broken down (become insane) due to one or more of the many causes outlined in Chapter 3. The human mind usually affects the cell mind positively and constructively or negatively and destructively to some degree. However, in some situations the human mind may be able to take a completely neutral position, in which case the effect on the cell mind would be neither constructive nor destructive. In Spiritual Healing, we are re-awakening the intelligence of each cell to an awareness of its oneness with the Divine Mind, the one source of all intelligence. This causes each cell to reform itself into its original perfection.

As we have seen, our physical bodies consist of millions of individual cells. We probably do not think of them as separate entities but rather as one complete body. So it is with God. We are each one tiny cell of His total Being, yet we are completely merged and unified with Him. The less we think of ourselves as separate entities, the more complete we will become in every respect, experiencing all the attributes of God, including perfect health, as integral parts of our selves. We will be At One.

The Total Person Is Involved

The beauty of Spiritual Healing is that it affects the total person—body, mind, emotions and spirit. Thus it is not essential for the healer to be a specialist in any one of these areas, nor to know in which of these the disease originated. Members of the medical profession, especially those practicing holistic medicine, are increasingly convinced that *all* disease is psychosomatic in origin. This does not mean that the disease is purely a figment of the patient's imagination, but rather that there is an intrinsic interaction between mind (psyche) and body (soma) in every case of disease or dysfunction.

In Spiritual Healing there may be a correction of the physical symptoms, a change in the mental attitude or thought process, a transformation of negative, destructive emotions into positive, constructive ones, a revelation of a need for deeper spiritual awareness, or a combination of any or all of these. The patient's own Higher Self knows what the greatest need is, and will use the love/energy received for that greatest need. It is important that the healer be completely open to this and that he make no attempt to impose his own will or direction on the other person, or have expectations of specific results.

Most experienced spiritual healers have found that as they tune in to the Spirit world and the sick person's Higher Self during the healing process they will often intuitively become aware of what is needed. This may consist of the simple knowledge of where to place their hands, not necessarily with any logical relationship to the designated area of pain or disease; it may be a realization of the deep seated cause of the disease which had not been apparent in the preliminary discussion with the one in need; it may be guidance as to specific physical or mental action which should be taken by the sick person to contribute to his healing; or it may be some other message or symbol that is coming to the healer from the Higher Self, Spirit Guides or Teachers of the other person or the healer. Sharing this intuitive, psychically received information with the other person can be a very important part of the healer's service.

Healing Is Not Limited to Physical Cures

Since Spiritual Healing works on the whole person it can be just as effective in cases when there are no physical symptoms of disease but the person is feeling ill emotionally, mentally or spiritually. Admittedly, real psychotic mental breakdowns are very difficult for Spiritual Healers to work with because it is usually difficult to communicate with, or obtain co-operation from, the mind of the sick person, but it must always be remembered that "With God all things are possible" (Matthew 19:26), and healings of this type of problem do occur.

One case of a non-psychotic, but mental/emotional healing which I recall was that of a 25-year-old girl who was depressed to the point of wishing to die. Her father had died under tragic circumstances five years before and her mother had committed suicide six months earlier for reasons that were not entirely clear to this young lady. At first she had imagined that in some way she had been responsible, but now she felt certain that she had resolved that difficulty, and no longer had any sense of guilt. Nevertheless life had lost all meaning for her. I therefore proceeded with a session of Spiritual Healing, just as for any physical disease, leaving the healing power to flow wherever it was needed. On the telephone two weeks later she said that she had felt happy and peaceful ever since, and had no trace of any death wish.

Another interesting situation started with a physical symptom and ended with a non-physical side effect. This lady, an artist, came with the complaint that as far as she knew there was nothing physically wrong with her except that she was greatly lacking in her normal ample supply of energy. A week after the Spiritual Healing session she reported that not only did she have greatly increased energy, but her creativity had multiplied enormously and she could not keep up with the new ideas that were flooding into her mind.

One young mother came to me saying that her second child was due to be born in two weeks' time and that she was terrified of giving birth because she had had a difficult experience with the birth of her first child. It had been breached, lying across her pelvis instead of being head down as it should have been. The first delivery was done with forceps and was extremely painful and traumatic. The memory of that trauma was constantly present during the second pregnancy, and this baby also seemed at times to lie across the pelvis, increasing the apprehension of another difficult birth.

During the healing session all of her fear left, while I silently talked to the baby asking it to move into the correct position, for its own sake as well as its mother's. She reported later that the baby did move to the head down position during the following week; that a normal birth had been possible; and that she had been completely free of fear throughout the remaining two weeks and during the delivery. Two years later she said that the burden of the original trauma had never returned.

These are just a few of the experiences which have taught me that Spiritual Healing affects people's lives in many different ways; it is not limited to the healing of physical disease. Before I started to be a channel for the healing power I received the following words during a deep meditation:

> As the power flows, so it will automatically clean up all discord and disease in its path; lining up bodies, minds and lives in accordance with the harmony and beauty of God's plan for His creation.

When I first received this message from the Spirit World I did not perceive the significance of the word "lives" in this context. As I entered into the healing work, however, I found that changing lives was indeed a very meaningful part of the whole process. People would come for a healing of some physical or emotional problem, and as the Love of God was shared with them, and we became in tune with the Spirit World, wonderful changes or events would occur in their lives. People have very often told me how their reactions towards life became more trusting and free flowing, and their attitudes towards people changed to include more love and service.

Is Belief Necessary?

The belief of the one who is ill has a tremendous effect on the results of any type of healing effort. The medical profession has conducted thousands of tests using placebos (inert pills) on half the patients being tested and curative drugs on the other half. The patients all had identical illnesses and they were all told that they were receiving the same effective drug. Nearly always there was no significant difference between the two groups in the percentage of people in each group who recovered.

A doctor's "bed-side manner" and level of self-assurance can give confidence to the patient that he will recover and that the doctor knows what he is doing, or he can cause the patient to feel uncared for, insecure and pessimistic about his recovery. The patient's resultant belief does much to contribute to the success or failure of orthodox medicine.

We cannot, therefore, ignore the effect of the sick person's belief in a spiritual healer's ability, nor in his belief in the efficacy of Spiritual Healing itself. There are numerous recorded cases of complete healings where the sick person had no belief in either, but was persuaded by friends or relatives to try this way in spite of his attitudes; so we know that belief is not absolutely essential. Nevertheless it certainly increases the chances of success and is often an important factor. Notice how often Jesus said after healing someone:

> Your faith has made you well.

It was also reported that:

> He did not do many mighty works there because of their unbelief.
> (Matthew 13:58)

I have been talking about the presence or absence of positive beliefs, but negative beliefs are just as powerful in the opposite direction. This has also been proved by the use of placebos given with the warning that "this drug will probably make you feel very ill". So if the sick person is convinced that Spiritual Healing will not work for him, it probably won't. It also seems easier to heal a young adult, unless it is a life long illness, than an older one, probably because the former has had much less conditioning by society, and has fewer preconceived ideas about the illness than the older person. He is also usually more willing to change his beliefs and be receptive to the spiritual healing power.

In addition to having faith in the healer and in the spiritual healing process, the sick person's belief in his own eventual recovery is also a powerful factor. I recall the case of a young boxer which was reported widely in the newspapers in 1977. He had been shot in the back and was not expected to walk again. He was in great pain, had lost all desire to live, and had become deeply depressed. He ate practically nothing and lost over one-third of his weight. Then a hypnotist planted positive thoughts in his sub-conscious mind and his whole conscious attitude changed. He ate ravenously, started to move his body, which up to then had been immobile, and quickly learned to crawl. Truth cannot be changed regardless of what we believe, but our life and what we experience can be changed by changing our beliefs.

Surrender by the One in Need

Willingness to surrender his total being, all he owns, his will and his very soul to his Creator is even more important than a needful person's belief that he will be cured. Whether he refers to God, the Universal Power, the Divine Source, All There Is, or any other title is not important as long as he is willing to acknowledge that there is "something" that is greater than himself, and is willing to let that "something" take over his life.

When a sick person surrenders to the will of God he is not merely letting God decide whether he will live or die, he is surrendering to His will in every respect, and therefore must of necessity be asking that God's will, whatever it is, be made known to him. If God wishes him to reconcile his relationship with someone he hates, this must be done. If God wants him to forgive someone who harmed him in the past, this must be carried out. If he wants him to change careers, or to serve humanity in some way in addition to his present career, an effort must be made to do this. Thus it is not an either/or proposition—it is all, everything.

When we try to run our own lives, ignoring the inner voice, smug in our assurance that we know better than our Creator that which is best for us, trouble of all kinds plagues us.

Does the One Being Healed Feel Anything?

During a Spiritual Healing the person to be healed may feel various types of activity in his body, or may feel nothing at all. He may experience warmth, cold, tingling like a mild electric shock, or a sensation of movement or disintegration within his body at one place, or internal movement from one place to another. Sometimes there may be some pain or numbness as the body resists the input of energy at the start, but this quickly disappears as the healing session continues, and nearly always has gone when the session terminates. Whatever the sensation may be, it appears to indicate that something is being unblocked or moved to permit the body to heal itself right then or later on.

Usually people presume that the heat they feel is emanating from the healer's hands; however, tests with a thermometer placed between the body of the other person and the healer's hands prove that there is no increase in temperature between the two. There is a powerful energy flowing from the healer's hands but it in itself has no heat. It is probably the activity within the body, a re-arrangement of atoms, that creates the heat, somewhat like a microwave oven.

I recall the case of a young woman who came to me because she was scheduled to have an operation in two weeks. She had a tumor on one ovary and her doctor had said that both the tumor and the ovary must be removed, and that if malignancy was suspected while she was under the anesthetic, he would probably decide to give her a complete hysterectomy. Since she was only 25 and hoped to have children someday, this was the last thing that she wanted. The next time I saw her she reported that while my hands were over the defective ovary she felt the tumor explode. However, she said nothing at the time because she found it hard to believe that it had actually happened, but she did return to her doctor five days later for a re-examination. He reported to his great surprise and her intense joy that there was no sign of the tumor, that everything looked perfectly normal, and that no operation was necessary.

If a person does not feel anything during the healing session, it does not necessarily mean that no healing has taken place. It may merely mean that for that particular situation and person there were no physical sensations accompanying whatever took place within the body. It is also possible that medication, particularly tranquilizers and pain killers, impair the body's ability to sense the healing energies.

Temporarily Feeling Worse

Sometimes a sick person who is exposed to Spiritual Healing finds that the healing is momentarily accompanied by pain or extreme discomfort, or that the next day they actually feel worse than before. Sometimes this manifests as irritation or itching of the skin. This appears to be because under the influence of the spiritual power the person's body is making some very rapid changes, such as the destruction, dissolution or renewal of tissue or other matter, which causes temporary pain or discomfort. However, this quickly disappears and the person finds that he is partially or completely healed.

It is usually safe to say that the new pain or discomfort will cease within 24 hours. However, I do recall one case of a woman whose uterus was full of fibrous tumors the size of lemons. During the healing she felt tremendous energy and activity and even a burning sensation in that area. She reported later that it continued for thirty-six hours. Afterward all discomfort ceased and she noticed that her abdomen was much flatter, and she felt sure that she had been healed.

Another reason for temporary discomfort after a healing session is that previously suppressed or denied emotions or traumatic experiences may have been brought into consciousness by the power of the Spirit, and this may prove to be painful until examined and dealt with. In these situations the pain is emotional, not physical, and may result in crying and sobbing or even screaming aloud during the healing process. I am still occasionally surprised at the rapidity with which this sometimes occurs. Maybe only a few minutes after the healing power has been invoked, the release of tension in this manner will appear and run its course. This release can be extremely valuable and can contribute much to the healing process. In most cases it seems wisest not to interrupt or stop the experience by trying to comfort the other person. No harm will result if the healer is careful not to impose his own will on the situation, but to trust in the power that has been invoked.

The Power of the Group

So far I have been talking about Spiritual Healing through the channel of one person, but there are also many situations where the power is channelled through several people at the same time. This can be very potent. For example, there are special regular healing services held in a number of churches throughout the world. It is really surprising that these are held in only a small percentage of the total number of churches, when we recall that Jesus spent such a large part of his brief three year ministry in healing the sick. He did this not only because of his compassion for all mankind, but as the finest tool for his teaching (actions speak louder than words) and a great demonstration that God is a God of Love, not anger.

In addition innumerable small groups meet in private homes for the sole purpose of Spiritual Healing for those who are present or for those not present who have requested help. Once more we can turn to the teaching of Jesus to understand why these groups can be so effective, for he said:

> If two of you agree on earth about anything they ask, it will be done for them by my Father in heaven. For where two or three are gathered in my name, there am I in the midst of them. (Matthew 18:19-20)

I remember one case where a frantic grandmother phoned to say that her one year old granddaughter had swallowed a powerful tranquilizer which the child had discovered in her mother's purse. The child, who had gone into a coma, had been put into intensive care at the local hospital, her stomach had been pumped but she was still in a coma. The doctor had said that the child would in all probability die within 24 hours since the liver, as well as the blood, would have absorbed the drug. The grandmother asked if we would please pray for the child. My wife and I did so. It also happened that within an hour I attended a weekly healing prayer circle in the house of another spiritual healer.

At the meeting I sat in the center as a substitute for the child, while another member of the group laid hands on me and led the group in united prayer for the child. Later we learned that within a brief period of time she had come out of the coma and by mid-afternoon she was fussing because the needle placed in her foot for intravenous fluids had slipped so that the fluid was swelling the tissues in her leg and causing her pain. She was awake and responsive during the evening and had a normal night's sleep. She was shortly discharged in perfect health. I feel sure it was the power of the group prayer that resulted in the happy ending to that crisis.

Those churches that are most successful with their healing services usually have strong prayer support from their congregations, not only during the healing service itself, but also throughout the week. This may be by individuals in their homes or by groups of members meeting together for the purpose of healing.

Spiritual Renewal

True Spiritual Healing needs to include the healing of the sick person's relationship with God, or the Source of All Creation. This does not involve a conversion to a specific form of religion or belief, but rather a recognition and inner awareness by the one in need that there is a force and intelligence that is greater than his own, and yet is within him and within everyone else.

I have found that healing of the physical symptoms may take place without a spiritual renewal, because of a transfer of the life force energy. Healing may also occur because of a change in belief structure in regards to the disease or its cause. However, unless the spirit is also healed by at least partial awareness and acceptance of the Divine within, the same disease or another one is likely to re-occur.

If a man is in tune with the Source of his life he will usually experience harmony, health and peace in all aspects of his being—body, mind, emotions and spirit.

Broader Implications

A successful, permanent Spiritual Healing of a serious ailment nearly always requires an important change in the life of the one who is healed, in order to eliminate the cause of the illness. Hatred is replaced by love, resentment changed to forgiveness, a critical, judgmental attitude is transformed into acceptance of others as they are, and so on. Since these changes all contribute to more peaceful, harmonious and loving relationships with others, Spiritual Healing of the individual frequently contributes in a small way to the healing of the nation and the world. Thus, like a pebble cast into still water, the Spiritual Healing of one person in body, mind, emotion and spirit, sends love-energy outwards in ever widening circles.

The only source of Spiritual Healing is the Divine Creator of the Universe and everything in it, so it is available to all regardless of race, color, religion, belief, age, sex, language, location or time. Thus it encompasses the complete brotherhood of humanity in Love and Eternity.

It is my feeling that there are no barriers to Spiritual Healing as long as Love is present and the possibility of God's intervention is accepted. I remember one old gentleman, visiting the United States from a Middle Eastern country, who was brought to me by a friend. He was 75 years old, had had diabetes for 25 years; his sister also had it and his mother had died as a result of it. His disease was getting worse, making it difficult for him to walk and gradually destroying his eyesight. He could speak no English and he was a Moslem by faith.

However, through his friend as interpreter, we learned that we both believed in one God, in the use of prayer and in the possibility of Spiritual Healing. He willingly opened himself to receive the healing power through my prayer and laying-on-of-hands. A week later his friend reported that the sugar in his urine had decreased from 0.192 to 0.162 per cent. (0.160 per cent is the top of the range for a normal count for a healthy individual); his doctor was amazed, and he was overjoyed. The count was still down three months later, and his difficulties in walking and seeing had also decreased markedly.

Magnetic Healing

Magnetic healing may appear at first glance to be the same as Spiritual Healing, but it is not. The difference is that in the former the healer is transferring some of his *own* electro-magnetic energy to the sick person, whereas in the latter the healer is channelling Divine power and not his own. While magnetic healing can be effective in some cases, it has several disadvantages.

(a) Its power is limited to the power of the healer instead of being unlimited.

(b) It depletes the healer of his own energy and therefore the number and frequency of the healings he can participate in is also limited. A spiritual healer, on the other hand, is never depleted of energy as long as he remains open as a channel and always remembers that it is God's power and not his own.

(c) A magnetic healer must use his own judgement as to where he directs the energy and how much is appropriate, whereas a spiritual healer leaves it to God and His Spirit Ministers to distribute and control this energy in accordance with their greater knowledge.

There is sometimes a fine line between these two types of healing and some healers may be using a blend of the two.

Psychic Healing

Psychic Healing may or may not mean the same thing as Spiritual Healing. Some people use the words "Psychic Healing" and mean healing by the power of God, or the Holy Spirit, as described earlier in this chapter, but for some reason are reluctant to come right out and refer to it as spiritual. Technically they may be correct, as the word "Psyche" means "Spirit" or "Soul". Others, however, use this word to mean healing by their own supernatural powers or psychic abilities, which is a little different from allowing the power of God to heal in accord with the Divine plan. Obviously there is a greater danger of the individual's will and ego being involved, and perhaps in control, in healing by one's own psychic abilities.

Summary

In Spiritual Healing, regardless of the exact procedure used, the healer attunes himself to the One Source of Infinite Love and Energy, and thus becomes an open channel to direct that power to another. The acceptance or rejection of that force is then the choice of the one who wishes to be healed. He may make this choice intentionally with his conscious mind, or unintentionally with his sub-conscious mind, or by means of his Higher Self.

Thus there are two variables in the healing process which have a bearing on its effectiveness:

1. The healer and his ability to attune to the Source and to be open as a channel.

2. The sick person and his capacity and/or willingness to receive the Life Force.

The result of the healing usually depends on the degree

and combination of these two factors *at the time of* the heal-ing effort. However, there are many other points to be con-sidered in this regard which are covered in Chapter 6.

There are also two key points to understanding the Spiritual Healing process itself, namely UNCONDITIONAL LOVE and COMPLETE SURRENDER.

UNCONDITIONAL LOVE is the unlimited healing power we receive from God, both directly and through other beings living on the earth and in the Spirit world. We enable ourselves to receive that love by ourselves expressing love to God and to others. Thus it is a two-way street.

COMPLETE SURRENDER is the abandonment by the sick person *and* the healer of their own desires, expectations and personal wills. This allows God's will to manifest itself, even if that means moving from the physical to the spiritual plane, giving up the physical vehicle by so-called death. Complete surrender eliminates all FEAR, establishes TRUST, and allows the power to flow without obstruction. It also opens both people to Spiritual Guidance, gives all the an-swers that are needed at the time, and establishes PEACE AND HARMONY.

After all, what could be a more beautiful and natural way of healing than just allowing the force of Life and Love, which created us in the first place, to flow through us and into us, restoring each cell to its pristine glory?

Notes for Chapter 2

1. Joel S. Goldsmith. *The Art of Spiritual Healing.* Harper and Row, New York. 1959.

2. John G. Fuller. *Arigo. Surgeon of the Rusty Knife.* Thomas Y. Crowell Co. New York. 1974

3. Many books have been written about the life of Edgar Cayce. For example: *Many Mansions* by Gina Cerminara. The New American Library, New York (paper) 1967. *There is a River.* Thomas Sugrue.

Dell Publishing Co. Inc. New York. 1942. *Stranger in the Earth* Thomas Sugrue. Holt Rinehart & Winston, Inc. 1948

4. Fritjof Capra. *The Tao of Physics.* Shambhala Publications, Boulder, Colorado. 1976

5. Teilhard de Chardin. *The Phenomenon of Man.* Harper and Row, New York. 1959. (First published in French in 1955).

6. *Edgar Cayce Readings (281–3).* Published by the Edgar Cayce Foundation. 1971. Reprinted by permission.

7. Catherine Ponder. *The Healing Secrets of the Ages* p. 1. DeVorss & Co., Marina del Rey, CA 90294. 1985

8. Harry Edwards. *The Healing Intelligence* p. 71. The Healer Publishing Company, Ltd. Guildford, England. 1965

NOTHING

CAN WITHSTAND

THE POWER OF

UNCONDITIONAL LOVE

CHAPTER 3

INNER CAUSES OF DISEASE

MOST OF US are well aware that there is a direct connection between mind and body from our own experience. If we get angry the blood will rush to our faces and our muscles will tense. If we are suddenly frightened the blood will drain out of our face and it becomes "white with fear." If we face a physical emergency our adrenal glands increase their output of steroids and we experience above normal energy and strength to cope with the situation; e.g., a parent lifts a car which has fallen onto their child. If we observe someone else in action we sometimes have a mental reaction which manifests in a bodily change, for example: someone eats something that we are especially fond of and the saliva in our mouth increases in volume; or a friend has a bad cold and our eyes water or our throat feels sore just from seeing and hearing their symptoms.

There are many other examples known to medical scientists. It is a known fact that the human body produces cortisone to fight inflamation but it has now been discovered that the amount of cortisone produced is connected to that person's mental outlook. Scientific tests have shown that an optimistic, positive, happy outlook on life produces more cortisone, whereas depression produces less. Medical history is replete with cases of hysterical pregnancies—women who are so desperately eager to conceive a child that they convince themsleves that they are pregnant. By means of their autonomic nervous system their minds create in their bodies all the symptoms of pregnancy for several months, until their doctor finally convinces them, by X-Rays, if necessary, that there is no foetus. Once the women are certain that they have no child in their womb, their bodies quickly return to normal status.

On the other hand there are thousands of cases where a couple has been unable to conceive a child after trying hard to do so for a number of years, and out of desperation they adopt a child. Then to their great surprise, within a few weeks or months they conceive a child of their own. The tension created by their desire to produce a child, and yet failing to do so, was blocking the normal functioning of their bodies. Once the emotional stress had been removed, or greatly lessened by adoption, their bodies were able to operate in the natural way.

Medical authorities readily agree that many illnesses are caused by the mind and can be cured by the mind with suggestions from another person, with or without hypnosis. These illnesses include many skin diseases, asthma, irregular heart beat, colitis, migraine headaches, impotency, high blood pressure and ulcers. For many years doctors have stated that 50-60 per cent of all disease is psychosomatic; that is, it is caused by the patient's own mind or emotions. In recent years many doctors have increased this proportion to 80 to 90 per cent, and I have heard a few state that they now believe that *all* illness originates in this manner. This relationship between the state of an individual's emotions or mind and the physical condition of his body has been well known in the Eastern countries for thousands of years.

Edgar Cayce, the gifted clairvoyant who diagnosed illnesses while he was in a trance, consistently maintained in his "readings" that disease originates within the body, and does not arise from external influences; he said that "The mind is the builder and the body is the result."[1] Current thinking is that in some cases the cause may be external (e.g. bacteria) but the mind prevents the body's natural defenses from destroying the foreign invader and thus allows it to multiply into a disease.

It is therefore very important for the one in need and the healer to try to discover the cause of the dysfunction, rather than just to eliminate the symptoms. If this is not done the chances are that the disease will return in one form or another.

Whether the illness is physical, mental or emotional, it is usually essential that the sick person make some drastic changes in their life. This need to re-orient one's life is beautifully described by Gerhard Adler in his book *Studies In Analytical Psychology:*[2]

> It happens only too often that the patient expects at the beginning of an analysis that the psychotherapist will, by some magical means, simply rid him of his symptoms without ever touching the rest of the structure of his life, with which he is quite satisfied. The analyst is only too often supposed to be a kind of "medicine man" who will make the symptoms disappear from the outside. The truth is that nobody can be cured unless he is prepared to accept the need for a more or less complete re-orientation of his life. To put it in a nutshell: the healed person is not the original person minus a symptom, but a newly orientated person in whom, through the new orientation, the necessity for the symptom itself has disappeared. It may even sometimes happen that the cure does not mean the disappearance of a symptom, but that instead it makes the suffering caused by the symptom disappear, because the original suffering has fulfilled its purpose.

Although Dr. Adler was discussing patients with emotional or mental ailments, his remarks can apply equally well to those suffering from physical disorders.

My own studies and practical experience to date lead me

to believe that the real causes of disease probably fall into several main categories: self-abuse, negative emotions and attitudes, stress, guilt, negative thinking, self-created disease, conflict with a life plan, Karma, Possession and lessons to be learned.

I am still exploring this complex subject and do not claim that my analysis of causes of disease is exhaustive. Nor does it cover all of the psychological ramifications that helped to create the causes themselves. It does outline the connection between cause and effect, mind and body, including some actual examples. Uncovering the origins of the cause can be a lengthy process of spiritual or psychological counseling and analysis; however, practical examples included in this and the next two chapters show that Spiritual Healing can often dramatically shorten this process.

Self-Abuse

Sometimes the cause is physical but is subconsciously self inflicted by the sufferer. Abuse of one's body by the excessive use of tobacco, alcohol, food, sex or work, or a lack of sufficient sleep, rest or recreation (re-creation) will eventually cause the body to rebel. By means of a pain, disease or malfunction it will say "Stop what you are doing to me and be grateful for all I have done and am doing for you."

When we contribute to the pollution of the earth, air and water of this beautiful planet that we share with billions of humans and other life forms, we are abusing that which has been given to us to maintain our good health, and this, too, may contribute to disease of our body. We need to accept responsibility for this.

Negative Emotions and Attitudes

Most frequently, the real cause of a disease is found to be some negative emotion or attitude, which, more often than not, has been repressed and remains unexpressed. However, it is sometimes found that a negative emotion that has been freely expressed is the basic cause of the disease, because in the very act of expression the body is subjected to strong negative vibrations which it has been unable to absorb without harm. There are numerous emotions or attitudes that are harmful to the mind and body, many of which are outlined in the following paragraphs.

Anger, hate, hostility, resentment, and various shades or combinations of these, can be incredibly destructive to the one who originates them. If expressed they may also do harm to the person to whom they are directed. Carried to the extreme of wishing someone were dead, or even wanting to kill them, may produce such powerful negative energy in the one holding these thoughts that he or she will experience a terminal illness, fatal heart attack, or deep depression.

It seems to be that anger or resentment directed at God or "Life" is particularly destructive to the individual holding these feelings. This may be because such anger becomes a self-created invisible barrier between the individual and the Source of life. Only the individual can remove it.

Jealousy, envy, greed or possessiveness create much internal misery. Buddha stated that possessiveness is the principal cause of sorrow. Another translator used even stronger words quoting Buddha as claiming that attachment is the source of all human suffering. Actually when we permit ourselves to become attached to some person or thing we are surrendering our freedom and our free will in proportion to the strength of the attachment.

Jesus expressed it in a slightly different way when he said: "Do not lay up for yourselves treasures on earth . . . for where your treasure is, there will your heart be also." (Matthew 6:19 & 20) These treasures may be material possessions, physical sensations, fame or dependent relationships. The ultimate experience of freedom is to give up attachment to our body and to all phases of physical life on this earth; then we have no fear of loss, disease or death.

Fear may be the greatest of all destroyers: fear of death, injury or disease itself; fear of the loss of loved ones or loved possessions; fear of the unknown. Worry and anxiety fall into the same category as fear but at a slightly lower intensity. I recall one man who had recovered from cancer with normal medical treatment but without seeking or discovering the cause. A few years later he developed multiple sclerosis. After living with this for some time he asked for Spiritual Healing at which time a search for the possible cause was started. This revealed excessive and continuous worry over almost every aspect of life, both large and small. He agreed that his state of mind had not changed over the years; so it was most likely also the cause of his earlier cancer. He did not listen to the message his body was giving him the first time, so it came back with a louder and more dramatic one the second time.

Judgement or criticism of others is frequently accompanied by resentment or frustration because the one who is judged ignores the criticism and refuses to change the way the judger thinks he should. The Biblical injunction: "Thou shalt not judge" is a Spiritual Law, which has its own consequences, often in the form of disease, if it is ignored.

Frustration or depression can also be caused by an individual's inability to achieve goals he has set for himself, or to maintain an established position in society.

Unresolved inner or outer conflicts create a tension which increases with time and causes blocks to the flow of the life forces in the body, followed by disease. One cause of an inner conflict which seems to be especially prevalent in women at this time is the promiscuous sex life in which so many are now involved. Consciously they want to be free to follow their instincts, or to comply with men's wishes in order to be popular, or to have lots of male companionship; so sexual freedom is embraced as a liberator. Subconsciously, or at another level, their inner being is not happy with this; it is contrary to their ideals and their spiritual nature or the conditioning of their childhood, and thus a conflict occurs at a deep level. They may or may not be aware of this inner tension, but frequently the result seems to be a disease of some part of their reproductive organs (including the breasts) which cannot be healed on a permanent basis without a change in their sexual life or their beliefs. Because, historically men in general have assumed greater freedom and different moral standards in this area, this type of inner conflict does not appear to arise so often for them.

On the other hand exactly the reverse can be true. Repressed sexual feelings can also create an inner conflict resulting in disease. The owner of such feelings does have other choices which could eliminate the difficulty. He may be able to find a way to express such feelings in circumstances which do not conflict with his ideals or other reasons for repression. Alternatively, he can mentally raise this energy up from the second chakra to the fourth chakra, transmuting it to unconditional love as he does so. Remember, there is only one energy and we can decide how to use it.

Lust can also leave its mark on the mind and body in many different ways. Lust might be defined as an intense craving for sexual intercourse with another, without love, affection, knowledge of, or even acquaintanceship with the other person, and without any consideration for that person's desires or feelings.

Depression is often the result of repressed anger, but can have many other origins. One of these is a loss of reasons for living—an absence of goals. This in turn may result from a failure to listen to the inner direction, or from listening but failing to follow that direction. The will to live is essential for healing or survival, because we have a free choice in the matter—if we want to die we can. That doesn't necessarily mean by consciously committing suicide; it may merely be abandoning all desire to live and all effort to be healed or to stay alive.

Unresolved grief, or repressed emotional or mental pain can be deceptive. Externally the one who has been hurt may give an impression of bravery or courage, but internally the grief or pain may be literally consuming some vital organ, or building an unwanted tumor. Self-pity is another form that this negative emotion may assume, and it can be equally damaging.

Dominance of others, the desire for power, misplaced aggression, rebelliousness against all forms of authority ("I can't stand anyone telling me what to do"), are various forms of the basic instinctual drive for power. If these are allowed to operate unchecked they can corrupt and destroy the one exercising that power, and often do great harm to the one being controlled. It is now known that this struggle for power can result, not in the desired survival, but in a heart attack and early demise. The connection between the power drive and heart disease is logical because the heart area is the Unconditional Love center, and the very essence of this love is to leave others completely free. This, of course, is the exact opposite of achieving power over them. If love is suppressed the energy at the heart center may be blocked, creating disease of the heart itself.

Desire for revenge, the wish to hurt another who hurt us, can only increase the pain and suffering experienced as a result of the initial action, even if the retaliation is successful. An interesting example of this was the case of a young woman who had a serious physical problem for which her doctor could promise no real cure. In searching for the cause she explained that she had been married at quite a young age but her husband had become very cruel to her, both mentally and physically, after the first six months of their marriage. She had tolerated this for two years and then finally left him and obtained a divorce. Since then she had lived with three different men, each for a period of two years, after which she broke off the relationship even though in each case the man wanted to continue, and, in fact, would have been willing to marry her if she had agreed.

When I asked her why she did this, she thought for a moment and then said: "I guess it was to hit back at my husband for what he had done to me," that is, a desire for revenge. When I pointed out that she was not in fact hurting her husband but had caused pain for three other men who had done nothing to injure her, she suddenly became aware of her error. She said she had never realized before that moment that she really hated men. She also became aware that her inner being knew the wrong she had caused these other men, and that the resulting emotional and spiritual conflict was probably the cause of her illness.

During the subsequent healing session she first visualized her former husband and then silently spoke to him and forgave him. She then visualized each of the other three men, one at a time, and silently asked each of them to forgive her for the way she had treated them. She then asked forgiveness of God and resolved to change her ways by expressing love instead of hate, and to remain open for a new relationship which would be free of all old hates and resentments. This cleared the way for her to receive the healing energy, which was far more apparent to her than during the previous session. The healing that she had hoped for then followed within a few weeks.

Frustration, caused by the action or inaction of others, or by our own failure to perform up to our own standards of perfection, or merely frustration at the circumstances in which we find ourselves, can create all sorts of tensions within our body leading to disease.

Insecurity, negative comparison of self with others, and general lack of self-worth show up from time to time in the search for the cause of a disease. This negative emotion is commonly called an Inferiority Complex. Edward F. Edinger, in his book *Ego and Archetype,*[3] describes this type of person as one who:

> assumes unconsciously and automatically, that whatever comes out of himself—his innermost desires, needs and interests— must be wrong or somehow unacceptable.
> With this attitude psychic energy is dammed up and must emerge in covert, unconscious or destructive ways such as psychosomatic symptoms, depression, alcoholism, etc.

This poor self image may cause the individual to become ill (see Self-created Disease). In others it may express itself in sexual promiscuity—a desperate search for love and importance. This is rarely, if ever, successful as it is usually met by rejection and contempt, and may in itself lead to disease of the reproductive organs.

It is interesting that exactly the opposite situation can also block the flow of life energy and cause disease, namely inflation of the ego. In psychological terms a Superiority Complex is assumed to arise out of a major unconscious feeling of inferiority. The superior attitude has been developed as a defense against either the individual or others becoming aware of that inner lack of self-worth. As such it may be very important in the development of the individual's ego, which is very necessary in certain phases of development.

From a spiritual aspect however, I feel it can be closely allied with pride, selfishness and self-importance, when the individual overlooks or ignores the fact that everything we have, including our minds and our talents, and the very life force itself, comes from God, the One Source. When our ego believes that it is the source of wisdom and that it provides us with all of these blessings, then trouble is not far away and often appears in the form of disease.

When any of these negative emotions occur they cause significant changes in the bio-chemistry of the body. When the emotions are limited in amount or duration, the normal homeostatic mechanisms of the body can handle the new conditions of increased stomach acids or higher blood pressure, for example. When the negative emotion is excessive in the energy or time involved, then disease or malfunction is likely to follow.

In some cases it appears that repressing a *positive* emotion may also create a disease. For example in talking to a man who had cancer in the center of his upper chest (directly over his 4th chakra which is the center of unconditional love) he told me that he had great compassion for anyone who suffered injustice, cruelty or poverty, even if he did not know them but merely read about them. However he never did anything about it. He had also badly abused his body with tobacco and alcohol, so it seems likely that his body chose to rebel in that particular place because of the inner conflict he had created by not acting on his compassionate feelings. In other cases repressing positive emotions may result in depression.

In Chapter 2 we looked at the many different life support systems in the human body. When one or more of these becomes blocked by negative emotions, then the body becomes susceptible to disease. Its immunization response can no longer handle the normal exposure to bacteria, cancerous cells, and foreign organisms, and disease follows. When Spirit Power unblocks the obstruction the body takes over and heals itself.

Stress

Modern research has also shown that frequently the cause of an illness is excessive or prolonged stress in the life of that person. Life today contains far more stress than it used to— situations where a person has to adjust to social, environmental or personal influences that involve either positive or negative change. Such adjustments are, of course, always necessary in varying degrees; that is how we grow. But when the amount of adjustment required of one individual by the circumstances of his life becomes more than he can handle, then the stress involved will probably affect his health.

Some examples of events which cause stress are:

Death of a loved one.	Birth of a child or grandchild.
Divorce or separation.	Marriage or reconciliation.
Injury or illness.	Release from hospital.
Imprisonment.	Release from prison.
Job loss.	A new job.
Retirement or demotion.	Promotion.
Change of occupation.	Move to new location—job or home.
Loss of money or valuables.	Sudden increase in supply.
Abortion or miscarriage.	Pregnancy.
Spending exceeds income.	Social climbing.
Loss of supportive relationships.	Excessive noise.

Child leaving home—at any age.

Child returning home.

Loss of privacy or living space.

There are many other causes of stress, depending on the individual's own reaction to life events. In fact there is no such thing as a comprehensive list of stressful events because anything that anyone finds stressful can be considered stressful for that person.

The underlying reason for any particular situation creating stress for an individual is his resistance to or failure to adapt to the change required of him by circumstances. If he flows with the situation and adjusts to it by accepting the new status as part of his life experience, there is very little stress and no danger of disease. In cases of extreme stress (created, for example, by the loss of a loved spouse of many years) acceptance instead of denial will at least reduce the stress and the chances of disease. In some cases, where there is a close dependency tie between two people in a family, one of them may be subject to excessive stress and the other produce the disease. This may take extra digging to discover since it is usually only the sick person who comes to the healer, but it is well to be aware of the possibility.

Note that the stress can arise from pleasant or unpleasant situations because either way it requires adjustment. It is when several of these events occur at the same time, and/or are stretched out over a long period of time that the stress may become more than the individual can absorb and he becomes susceptible to disease or disorder. Of course, disease itself is a stressful situation and may delay the healing, whether the original cause of the disease was some other form of stress or nothing to do with stress. In these cases it seems possible that acceptance of the disease in the sense of non-resistance (but not resignation) may aid the body to heal itself by eliminating the stress of resistance or denial.

We will discuss how to stop stress from creating disease or preventing healing in chapter 5, but there is one situation where a desire to avoid stress can in itself initiate a disease.

This is where an individual is so eager to avoid or postpone a major change in his life, such as moving to another part of the country, that he subconsciously creates a disease which makes the change impossible.

In my experience the stress or repressed emotion that has caused an illness often itself turns out to be caused by an unresolved domination by a parent over an adult child. Usually the controlling situation is mother over daughter, but sometimes it is mother over son, and much less often, the domination by father over son or daughter, that is involved.

Sons, and daughters (sometimes with the help of their husbands), usually seem to be able to release themselves physically, emotionally and mentally from a domineering father. Maybe it is because the tie is never so great in the first place, as it is with the mother who carried the child in her womb for nine months, and then had almost complete control of the child for the first few years of its life. If the mother is not willing to grant her child the freedom it needs to grow into an independent, free thinking adult she is often able to extend that control into maturity and beyond, right up until her death, and even after that in some cases.

The mother-daughter conflict is tragically frequent, creating untold misery and disease, particularly for the daughter, but often for the mother also. Why is it that so many mothers are unwilling to let their daughters be free? One reason is the basic instinctual drive for power and possession that is in all of us. Another is the fear of the loss of meaning in life when the child no longer needs her. She knows instinctively that she has much less chance of controlling her son; so she may concentrate all of her efforts on her daughter. Often there is also a streak of jealousy involved when the daughter becomes more attractive to men (possibly including the father) than the aging mother. Usually there is a desire for her child to have the best out of life (especially for a daughter who reminds the mother of herself) and she wrongly believes that control must be exerted to ensure that this happens.

The result of this *conditional* love may be arthritis or heart disease for the mother, particularly if the daughter rejects all such efforts to control her. The daughter, on the other hand, may either rebel against the control or submit to it. If she is to establish her own identity as an individual adult, making her own decisions for her life, she must refuse to accept her mother's demands. If she can do this with love and forgiveness her body will not be affected; however, if, as often happens, she reacts with anger and resentment and holds onto this, her body may manifest this as cancer. This is especially true if her anger is coupled with guilt feelings because of her rebellion. If she submits passively to the control without outward disobedience, she may feel a great deal of resentment and frustration at not being able to make her own choices and live her life as she wants to. This too may result in disease for her.

Sometimes, in the case of adults, the control is being exercised by the child over the parent, and the latter is deeply resentful of this. However, because of old age, the parent is physically or emotionally not strong enough to break away from the control, or financial dependency makes this impossible. As a consequence the parent has arthritis or some other disease.

Control by one spouse over the other can be just as disastrous and disease creating for both husband and wife. The one who is controlled may repress a lot of resentment and anger, which, as we have seen, are prime sources of disease. Alternatively, if he or she resists the control and fights back, the resulting conflict may create such negative feelings on both sides that these may manifest as disease for either or both. If the conflict ends in divorce, as frequently happens, the one who was being controlled may experience a great sense of freedom and release from tension, and healing of any disease caused by the conflict will probably follow automatically. However, the one who was trying to control may have lost an important (to them) reason for their existence and disease may arise, or be aggravated if it already exists.

It makes me sad to see the unhappiness caused by these conflicts but I feel a great joy when the control is changed to letting go, and the resentment and hostility are transmuted into love and forgiveness by both, thus dissolving the frustration. Usually healing will follow this change.

To love is to allow
To allow is to Love
God loves
God allows

Guilt

In a unique category by itself as a creator of physical and mental disease or dysfunction, is the feeling of guilt. This may not be justified if, for example, parents get divorced, or a parent commits suicide, and their child feels that he is in some way responsible. This is probably completely unwarranted but unless the feeling is uncovered and resolved with the help of responsible adults, the child may grow up and carry this feeling of guilt for years, consciously or subconsciously. The resulting inner, repressed conflict may then manifest in the form of a disease.

On the other hand, the guilt may be properly justified. For example, if an individual has injured someone physically, mentally, emotionally or materially, and has done nothing to offset this, he will carry some sense of guilt for this act, however hardbitten and insensitive he may appear to be on the surface. The more sensitive and spiritually advanced the offender happens to be, the more aware he will be of his conscience, and the greater will be his sense of guilt. Since in this case the guilt is justified it will have greater power to create a disease.

Then, too, a person may feel guilty because he has *not* done something that his conscience or inner voice tells him he should have done. Maybe he failed to give an aging parent the care and support that the parent needed; or did not love someone who deserved his love; or failed to inform the appropriate authorities when he knew that a child was being abused, or "did not want to get involved" and thus indirectly supported a crime. Possibly, his Higher Self or the Spirit of God has been urging him for years to respond to the Divine call to seek the Source of all creation, and he has failed to act on this. Perhaps he has spent his whole life indulging himself in physical pleasures and ignoring people around him who were in need, knowing full well that his inner voice was telling him that he ought to share and serve at least part of the time.

One man who came to me with several physical problems revealed that he had spent much of his working life in a type of work he enjoyed and was skilled at. However, in his later years he had worked for an organization which made him cut corners to save money, with the result that he knew that his work was defective and would not last. His guilty feelings finally created a disease which forced him to retire early.

Guilt feelings are also sometimes created by a conflict of conscience arising out of teachings of spiritual, moral or ethical principles received during childhood, which are no longer being observed. Even though current mores and the environment or society in which the person is now living leads him to the conclusion as an adult that such principles no longer apply to him, guilt may still arise at a deep level.

Any of these possibilities may create guilt feelings which eventually erupt in some form of physical or mental illness.

Negative Thinking

Thought is the most powerful force in the world; in fact the Universe and all that is in it were created by the power of God's thought. We are each a manifestation of His thought. Even if science is correct in maintaining that man evolved from a single cell over billions of years, that single cell must have been created by the thought of the Divine Intelligence that created this orderly Universe. Also the pattern for man's evolvement must have been established by the thought of that same Intelligence.

Those things which we consider to have been created by man have been created by man's thought. For example, think of a table, a building, an automobile or an airplane; the concept, the idea was first formed in some individual's mind and was then constructed by some person's hands which were controlled by that person's thought.

Nor must we overlook the power of thought as a cause of disease. It is becoming more and more widely accepted that our minds control our bodies in every respect. The *Upanishads,* the ancient Hindu scriptures, say: "What a man thinks, that he becomes." Other great religions and spiritual teachings contain similar statements. This consequence is nowhere more evident than in the case of health and disease —what your mind dwells upon will be manifested in the physical body. Scientific proof of the extent to which the mind controls the body is now available through the use of Bio-feedback instruments, by means of which a person connected to an instrument can see for himself that he can mentally control his autonomic nervous system, his blood temperature at different parts of his body, his brain waves, his blood pressure, and other supposedly involuntary processes.

A simple but rather dramatic exercise, which you can perform with a friend in your own home, can demonstrate the instant effect on the body of a change in thought:

> Ask your friend to stand up and hold one of his arms straight out to his side, horizontal to the floor with his thumb turned down. Now ask him to resist you as you firmly attempt to push his hand down. This is not a test of strength, but you should push down enough for you both to feel his ability to resist some pressure.
>
> Now ask him to close his eyes and think of something that makes him feel very sad. If nothing that makes him feel unhappy comes readily to his mind, suggest that he imagine someone he loves has been killed in a motor accident. Ask him to say "O.K." when he has really entered into the feeling of sadness.

When that happens, ask him to raise his arm into the same
position as before and then to resist you as you again try to press
his hand down. You will both find that he cannot do so, or at
least his resistance will be considerably less. Now, in order to
allow him to restore his strength, ask him to think of something
which makes him very happy, and to signal you with an "O.K."
when he has achieved that feeling. When he does so, ask him to
again raise his arm into the same position while you try once
more to push his hand down while he resists you; you will find
that he is now able to resist with ease.

Actually in the first part of the experiment you were combining negative thoughts with negative emotions, and this
combination creates a devasting force which makes one
vulnerable to disease and disharmony. Likewise in the second
part you were combining positive thoughts with positive
emotions which is equally powerful, but in a healing, constructive manner. Frequently, it will be discovered that this
combination of negative emotions and thoughts is involved in
the cause of a disease and it is not easy for the one in need to
overcome this.

For example, they may be carrying a strong resentment
towards a parent who had treated them cruelly, or rejected
them during childhood. At the same time they may often
think about the situations which caused their suffering, reliving them over and over again, and thus constantly rein-
forcing the negative emotion of resentment.

There are some situations where a negative emotion can
temporarily *increase* the muscular strength. For example,
where a mother finds her child lying pinned under a car, and
without thinking she rushes forward and lifts the car off her
child, even though she badly injures her back in the process.
However, this is a momentary change and the muscle tone
quickly returns to normal, or weaker than normal, once the
crisis has passed; whereas it is the constant or repeated negative emotion or thought that makes one vulnerable to disease.

There is another aspect to the power of thought, and that
is the effect on the thinker of negative thoughts directed at
someone else. One way of describing this is found in the

picturesque words of an American Indian Medicine man named Mad Bear, who is quoted in Doug Boyd's book *Rolling Thunder*[4] as saying:

> The principle of cause and effect is at work everywhere, and somebody has to receive the results of everybody's doings. Every sentence or thought or act has an effect on somebody. If someone has a destructive thought or wish, it has to have an effect on someone. If it doesn't work on someone else, it works back on the person who created it. Of course, in the end everyone gets his own earnings and accounts for his own debts; but just like money it can go around and around and involve many people, and it can get very complicated. The purpose of good medicine is to make it simple.

We also must not overlook the fact that negative thoughts and emotions can be infectious, and may adversely affect those with whom the negative person is in contact. We have all experienced the situation where our own mood of cheerfulness or positive outlook has been altered by coming into the presence of one who is depressed or expressing negative thoughts. It doesn't *have* to affect us this way if we remember to protect ourselves (see Chapter 8) but it is easy to forget to do this, and then to suffer the consequences.

Self-created Disease

There are a number of situations where the disease may actually have been subconsciously or consciously created on purpose by the sick person.

It may be to avoid or postpone a change in the person's life which they very strongly resist, such as a change of job or location that is being required by an employer. Here the employee may develop an illness which will make the change impossible. I remember one woman who became very ill after her husband was promoted to a better job in a new location. She did not want to leave her old environment and did not like the new one, so she said that the climate in the new area made her ill, and she proceeded to demonstrate various symptoms to prove it to her husband. Finally he had to ask for a transfer and demotion back to his old job in order to pacify her. Sure enough, once back in her old location all the symptoms disappeared.

It may be to extricate himself from an unpleasant situation. For example, a migraine headache may help to avoid trying to satisfy a demanding family; a stroke may eliminate the need to serve a tyrannical employer.

It may be that the individual has grown up with a great sense of unworthiness. He feels that he does not deserve success, plentiful supply or happiness. His self image, created in childhood, is so poor that he just can not feel comfortable with such blessings. So, when these things occur and life is going well for him, he creates a disease to make him miserable. This proves to him that he was right in his belief that he was not worthy enough for the good life, and this makes him feel satisfied in spite of the disease.

Then there is the man (or woman) who has been conditioned to believe that he must always work hard to justify his existence in the world. This drives him to work too hard and he has a heart attack. This enables him to take it easy with a clear conscience, or to depart from the earth and eliminate the whole problem.

Conflict with Our Life Plan

Any one who studies science, whether it is anatomy, biology, astronomy, mathematics or any other, is aware that there is a definite orderliness in this Universe. There was an Infinite Intelligence involved in the Creation, and it is still concerned, even down to a plan for each of our lives. Although we have a free will to do whatever we want, there are blue-prints for our lives which we chose in order to further our soul's growth and to teach us the lessons that we need to learn in order to evolve.

We each have a Higher Self, the Divine Spark within us, that knows what environment and what circumstances will best enable us to gain the knowledge and experience that we need in this particular lifetime. These situations may not always be to our liking, and may in fact seem very adverse. They may possibly include a disease from which we are to learn a particular lesson. However, whether they seem favorable or not, if we are led astray from the path laid down for us by our Higher Self, either by our own worldly desires, or by the influence of others, then an inner conflict arises. This conflict can be a root cause of disease and unhappiness. Two published examples of this type of disease creation are included in Chapter 5.

A very common conflict with a Life Plan is a denial of any need for the Divine Creator, or the very source of our life and being. Even if we do not realize it, we have an inner drive or longing to be fully aware of our One-ness with that which created us. The more that this drive is repressed or denied, the more powerful it becomes. This is a basic cause of much illness and failure to heal. Carl Jung said:

> Among all my patients in the second half of life—that is to say over thirty five—there has not been one whose problem in the last resort was not that of finding a religious outlook on life[5]

There is another factor to consider that is not unrelated to our Life Plan: that there is a unity of all things, and the Creator of all things is Love. Everything of which we are conscious is, in all its infinite variety of forms, a manifestation of that Love. Separation is impossible, and any action against ourselves, or against another, affects the whole. This too brings conflict and creates disease.

These causes are more esoteric than negative emotions and stress, but they should not be overlooked in the search for a cause for a disease.

Karma

In some cases the disease or pain may be the direct result of that person having earlier in their life caused pain and suffering to someone else, although they are probably quite unaware of the connection. Not only does the Bible say

"Whatever a man sows, that he will also reap" (Galatians 6:7), but all other major religions of the world include this basic spiritual law in their teaching. Jesus also phrased it in a slightly different way when he said "Whatever you wish that man would do to you, do so to them; for this is the law" (Matthew 7:12)

But what about those cases where it seems apparent that the one in need has done nothing to cause pain or suffering to someone else? What about children who have not had time to cause distress to others? Maybe they were born with a severe physical handicap. Does this principle or explanation ever apply to them? Yes, because in no case do the above teachings say that the harvest will necessarily occur during the same lifetime in which the seed was sown. Thus in these situations we need to examine the possibility of Reincarnation. This is the belief that over a period of thousands, or hundreds of thousands of years we have lived many different lives on this earth, each one providing opportunities for growth and learning.

More than half the world accepts this theory as factual; even the early Christian Church believed in it until the sixth century. Some of the church leaders of that time who spoke positively about the belief in Reincarnation were Origen, Nemosias and Hilarius. The contemporary historian, Justin Martyr, wrote of the same belief. However, the doctrine was unfortunately outlawed as heresy by the Second Council of Constantinople in 553 A.D. because it tended to dilute the authority of the Church. It also conflicted with the idea of repentance which was central to Christian teaching at that time; it was too easy for people to postpone the decision to repent, because there was always another life in which to take care of it—"Mañana" carried to the extreme!

Nevertheless it is not the purpose of this book to convince the reader of the truth or falsity of Reincarnation; there are a number of good books on the subject which include evidence in support of this theory (see bibliography). It is included here merely as one more possible explanation for disease and disability. If the cause of the disease originated in an earlier life, the lesson must now be learned by experiencing what the sufferer created for another person in that life. This is not punishment—it is a spiritual law known in esoteric teaching as the law of Karma. This is really the same spiritual law as the Christian teaching that you reap what you sow, except that Karma extends the harvest beyond one life in some cases.

Science teaches genetics as a physical explanation for the inheritance of a disease or physical defect, or a tendency towards one of them. Reincarnationists explain that we incarnate with subconscious memories and patterns from previous lives, and that we choose our parents and birth environment so that we will be able to experience what we need to learn for our soul's growth. In some cases a disease or physical handicap may be necessary for this lesson.

Acceptance of the scientific explanation alone tends to make a person who "inherits" a disease or handicap blame fate, bad luck or God. Acceptance of the reincarnationists' theory encourages the individual to accept responsibility for his situation. This does not need to be with a feeling of guilt, but rather with a determination to learn whatever lesson is involved so that he can move beyond the necessity for the disease or handicap.

One aspect of Karma which we all should be aware of is that we do not need to bear another person's Karma. Some people are full of fears, worries, and real mental pain because when they see or hear about someone else's illness or misfortune they think, "that is terrible!" even though they do not know the other person. A Spirit Teacher gave me a warning on this, speaking through a Medium, saying:

> It is neither bad nor good, it simply is. Let it go by, do not stop it with feelings. It is as much a judgment to say 'isn't that awful' if one were to see someone shot in the street, as to say 'that man is a fool'. The admonition 'Judge not' covers every kind of judgment there is. Fear is not at the bottom of the troubles of the earth—judgment is; without judgment there would be no fear.

This does not mean that we should not have compassion for our brothers and sisters, or that we should not render aid where this is possible; only that we must not take upon ourselves the suffering of a lesson that is meant for another.

However, the cause of a disease, pain or malformation that originated in a previous life may not always require that a lesson has to be learned or a balancing situation experienced. It may simply be from a subconscious memory of some problem or traumatic experience in that life which has not been released. For example, death from starvation, war injury or torture, or a life of extreme poverty or in a handicapped body may leave such a memory.

In analyzing the many cases in which I have regressed people into past lives in order to find the cause of a problem in this life, I have found that they fall into three main categories.

1. Those which are clearly karmic; the individual killed or injured someone in a previous life and is now suffering in this life in a way which seems clearly connected, and is meant to teach the error of the previous action. For example, a woman who killed her husband in a previous life and has lost two husbands by early death in this life.

2. Those where the problem in this life seems to arise out of a subconscious memory of past life events. For example one woman lived alone all of her life in two previous lives and now has a compulsive need to be always with someone in this life. Another felt helpless in three previous lives because of the events in those lives, and now in this life still has a great feeling of helplessness. Another had a great dislike of people in three previous lives and has the same feelings of dislike in this life.

3. Those where problems in relationships with parents, children, spouses or lovers in previous lives were not resolved during those lives. Now in this life they find themselves in a relationship of some kind, sometimes similar and sometimes different, with the same person or persons and the problem has still not been resolved. They may even have subcon-

sciously chosen a terminal illness to avoid a resolution. The majority of the cases have fallen into this category.

Information on how to get in touch with past lives and how to work with what is discovered is included in Chapters 4 and 5.

In this connection it is interesting to note that an individual's experiences of life fall into two main categories, each with an infinitely varying degree of intensity.

(a) Some appear to have a heavy cross to bear; it may be a retarded or severely handicapped child; the death of a child or children; the loss of a dearly loved spouse by death or separation; severe illness, pain or physical handicap in their own body, or constant poverty or deprivation of material needs.

(b) Others have healthy bodies, happy marriages, healthy and intelligent children, and all their material needs are supplied with only a reasonable amount of work on their part.

The manner in which each type of experience is handled is also two-fold. Of those with a heavy cross to bear: Some accept it patiently and without complaint, doing their best to overcome it quietly and to live a productive and helpful life in spite of their difficulties and suffering. Others complain bitterly, are unnecessarily burdensome to their friends and relatives, make no effort to assist others to the extent that they are able to do so, and are in general a miserable and depressing influence for those around them.

Of those who appear to have all of life's blessings: Some are deeply grateful for their good fortune, and seek to share it with those who are less fortunate. They use their healthy bodies to assist the sick and handicapped; they share their happy family life with those who are lonely or deprived of such an environment, and they share their material possessions with those who are in need. Others take full advantage of their situation to indulge themselves and to lead a thoroughly selfish and self-centered life, thus abusing the privileges which are theirs.

If we believe in reincarnation, it is easy to understand why some people have heavy burdens and some seem so blessed. Surely it depends on how they handled the circumstances in which they found themselves in their previous lives. Let us take a hypothetical example of three lives for one soul. In the first of these lives this person was cruel to others thus creating a Karmic debt or future lesson to be learned. As a result, in a later life he experienced much suffering himself. If he carried this heavy cross with cheerfulness and fortitude he may have succeeded in learning the lesson and paying off the Karma. Then in a subsequent life he will experience the harmony and well-being that has always been the will of our Creator for all of His children.

On the other hand, if in the first life this soul had led a life of concern and kindness for others he would probably be richly blessed in later life. However, if in that life he led an essentially selfish existence, using these blessings solely for his own pleasure, it would become necessary for him to be deprived of some or all of these advantages in a subsequent life. In this way he will learn to be grateful for them and to share them with his brothers and sisters in the one family of God.

Many schools of psychology recognize three major, very powerful, instinctual drives or forces in all human beings:

1. The drive for sexual expression. Sigmund Freud maintained that when this is repressed or distorted it becomes the cause of all neuroses and psychoses; by his interpretation he found symbols to prove his theory in *every* patient's dreams.

2. The drive for power to control others and one's environment. Alfred Adler considered this to be the reason for all mental illness and all evil in the world.

3. The need to survive. Men are driven to heights of heroism and feats of endurance and strength, and also to depths of depravity, by this basic instinct. Out of this comes the desire for power, because of the belief that the more power we have the more likely we are to survive.

While Carl Jung and other noted psychologists have maintained that there are many other important influences in people's lives, the drives for sexual expression, power and survival still remain dominant for most people. In fact these three forces are all based in *power* which may therefore be considered to be the primary force.

Closely allied with this is an observation that I have made which is that the two most common negative Karmas, or lessons to learn, that individuals seem to have brought forward from their previous lives seem to be:

(a) How to handle their sexual drive in a balanced and reasonable manner, without harm to others or themselves and yet without artificial repression, and

(b) How to use their innate drive for control as a means for controlling themselves and not for controlling others.

It also seems to be true that these same two areas are often ones in which people are creating negative Karma for themselves in this lifetime which will have to be corrected or offset later in this life or in a future one. Taking this one step further, the above analysis of the root cause behind the diseases or illnesses of those who come for Spiritual Healing shows that these two forces are very frequently involved, with the sick person being either the aggressor or the recipient in each case.

Possession

Another possible cause which is being given more credence by some psychologists, therapists and spiritual healers is that of possession or attachment by a discarnate entity; that is, a soul that no longer has a physical body but remains on the earth plane and enters into, or attaches itself, to someone who is still in a physical body and makes them ill as a result. This is not necessarily a demonic entity that must be exorcised, although this does happen.

The most common origins of non-demonic possession or attachment (which may be accidental or intentional) are:

1. Where the spirit entity enters out of love for the other individual.
2. Where the spirit entity is lost on the astral plane and does not know how to move on into the Light. They often do not realize they are dead or know where they are, and they find a comfortable home by entering someone else's physical body. Strong feelings of anger, hate, fear, guilt or even love at the time of death can interfere with a normal transition into the Light.
3. Where the spirit entity has a craving for some physical sensation such as tobacco, alcohol, drugs or sex, which they were addicted to when they had a physical body. By entering the other person they can experience the desired sensation vicariously through the sensory apparatus of that person's body.

The opening by which the entity enters the individual may be created by repressed negative feelings, severe stress or shock, drugs, alcohol, loss of consciousness or even sleep, especially if accompanied by a nightmare. This is another reminder that we all need to protect ourselves with white light and God consciousness.

Chapter 4 describes some of the ways by which this type of cause can be recognized.

A Lesson to Be Learned

There is one other more subtle cause of disease which may be involved in some cases. At a deep level our Higher Self knows what lessons we need to learn for the growth of our soul and our spiritual evolvement. It is conceivable therefore that in some situations we unconsciously choose a specific disease or injury because we know that it will bring us the opportunity and conditions in which to learn that lesson. Deep down we know that if life continued at a placid level with no challenges or difficulties we would stagnate and fail to grow. However, there is an inner drive in all of us to evolve, and sooner or later it will gain the upper hand and motivate us to choose some path that will move us forward. It does not necessarily have to be a disease or injury, there are other less critical ways, but most of us seem to choose the former or some other traumatic crisis. Consciously at the time we will strongly deny that we could choose pain, suffering and inconvenience to learn a lesson, but after it is all over, if we are honest with ourselves, we will realize that we have learned a valuable lesson, or maybe several lessons, from the experience.

Mental Illness

Mental illness can be caused by any of the factors discussed in this chapter, however there are other possibilities.

One interesting theory is that mental illness, including schizophrenia, is frequently only the initial sign of developing mediumship or psychic abilities. The possibility that these people are becoming psychic is validated to a degree by the fact that clairvoyants report that the aura of a schizophrenic person is very similar to that of a psychic. It has also been observed that schizophrenics often have greater extrasensory perception than the average. The 'voices' they hear and the 'people' they see may be from the Spirit World, but are incomprehensible to them, and therefore inexplicable to others. In the Western world these signs are presumed to indicate mental illness and the subject is usually treated with electric shock, insulin or tranquilizers and other drugs which effectively block these natural phenomena, and destroy whatever it is that makes these psychic abilities possible.

Others believe that much mental illness is caused by invasion of the subject's psyche by a low level spirit entity which literally takes over control of the person's body and mind. Exorcism of the spirit entity and infusion of healing power through Spiritual Healing would seem to be the most appropriate remedy in these cases.

There is also the possibility that in some cases mental illness may be a form of natural healing in process. For example an individual may retreat from the outside world because he finds it too difficult. The self imposed isolation increases his fear and his sense of disorder multiplies. Orthodox medicine then applies heavy doses of medication. A psychiatrist who has done much work with psychotics found that when medication is avoided, nature's own healing process is allowed to operate. Patiently working with the images that came from the subjects' psychic depths provided the psychiatrist with the means for helping them through their difficulties. (See *Roots of Renewal in Myth and Madness* by John Weir Perry[6].)

In other cases, merely being placed in a mental institution, where the individual escapes from the emotions and demands of "normal living", is sufficient. In this less stressful and undemanding situation he enables his body, emotions, mind and spirit to become healed.

All healers seem to agree that mental illness is usually much slower, or less likely to respond to Spiritual Healing than is physical illness. This is also my own experience, although healings of mental illness have occurred. One day when I was thinking about this, I asked for guidance and received the following message from my Spirit Guides:

Mental Cases are very hard to deal with because the mind creates the body and the reality that the soul experiences. "As a man thinks in his heart, so is he." So, until the person is willing to change his thinking from that which has made him mentally ill, he cannot get better. In other words the tool to be used for recovery is itself out of order or in disrepair.

However, never doubt that Spiritual Healing can reach the mind also, at both subconscious and conscious levels, and your mind can be the channel. You need to hold to the thought of perfection of their mind and yours, and of perfect communication between the two. Visualize an open circuit between two centers of power, with your end connected to the Universal Power. As the Power flows through you to the other person it will provide nutrition, light, energy and balance to the other person's mind, and connect that person to the Divine Mind which is already within him, but buried under a load of negativity, past experience and mental input, hopelessness and fear. Teach them to release these and to know that the other is underneath. Even though they come to you for help, they seldom believe that their mental difficulties can be healed because they have been conditioned to believe otherwise. You need to get in touch with that inner strength and wisdom and harmony which is there in their Temple, if you will seek it.

We have specialists in this Spirit World who can help in these cases, if you will *ask* them to do so. The color they use is pure white.

In some cases people who are mentally ill by your standards are really more in tune with this plane but do not know how to interpret, or bring through to daily life on the earth plane, that which they see and hear with their inner senses, and so they are confused. In these cases ask them to tell you what they are experiencing in their minds and you may be able to help them understand the significance, and how to apply it to their daily life.

Sometimes the desires and conflicts they have brought with them from previous lives are so strong that they find them to be uncontrollable; to that extent their mental illness is Karmic, but that does not mean to say that it cannot be helped. The Healing Power can help them to see what they need to work on, to change, to transmute, and if they will follow that guidance healing of their mind will occur.

In general, of course, the same rule applies as it does to any physical disease or deformity—just allow the Power to work in accordance with the Divine Plan, and do not get in the way with your own ideas. Surrender and Love are the keys, as always, with no preconceived ideas or expectations as to the timing or the extent of the results. It is the overall picture of the WHOLE in Eternity that is important, and that will take place, not the effect that you see with your time and space bound consciousness.

Phantom Pain

Phantom pain may occur when a part of the body, such as a leg or an arm, has been amputated and the individual continues to feel pain in the limb which is no longer there. This may last for years, sometimes for the rest of their life.

As with all other pain or disease, the problem is unlikely to be resolved unless the cause is discovered and corrected. In the case of phantom pain it has been found that there is usually some mental, emotional or spiritual "unfinished business" connected to the original injury.

For example, if the injury was caused by another individual, either on purpose or accidentally, they need to be completely forgiven and loved unconditionally by the injured person. If other people died in the accident or disaster that caused the injury, their souls need to be prayed for, blessed and surrounded with Light and Love. Sometimes a sincere memorial service with the aid of a minister or priest may be called for.

When an amputation has been necessary because of cancer or other disease, then a search for the cause of the cancer or disease, as previously outlined in this chapter, needs to be undertaken and resolved in ways described in chapter 5.

Notes for Chapter 3

1. Edgar Cayce. See Chapter 1 reference notes.

2. Gerhard Adler. *Studies in Analytical Psychology* p. 49–50 G.P. Putnam's Sons, New York. 1966

3. Edward F. Edinger. *Ego and Archetype.* p. 56–57. G.P. Putnam's Sons, New York. 1972

4. Doug Boyd. *Rolling Thunder.* Random House, New York. 1974

5. This statement by Carl Jung has been quoted many times in many publications, e.g. P.W. Martin. *Experiment in Depth* p. 188. Routledge and Kegan Paul, Carter Lane, London, England. 1955. The date and place of the original statement are not known to the author.

6. John Weir Perry. *Roots of Renewal in Myth and Madness.* Jossey-Bass Publishers, San Francisco, California. 1976

GOD IS LOVE

THEREFORE

WE WERE CREATED BY

AND

ARE SUSTAINED BY

LOVE.

CHAPTER 4

SEEKING THE CAUSE

How can a sick person discover the cause of his disease? If he goes to an orthodox medical practitioner the chances are that the search will be limited to physical causes such as climate; pollution of air, water or food; exposure to diseased persons, bacteria or viruses; or it will be diagnosed as hereditary, or an internal breakdown of the normal function of some part of the body. Thus, as a general rule, the body is considered by itself apart from mind, emotion and spirit.

If the doctor suspects that the illness is psychosomatic he may give his patient a placebo. If he feels that the problem is deeper than that, he may refer him to a psychiatrist or psychologist who will then include the emotions and the mind in the search for the cause. Occasionally the patient may be referred to a priest or minister for spiritual counseling.

Sometimes the crisis created in the patient's life by a need for surgery will cause the patient to work on the emotional, mental or spiritual aspects of his life by himself. This may result in the elimination of the deeper cause with or without the aid of a counselor, psychotherapist or spiritual healer.

Unfortunately many spiritual healers are also satisfied with treating the symptoms, and if these clear up will consider the subject to be healed. All too often the symptoms will reappear in the same or a different form, because the underlying cause is still there. That cause may be physical, emotional, mental or spiritual, and unless it is discovered and worked with, the desired healing will not take place, or if it does it will probably only be temporary.

A good way to introduce this concept is to ask the individual if they can accept the idea that their pain, disease or malfunction is a message from their body that something in their life needs to be changed to bring it into balance or harmony with physical or spiritual laws. A very simple but easily understood example is to say "If you put your hand on a hot stove you will quickly receive a message from your body to remove your hand before it is burned or destroyed."

If the one who has asked for help is willing to accept this idea, and I find that nearly all those who seek the help of Spiritual Healing are open to this concept, then they will probably be motivated to seek the cause on their own or with the help of the healer. They may even come to see that a serious disease such as cancer, can be a positive force for good rather than a negative force for evil, if an honest effort is made to discover the cause and to work on eliminating it, and this results in the transformation that the individual needs for his soul growth.

One of the difficulties (or *side effects,* as the medical profession calls them) of the use of pain killer drugs is that they mask or conceal the symptoms that our body has given us as a warning that we need to change something in our life. The result may be a stronger message in the form of a more violent or dynamic symptom or serious disease that the drug is unable to conceal. If the body's warning continues to be ignored the new symptoms may be supressed by a more powerful drug. Eventually there is a point beyond which drugs will not work, because the body is more powerful than the drug and the body insists on giving its message, even to the point of terminating life in that particular body. The same holds true if a healer "releases" pain from the body before the cause of the pain has been uncovered.

I find that people seeking help often already *know* what the cause is, see the connection and are eager to be shown how they can eliminate it. If they are not aware of the cause, there are a number of ways, or clues, by which the cause can be identified as follows:

Timing Can Be Important

One of the first clues to look for is to ask what happened in their life that was new, different or traumatic shortly before, or possibly as long as two years before, the onset of the disease. Maybe there was a big increase in stress, or someone did something which caused deep resentment, or the individual harmed another and created guilt feelings in himself, or there was some other event which gave rise to one of the causes already outlined.

Location of the Disease May Help

The location of the disease in the body may give an important clue as to its cause. For example:

Heart disease may result from an inability to receive and/or to give love. Thyroid or throat trouble may point to stifled creative abilities, or repressed communication with others.

A brain tumor may reveal that the brain has been used in a way that is contrary to the life plan for that individual.

If the hands are crippled with arthritis, the owner might consider whether or not his hands have been used in accord with the spiritual laws of the universe. Arthritis of the jaw may indicate an overly aggressive nature.

Hearing difficulties or eye trouble may hint that there is something that person does not want to hear or to look at. This could be physically or mentally.

One woman told me that her immune system was very weak and that she caught everything that was going around; her body was also irritated by many things in her environment which created asthma and allergies. I asked her if people irritated her also. "Oh yes," she said, "I know what they should do or be, and when they do not comply I get irritated". Saying this she immediately saw the connection and agreed to try very hard to take full responsibility for her own life, and not to judge or interfere with anyone else's—to let them make their own choices and to exercise their own free will. It was quite a struggle for her to change a life long pattern, but she tried hard and her health showed definite signs of improvement. Unfortunately she moved away before I was able to know the final result.

The connection may be even more subtle than this, and only discovered unexpectedly during the course of a healing session, as happened in the case of Sally. This lady came to me with the complaint that her right arm had been very painful for over a year and that her doctor had been unable to correct it. During the first visit she confided that she had been in and out of therapy for sixteen years, mainly because she had been too aggressive and insensitive, over-developing her masculine side, but now she felt confused and undecided about the direction her life should take. As we talked it became apparent that she needed to balance the feminine and masculine sides of her personality, as she had now swung too far to the feminine, passive, receptive side.

Two weeks later Sally returned and said she felt much more balanced and had a better sense of direction, and was able to make important decisions for her life; however, her arm still hurt. This time during the healing I placed my hands directly on her arm, and almost immediately she started to cry and sob with considerable emotion, none of which had occurred during the first visit. Afterwards she shared that when I touched her arm it brought back strong memories of her father whom she had loved greatly. She grew up on a farm and often helped him with the farm chores. "In fact," she said, "I saw myself as his right hand man." As she said this we both recognized the significance of the phrase in connection with the pain being in her right arm, and her previous tendency to be too masculine.

When he died seventeen years ago, she now told me, she had never permitted herself to feel or express any grief for him, as she felt this would have been contrary to the masculine side of her personality which was in control at that time. Thus she had never really accepted his death, and the fact that she was no longer his "right arm"; a year ago the grief had finally manifested in her physical right arm.

We were both convinced that we had found the key to healing the pain in her arm, and with the understanding of the connection to her father, and the expression of her grief during the healing session, we expected the pain to rapidly disappear. However, when she returned two and a half weeks later the arm still hurt, so it was apparent that there was still some block to her healing. We continued the search and found that she was harboring a lot of resentment towards three different people:

(a) Her psychologist whom she felt had charged her too much and then had left town before the therapy was complete.

(b) A doctor who had operated on her in what she felt was a most unsatisfactory manner, and

(c) Her ex-husband whose behavior had been devious and manipulative.

These resentments might also be connected with pain in the right arm. Sigmund Freud found that often when a person is angry they want to hit someone else, but as this would be unacceptable behavior, they restrain the arm in some way such as by pain or paralysis.

The hostility towards her former psychologist and the surgeon was handled by her forgiving them during the healing process. That towards her ex-husband needed a little more understanding. When I reminded her that she had told me that they had really reversed normal roles in their marriage, she acting out the masculine aggressive part, and he being passive and receptive, she could see that his devious behavior had been the only way he could operate under the circumstances. I pointed out that in the past, women have always had to be more or less devious and manipulative in order to survive, because men have controlled the purse strings and had the superior physical strength. She immediately saw the truth in this and was able to forgive him too.

These resentments were apparently the remaining obstructions to healing, because within a week the pain was gone and it was not necessary for Sally to return for any more healing sessions. There is no way of knowing for certain if the unexpressed grief or the repressed anger, or both of them, were the basic cause of the pain in the arm. I feel sure that both were involved in blocking the healing and that if the anger had been discovered and dealt with first there would have been no healing until the grief had been exposed and expressed. However, the latter was apparently closest to the surface, as this is what was triggered when I touched her arm.

This case not only illustrates how the location of a pain or disease can help to uncover its cause, but it also is a good example of the complexity of cause—it is seldom just one thing. Sometimes the one asking for help is convinced that they know the reason for their problem, but they are really aware of only part of it; there is much more below the surface.

Sometimes it is difficult to discover where someone is blocking the healing. After one particular person had visited me several times, uncovering and releasing much emotional material, but failing to receive the desired healing, my Guide directed me into an interesting technique. The sick person and I both felt that it was necessary to open up the heart chakra (the energy center in the middle of the chest) in order to allow more of the unconditional love-energy to move in and out. So after the overall general healing process (described elsewhere) while she was still lying down on the table, face up and eyes closed, I held my right hand a few inches above her root or first chakra (located at the very base of the spine) and asked her to feel her own energy in her body at that point.

After two or three minutes of this I placed my other hand above her heart chakra, informing her that I was doing so. I asked her to visualize moving the energy up from the root to the heart and told her that I would visualize the energy moving from my right hand to my left hand, thus assisting her in this transfer. After another two or three minutes I placed my right hand above her second chakra and repeated the process, continuing on with each step for each chakra, always directing the energies to the heart chakra.

In this particular case, the entirely unexpected result was that when my hand was above her sixth chakra (slightly above and between the eyes) she burst into tears and finally said, "I feel absolutely defenseless when I move the energy away from that point." I explained that in our relationship with God we need to be defenseless; we need to surrender everything to Him if we are asking for Spiritual Healing and guidance. This does not mean becoming vulnerable to other people, only to the Source of our being. Understanding this, she tried hard to allow the energy to move down from the sixth to the fourth chakra, but it was not easy and the process had to be repeated.

Afterwards she explained that she now realized that she had hidden herself behind her knowledge of psychology and esoteric learning, using this as a defense against becoming aware of her own inner needs. The result was disease in her body.

Does the Disease Bring Any Benefits?

Another way to establish cause is by asking the one seeking help to consider carefully what benefits he is gaining from the disease. At first he will probably say that there are none, and may even be insensed at the suggestion, but if he is honest with himself and the healer, and there is some positive value for him in the disease, he may admit that he is getting more attention, or avoiding a situation that he does not like, or postponing a move that he does not want to make.

Brugh Joy, who is a highly skilled physician and healer with a deep understanding of psychology and of the connection between mind and body, made the following comment after reading the above statement:

> There is *almost* always a secondary gain from disease. This is not a minor point, but is truly a major aspect of disease.

Review Possible Causes

Another approach is to make a fairly systematic review of the various possible causes outlined in Chapter 3. For example the healer might ask "Do you hate anyone, or bear any resentment or hostility towards anyone?" If the answer is a clear and sincere "No" it will probably be in order to proceed to ask about other negative emotions. If there is some hesitation or uncertainty in the reply, I find it is helpful to ask about specific relationships in this connection.

For example: "How do you feel about your father?", then in turn, mother, brother, sister, spouse, former spouse, children and so on. This will often trigger a response acknowledging anger or resentment towards one of these. If inquiry about negative emotions fails to produce a clue as to the cause, the discussion can move on to excessive stress, guilt feelings, negative thinking and conflict with life plan. This may sound like a very lengthy process, but in actual practice answers or chance remarks given during the discussion on negative emotions may lead directly to one of the other causes and thus shorten the time involved.

Sometimes during the dialogue the sick person will notice that the pain increases, or it suddenly returns even though it had been eliminated during a previous healing session. This nearly always seems to indicate that the discussion at that moment had zeroed in on the cause, or at least an aspect of

it. This is an extremely valuable clue, and further exploration can be made as to the situation or facts surrounding
the point being discussed at that time.

If this line of enquiry does not produce results then the
healer can offer to help in the search by using one or more
of the other methods that follow.

Sick Person Asks Their Higher Self

In my own experience I have found that one of the best
ways to help the other to discover the cause is to ask them to
ask their Higher Self (or the God within them, if they prefer)
to show them what they need to know for their own guidance and healing.

During the preliminary discussion I explain that I am going to ask them to do this after the healing process has started,
when they will be in a really relaxed and receptive mood.
Then about two-thirds of the way through the "laying-on-of-
hands" channeling of love-energy (when my hands are over
their heart chakra) I quietly remind them to ask this question
silently and to be open to whatever may come. The answer
may be received in the form of a vision, symbols, spoken
words, inspirational thoughts or in some other way. Also it
may come then, later that day, in a dream that night or any
time subsequently. I explain that they will not have to reveal
to me the guidance they receive, but if they wish to talk about
it afterwards they are free to do so.

The wonderful thing is that in the majority of cases they
receive some sort of guidance as to what they need to do. It
is, of course, then up to them whether or not they follow that
direction. If they do, the healing they seek will probably be
accomplished, or at least started, in which case further
guidance will frequently follow at a later session. Often the
answer they receive is directing them to the cause of the
disease, rather than merely to a cure for the symptoms; discovering the cause is so important if a reoccurrence of the
disease is to be avoided.

Then, too, because this advice comes from within the person himself, he can take full responsibility for his own recovery, and know that the power is within him, and he need not be dependent on someone else. This does far more for his own growth and development than believing that he must be helped by, or follow the advice of, another. He is also far more likely to obey the instructions of his own inner voice than he would those given to him by the healer or someone else.

Correspondingly, it relieves the healer of the responsibility which is not really his to take, but which it is so easy to assume either because of unconscious egotistical or power drives, or simply out of a sincere desire to be helpful.

Simultaneously with instructing the other person to ask their Higher Self for guidance, I silently pray that the Holy Spirit will speak to them through their Higher Self, and will speak to me through my own Higher Self and tell me if there is anything further I should do or say that would be helpful and in accord with God's will. Quite often I will receive guidance in this way, and will share it at the appropriate time.

Alternatively one can attempt to tune in to the other person's Higher Self and receive information in that way. If this method is used, breathing synchronistically with the other will help to make the connection.

The answers that those asking the question receive are seldom, if ever, alike. A few examples may be of interest.

Alice had been in a state of depression for over twenty years; she had been to many doctors and tried many kinds of therapy, including two years of analysis with a psychiatrist, but all to no avail. Spiritual Healing helped temporarily, sometimes quite dramatically, but the fears and insecurity quickly came back. As the healing sessions continued, her Higher Self made it clear to her that the original cause lay with her mother who was a very controlling individual, full of her own fears and lack of self worth. The mother seemed to be determined to keep Alice in a state of dependency by being angry, by alternately giving and withholding love, and by implanting fears and thoughts of Alice's incompetency. Alice also began to realize that the mother's neurosis originated in her own mother's similar character. This grandmother was still alive, and doing her part to add to Alice's insecurity and depression.

On the other hand it also became apparent that Alice, who was forty years old, was still terribly dependent emotionally, but not financially, upon her mother and grandmother. She constantly asked them for moral support in spite of the fact that they nearly always gave her just the opposite. This caused Alice many a relapse into deep depression and anxiety just as she was beginning to surface above it. When she understood the connection she moved many miles away, established a new life for herself, discontinued asking for approval of her actions, and became much improved.

In another case a very overweight lady, who was frightened because she could barely breathe as a result of emphysema and asthma, found that after the healing session she could breathe freely and was much less frightened. The guidance that she received from her Higher Self was that she must lose at least forty pounds. I could have told her that from normal observation and common sense; however, if I had done so she would have either resented it, or agreed with me and then done nothing about it. But, because the advice came from within her own being, she determined to do something about her weight.

A very psychic young woman who had suffered from arthritic pains since she was twelve years old, when she had been in bed for one year with rheumatoid arthritis, received guidance which surprised her, but which she felt made a lot of sense. She was told that the reason for that illness was to force her parents to delay the adoption of a baby boy for a year and thus receive a different child than would otherwise have been the case. Although the difference in ages between this young woman and the boy that was eventually adopted was such that she became more of a second mother to him than a sister, the boy was an old soul with a very strong connection to her in a previous life. Once this explanation had been received and accepted, the arthritic pains disappeared within a few days.

In answer to the question to her Higher Self, another woman, who had been fighting a serious illness for a long time, received a very interesting series of visions. In the past she had rejected all religion and had been an atheist for many years. Before coming to me others had enabled her to see that she needed a spiritual awakening. This had been happening slowly, with considerable reluctance on her part. After several healing sessions she experienced the following visions on consecutive visits when I asked her to ask silently for guidance.

1. She saw Jesus. This she rejected and the picture was replaced by a fish, which was the early Christian symbol for Christ. We interpreted this as saying to her that it was O.K. to reject Jesus, the man, if she insisted, but she needed to accept the Christ within her.

2. She saw a white dove with a red rose in its beak, which we interpreted as a symbol of the Holy Spirit.

3. She saw the Buddha, which she also rejected, this was followed by many other religious images or symbols.

4. Nothing special this time.

5. She heard a voice saying; "You must fully experience the fact that it is I, Jesus, who is healing you."

About four weeks later she telephoned to say that she felt under a great deal of pressure in regards to her spiritual life and therefore wished to discontinue the healing sessions. Apparently she was not yet ready to accept the guidance she was receiving from her own inner being or Higher Self.

The guidance another person received was a vision of a rock being rolled away from a cave, with a white light streaming out of the cave, and she heard the words "Be not afraid, I am with you always." During the next healing session I suggested that she recreate the image of the open cave and then ask whatever was in the cave to come out. This took some courage on her part, but when she did this she saw a giant angel come out, followed by a normal sized human figure—both were full of light. I then suggested that she enter the cave and ask the human sized guide to go with her. She did this with some trepidation and found it was filled with white cloud-like stuff and nothing else. This experience put her in touch with three spirit guides who have helped her ever since. It also enabled her to face subsequent, possibly unpleasant situations by moving into them without fear.

One man who came because of severe depression and a loss of Spiritual beliefs, was shown the parable of the Prodigal Son and many Spirits welcoming him back. From this he experienced a real Spiritual renewal and a lifting of his depression. Other examples from the wide variety of messages received are:

"Don't pretend to be strong in the areas where you know you are weak; let others help you."
"Don't be so hard on yourself."
"Let the tears come."
"Play the piano even if there is no audience."
"Go through the third door"—accompanied by a vision of three doors—two open and the third one closed."
"Watch your diet." (A frequent message)
"Resolve the conflict with your mother." (also frequent)
"Relax."
"Meditate."
"Express gratitude for all your blessings."
"Trust—let go."
"Cut the ties to both of your parents." (A 32 year old)
"You are attractive and intelligent. It is not too late to change."
"Listen to your body."
"Love."
"Go forth and shine your beauty."
"Slow down." (Repeated twelve times)
"Confront the fear."

Influence of Past Lives

If the individual was born with a disease or malfunction (e.g. cerebral palsy) or medically speaking the problem is hereditary, then it is clear that it has not been caused by the person's own emotions, thoughts or stressful activities in this lifetime. Therefore it is necessary to explore the possibility of the cause having originated in a previous life or lives. This can be attempted, usually successfully, even if the individual does not believe in reincarnation but is willing to be open to such an exploration.

There are two ways I have used for this purpose. The first is to simply ask the individual during the healing to ask their Higher Self to reveal to them any past life which will help them understand the original cause of their problem. For example, one 40 year old woman had a severe pain in her right arm which neither a doctor, acupuncturist nor spiritual healer had been able to cure. She received a vision of herself being attacked by a soldier who mangled her right arm with his sword. At first she was very angry at the soldier in the vision but then decided to forgive him and the pain left and did not return. Research has shown that the reason the pain did not occur in this life until the woman was 40 years old is probably because that was the age at which the injury occurred in her previous life.

The second way of discovering any past life that is the cause of this life's problem, is to use a past life regression technique to lead the individual into seeing and experiencing the appropriate life. It is not necessary to hypnotize them, although some therapists prefer to do so, but a guided meditation will usually be sufficient. (See the Bibliography for books and tapes on this subject.) I have found that about five out of six people are able to visualize past lives successfully in this manner. The ones who cannot do so either block the process out of fear or because they really do not want to find out the answer. Also it may not be right for their soul growth to have the information at this time and the spirit forces prevent the flow.

Sometimes people will experience a past life which does not seem to have any connection with their problem in this life, although we have specifically asked for a life that does help. One reason for this is that the life shown to them is fairly uneventful and with no special meaning, in order to calm their fears of exploring their past. On the next visit, when regression is tried again, the life revealed to them is very traumatic and disastrous and would have frightened them into stopping the "movie" before it was complete if they had been shown it the first time. But having experienced the first one without fear, they can now handle the more dramatic one.

Another explanation is that the person blocks looking at the important life because they really do not want to look at it. Maybe they are intuitively ashamed of it, but they have no objection to allowing "harmless" ones to come through.

Because of these built-in defenses it seems most unlikely that any harm can come from exploring past lives provided that the counselor brings them out of the altered state of consciousness and helps them to work with their experience. Then too, the individual (unless deeply hypnotized) is always conscious of where they are and what they are doing, and can stop the process at any time that they feel it is more than they wish to handle. Once the individual is guided by an imaginary journey to a point where they see some stage or event in the past life, no suggestions are made, only questions are asked such as "What are you wearing?" or "What can you see?" or "What are you doing?". When nothing further of value seems to be transpiring at that stage in that life, they are instructed on the count of three to move on to the next important stage in that life, then again questions are asked. In other words even if I psychically pick up some impression of a past life I never pass that on as a suggestion or possibility. Everything must come from them. When the vision of that life is ended, they are instructed to move on into the space all go to in between lives. Once there they are given the option of looking at another past life to add further understanding to their problem if they wish. When the reviewing is complete they are gradually brought back to a normal state of consciousness, whole and complete.

Possession or Attachment

Some of the signs which *may* indicate possession or attachment are:

1. The individual has taken on the characteristics of a deceased person, especially if it occurred shortly after the death.

2. There is a sudden change in personality. For example, if they started taking alcohol or drugs whereas previously they had no interest in these, especially if this occurs after a period of unconsciousness as in anesthesia (which usually is administered in a hospital where there are many recently departed souls), an accidental blow on the head or a drug overdose.

3. The individual has unexplained headaches or pains. However, these could also be sub-conscious memories of past life injuries or death.

4. A sudden onset of a phobia which has never caused difficulties before.

5. An individual has multiple personalities. Possession is not the only cause of such an aberration.

6. Constant fatigue or lapse of memory for which there is no medical explanation.

7. An urge to commit suicide.

8. Simply a feeling by the individual that they are not in sole possession or control of their body.

The possessing entity can cause the individual to take on the disease from which the entity had died, and/or the pain which it had experienced. There are many other ways in which the entity can drastically complicate the mental, emotional or physical life of the individual, including taking on the habits to which the entity was addicted during its previous incarnation.

Meeting a Spirit Guide

Sometimes the one who is seeking help will find it easier to receive some inner guidance if he is led by the healer on an imaginary journey to meet his Spirit Guide, who can then be asked to help. Either at the end of the healing session when the one in need is completely relaxed, or on a separate occasion after some preliminary relaxation process, the healer can quietly ask the other person to imagine himself going for a walk alone in the country, by the sea or in the mountains. For example:

"Imagine yourself walking across a field—it is very quiet —the sun is shining but it is not too hot—you see some beautiful wild flowers in amongst the soft green grass (longer pause). As you continue you become aware of the gentle murmur of the sea in the distance—it increases slightly as you approach the edge of a cliff (longer pause). Now you are at the top of the cliff and can see the ocean below you—it is a beautiful blue-green with white crests on the waves as they roll up the beach—Slowly you wind your way down the zig-zag path in the side of the cliff—when you reach the bottom kick off your shoes and feel the soft warm sand between your toes. (longer pause) There is no one else on the beach—you are all alone—as you walk towards the edge of the water you notice a small sand bank near the water. This is just the right height to make a comfortable back rest—sit down—lean back and rest and relax in peace. (longer pause).

Now, as you look out to sea you become aware of a small sailing boat coming towards you. (longer pause) As it gets closer you notice there is a figure in the boat; at first you cannot tell if it is a man or a woman—but as the boat gets closer you can see which it is and gradually you become aware of the person's build and the clothes they are wearing. (longer pause). Notice the color of the hair and the expression on the face. (longer pause). Now the boat has drifted onto the sand and the occupant is getting out and walking towards you—stand up and move forward to greet this person—this is your guide. Ask your guide to tell you the cause of your disease, and then tell you what you need to know for your healing."

At this point the healer should remain silent for five or ten minutes, allowing the other to continue a silent dialogue with his guide. Then quietly suggest that he say goodbye and permit the guide to leave, if the guide has not already done so, and then retrace his steps up the cliff and across the field. If a dialogue was accomplished, suggest that he write it down before any further discussion with the healer takes place. Just as we can lose the details of a dream, if it is not recorded promptly, so it is easy to forget much of what took place that could be invaluable later on.

No one, in my experience, has met anything but a friendly guide using this process, even if at first they were frightened at seeing someone. Usually the dialogue with a guide is meaningful and helpful. As an example, I would like to share my own experience which occurred during a conference of 500 people, not during a healing session. The lecturer led us in active imagination through a forest and meadow to a small lake; she then asked us to look into the clear water for a few moments and then look up and see who was on the other side, then we were to share with that other person our deepest wish.

Looking down into the water I saw many small people; all were laughing, happy, embracing each other and moving around; all was joyous. I looked up and to my surprise saw Jesus with his arms outstretched to all the people and to me; blessing, loving, forgiving and healing. I then expressed to him my deepest wish which was to be used as a channel for healing. Jesus said "Look into the lake again". I did so and saw people who were sad, unhappy, sick and crippled; they were left beside the way, unable to progress; obviously the need for healing was great.

I looked up again and saw Jesus with hands outstretched directly to me; light rays of energy were coming towards me from his hands; I actually felt the energy coursing through my body like an electrical charge. My heart filled with gratitude as I realized that Jesus was promising to fulfill that wish, although he did not speak any more words. The promise was implemented ten months later when people started to come to me and ask for help, and many healings occurred.

Listening to the Inner Teacher

We all have an Inner Teacher, Guide or Voice and it is not always necessary to be led on a visual meditation in this way if one wants to meet or receive advice from this source. Sometimes all that we need to do is to sit quietly and meditate on the problem for a short time, silently asking to be shown the cause, and then listening for our Guide to answer.

Dreams

Dreams often tell the sick what the cause of their disease is, but they ignore or forget them, or do not know how to interpret them. In cases where the cause is not quickly discovered by one of the foregoing methods, I encourage the person to keep a Dream Journal, and to share with me any dreams that he does not understand. Sometimes the cause, and even the cure will be discovered in this way. Chapter 10 contains some guidelines on how to interpret dreams, and further information on this subject.

If the one in need is able to remember his dreams, but no dream seems to reveal the cause, you can suggest that just before going to sleep he *asks* for a dream to show him what created the disease. This is, of course, not an original idea, or even a modern one; you will recall that in reviewing the history of Spiritual Healing we noted that three thousand years ago in the Greek Temples of healing the patient was instructed to ask for a dream to show him the cause and the cure of his disease, and the priest helped him to interpret it the next day.

Drawing a Picture

Another technique that is sometimes helpful in understanding the cause of a disease, is to ask the one who is sick to draw or paint anything that flows from his pencil or brush —not a reproduction of something that he is looking at or has seen in the past, but a real free flow without logical thought, so that his innermost feelings or drives may be expressed. Alternatively, especially if the sick person is a child, ask them to draw or paint their feelings, the pain or the disease itself. When this has been accomplished the

healer and/or the creator can contemplate the picture med-
itatively, not with the idea of analyzing it as a psychologist
might, but so as to let the creator's intuition work on it, and
maybe to reveal to him some clues as to the cause.

A Psychic Reading

In really difficult cases where none of these methods seem
to work (maybe because the ill person is resisting the search),
the healer can suggest that they request a psychic reading
from a reputable Psychic, with the specific objective of trying to discover the cause, however, they can silently block
that too, if they wish.

Hypnotism

As a last resort, the sick person can request the help of a
reliable and trustworthy licensed Hypnotist who may help
them to find answers to specific questions while they are
hypnotized.

Prayer

During the healing process the healer can pray that the
person seeking help will be shown the cause and be given
the strength to make the necessary changes in their life.
Also the healer can counsel the one in need to pray for guidance as to the cause, explaining that this is better than
simply praying to be healed. Continually praying about the
disease or its symptoms simply tends to reinforce their existence in the person's conscious and subconscious mind,
whereas asking to be shown the cause, and remaining open
for the answer, creates no such negative impressions. Once
the cause has been discovered, the sick person can pray for
the strength and the will to transform it.

After Discovering the Apparent Cause

Once the cause has been discovered, the sick person still has a choice as to whether he does anything to correct it or not. Ultimately, therefore, he is choosing whether to stay sick or to get well; he may even choose to die. As pointed out in Chapter 6, there are many reasons why some people do not respond to Spiritual Healing and nearly all of these reasons involve the choice of the sick person.

An interesting observation that I have made is that until the true cause is discovered and dealt with by the sick person, they sometimes do not sense anything happening in their body during the healing process. Nor do they feel any warmth, pressure or tingling resulting from the energy being channelled to them through the healer's hands.

However, when the real cause has been pinpointed and the individual has at least started to make the necessary changes in his thoughts, attitudes or beliefs, then they will frequently feel the effects of the power being channelled to them. This is a further valuable clue that the cause being dealt with is the right one. This is not always the case, as many people feel the effects of the love-energy from the very first, and others never feel it even though they are healed; but it happens often enough to be worth noting.

Discovering Reasons for Living

I have found that most of the techniques for discovering the cause of an illness can also be used for helping the sick person to become aware of their life goals, or their reasons for living. This is very important, especially for those who have been told that their disease is terminal or incurable. For healing to be successful, the sick person must, consciously and un-consciously, want to be healed and want to live; without goals and purpose this is seldom the case.

Thus, for example, where there seems to be an absence of this motivation I will ask the one in need, near the end of the healing session, silently to ask their Higher Self, or the Holy Spirit, to reveal to them the will of God for their life—how can they be of service in this world? At the same time, or during my own quiet time when I am alone, I ask my Higher Self, or the Holy Spirit, to inform me of anything that would be of help to the other person in this regard.

On several occasions new goals have been discovered, or a new purpose in living has been realized; this often appears to be the turning point in their recovery.

Terminal Cases

Is it worth troubling a dying person to discover the cause of their fatal disease? I believe that unless they are so weak or semi-conscious that the effort would cause them greater discomfort, an offer to help in such exploration should be made for two reasons:

1. With God all things are possible, so regardless of the circumstances, appearances and medical diagnosis, a recovery by means of Spiritual Healing is always a possibility, and the chances are increased if the cause is discovered.

2. Understanding the cause may make it possible for some correction to be made by the sick person, allowing them to die with peace of mind. For example, if the cause is hatred or resentment towards some individual, an opportunity to love and forgive instead can be offered. If the problem is one of guilt the sick one can ask forgiveness, either directly from the injured party or in silence with visualization of that person, and then to ask forgiveness of God. (See the next Chapter.)

THE KEY

TO SPIRITUAL HEALING

IS

UNCONDITIONAL LOVE

CHAPTER 5

ELIMINATING THE CAUSE

HAVING DISCOVERED THE cause, it is necessary to do something about it. The sick person had a choice as to whether he wanted to find the cause, and he was willing to co-operate in the search; now he has a choice as to whether or not he is willing to make the necessary changes in his life. Often the action that needs to be taken will be obvious to him once he is aware of the cause, but in other cases it may not be clear to him. One thing is certain—the cause arose from within him and the potential for cure is there also. So let us review the causes and how they can be overcome.

Negative Emotions

If the cause of the disease appears to be hatred, anger or resentment towards another individual, the first step is for the sick person to forgive the other person for whatever they did or did not do, which resulted in the negative emotion. Forgiveness is an essential part of the healing process and is a lesson that most of us have to learn in this life to one degree or another.

The need to forgive is a spiritual law. When Peter asked Jesus "How many times should I forgive my brother if he keeps offending me, seven times?", Jesus said, "No, seventy times seven" which is in effect saying "Just as many times as he offends you." (Matthew 18:22) Jesus gave us the supreme example (he always practiced what he preached) when he said "Father, forgive them for they know not what they do" at the very moment he was suffering the agony of the nails being driven into his hands and feet. (Luke 23:34)

When the forgiveness is complete, and the incident, to all intents and purposes, is forgotten it becomes possible to transmute the energy of the negative emotion into positive energy and to radiate unconditional love to the one who caused offense and thus complete the healing.

To implement the willingness to forgive I wait until near the end of the healing process by which time the individual is very relaxed and their energy field has expanded. With my hands over their heart chakra I ask them to visualize the person with whom they feel anger standing in front of them. I ask them to tell me when they have done this. (If they find visualization impossible I ask them just to imagine, feel or sense the presence of the other person.) I then ask them to tell the other person silently, and as sincerely as they can, that they forgive them for everything that they did, or did not do, or said, that made them feel angry or resentful. They are then asked to listen to what the other has to say and this may create a new understanding.

I then pause for a few moments so they can do this, and I then ask them to radiate unconditional love to the other person, visualizing it, if they wish, as a purple light going from their heart center to the other's heart center. I then ask them to forgive themselves, which is equally important. In fact some people have told me that they could not forgive the other *until* they had forgiven themselves. I then suggest that they repeat this process daily for 21 days, after first relaxing and meditating for a short time. It seems that doing it once during the healing session is insufficient to change a pattern of anger which has been followed for months or years. However, transmuting the anger to love in this way for 21 days completes the change and the problem is resolved. People sometimes ask "Why twenty one days?" I think it is because 21 is 3 x 7 and both of these numbers have a deep spiritual significance, and appear in the scriptures of many religions and in nature. The idea of repetition for 21 days to change a pattern has also appeared in a number of other recent writings.

After the 21 days has been completed, the individual may wish to verbalize the forgiveness by letter, telephone or in person, or even take the specific steps to demonstrate their love. The interesting part is that even without such external activity the person who is forgiven will usually sense the change subconsciously, and without knowing why, will initiate some act of reconciliation on their own.

I was very touched by two beautiful examples of true forgiveness given to a Time magazine reporter by two Cambodian 10-year-old boy refugees whom he interviewed. Two years before, each had lost both of their parents to enemy action, in one case in front of them. Then they were forced to work in the fields and nearly died of starvation. When asked if they desired revenge they both said "Yes." However, when they were asked what they meant by that one said "That means I must make the most of my life"; the other said "It means to make a bad man better than before".

Sometimes when the negative emotion causing the disease has been acknowledged it is necessary to search further as to the origin of that emotion, in order for a change to take place. For example, if the one who is ill is suffering from fear, and yet there seems to be no current reason for that fear, he can be encouraged to think back over the years, maybe into childhood, for traumatic experiences which have left a residue of fear. If he is able to recall such an event, then he should examine it carefully and relive it in his mind without resistance, however painful that may be (remember that resistance increases pain). If there is a complete or partial resistance to reliving the experience it may be necessary to repeat the process on two or three occasions; by doing this the cause of the fear will be brought into full consciousness and its energy will be dissipated.

The past is only real to the extent that it is carried in the consciousness of the individual in the present. This means that it can be changed or transformed by the individual if he wishes to do so. Using his imagination he can recreate the experience in his mind as he would have wanted it to be, thus withdrawing the energy from his memory of what actually happened.

Sometimes the underlying reason for fear is that someone who has a poor opinion of themselves has created a false facade to their personality, endeavouring to cover up what they believe to be their inferiority. They are well aware of their life of deception; so they are constantly afraid that their act will be discovered, and that they will be exposed and rejected. One of the big problems with falsehood is that one has to remember the falsification which was used or created, so that it can be maintained. If the person can be brought to recognize the futility of the false front with the fear of discovery that this creates, maybe he can learn to replace this facade with the realization that he is a child of God with unique talents and a purpose in life that only he can fulfill. Meditation on Truth as an attribute of, or a synonym for God will also help to raise the individual's consciousness from one of fear and falsehood to one of trust and truthfulness. Having accomplished this change in consciousness the cause of fear and the disease it has created can be eradicated.

The cause of the fear may, of course, be more obvious than that. For example; just being told that one has cancer immediately causes great fear in most people. In fact it has been said that eliminating the fear is harder than destroying the cancer itself. My wife discovered for herself an interesting technique for eliminating such terror when she feared that she had cancer. This was based on symptoms, not on a medical diagnosis and was fortunately later proved to be unfounded in fact. I have since successfully used this method with a number of people, in several similar and different situations.

After the laying-on-of hands healing process previously described, when the ones who are afraid are very relaxed and receptive, I ask them to close their eyes and to make a mental image of the word FEAR, painting or drawing it in large letters in any color and on any surface that they choose. Then I ask them to examine it carefully to see how and where it is connected to them; usually they will see ropes or chains, or some other material, tying the word to some part of their body. Then I ask them to take an appropriate imaginary tool and visualize cutting through the ties and watch the word float away. If this does not happen, they are invited to do whatever seems appropriate to them at the time to eliminate the word.

In the case of cancer, this process may be followed by asking them to paint or draw the word CANCER in large letters, and then we follow the same procedure as we did for FEAR. The process may have to be repeated once or twice on subsequent visits but will eventually leave a sense of peace and trust which will contribute much towards a successful healing.

The point or points at which the word is connected to them, and the surface on which it has been placed in the vision, are also significant clues as to what part of their body or bodily function, or what emotion or mental attitude is connected with the word they are visualizing. This gives them valuable information with which to continue to work for the final transmutation of whatever it is that they are trying to release. For example; one woman painted the word on an image of her own house, and this puzzled her. When I pointed out that the house was her own home, she immediately realized that her fear of the cancer was not for herself but for her young children. She had lost her own mother in a motor accident when she was three years old, and had a very unhappy childhood after that. Her fear was that her children would suffer in the same way if her cancer should prove to be fatal.

In another case of fear, that was not related to cancer, the words FEAR and ANGER, were visualized separately, and yet each was seen to be attached to the woman's birth canal. It dawned on her that the origin of her fear was her own mother's fear at the time of her birth, which had been a very difficult one. The origin of her anger was the frustration she felt at the time of her birth because of her prolonged, agonizing entrance into this world.

In another case the problem was extreme insecurity created by a young woman's father while she was growing up. The woman had no difficulty visualizing the word INSECURITY and cutting the few ties that she saw. However, when I asked her to visualize the word TRUST she found this to be very hard to do—the first letters kept fading away before she could write the last ones.

Another way of transmuting fear is for me to ask the person simply to visualize their fear and tell me what they see. The resulting picture or pictures that appear before their closed eyes may reveal the underlying cause for their fear to an extent they had not previously realized. I point out that these pictures are a part of themselves and suggest that they try radiating love to the picture and the symbols it includes and then let me know what happens. Nearly always they will, after a few minutes, report that the images have changed into something less threatening or even beautiful and loveable. This gives them a further understanding of what lies behind their fear and hopefully a resolution.

When their own psyche has changed the picture in this way, the emotional and mental attitude changes also, and after the session much or all of the fear has gone. It has been transmuted into a positive energy along with the changed picture.

During the whole time that these visualizations are being experienced by the other person I hold my hands a few inches above their heart center and continue to channel the healing energy to them. The combination of their own new direction of energy and the energy that is coming through me provides a force of greater intensity than the forces which are holding onto the negative emotion. This enables the transmutation to take place.

In other situations the underlying cause of anger may be the experience of much physical or mental cruelty during childhood. Unfortunately in this age of rapid change, high divorce rate and over-riding fear of a nuclear holocaust, the incidents of child abuse are escalating. Bringing these experiences to light, examining them without repressing them, and then transmuting the anger by sending love and forgiveness to those that caused the pain—however difficult it may be to do this—is the quickest way to eliminate the cause of the disease.

Anxiety is often caused by tension which in turn may be caused by shallow breathing. The statement "I was so anxious I held my breath. . . . " dramatizes this fact. The cure is to breathe deeply and slowly, releasing the tension and the anxiety. The breath can also be used to forestall a negative emotion if a person is sufficiently aware to sense its approach. At that time he should breathe deeply, holding the breath for a few seconds after each inhalation, and then exhaling slowly.

Brugh Joy, a spiritual teacher of higher consciousness, and the author of *Joy's Way,* teaches that the energy involved in negative emotions is centered in the solar plexus area (the third chakra) and may be transmuted to the energy of unconditional love, which is found at the heart level (the fourth chakra). This can be accomplished by mentally visualizing that energy moving up the spine from the third to the fourth level and being transmuted as it moves up. This same technique can be used to move excess energy from other chakras (e.g. sexual energy from the second, or mental or psychic energy from the sixth chakra) to the safety of the fourth.

If the cause seems to be unresolved grief, the individual should be informed that while it is perfectly normal for someone who has suffered the loss of a loved one to experience shock, anger, self pity and grief, it can be destructive to their physical body if the grief continues too long. Three to six months is considered a fairly safe period to release the emotion, and this in itself is healing. It is certainly preferable to repressing the emotion, refusing to confront the loss, and pretending to oneself and others that the loss did not make any difference.

However, after this release period is complete it is important to *accept* the fact that the loved one is no longer in a physical body, but is very much alive on the Spirit Plane, and will be seen again when the individual also passes on to that Plane. Meanwhile the griever is still on the Earth Plane, has service of some kind that they can perform for humanity and lessons to learn. The more they can involve themselves with *living* the less they will mourn the loss. It should also be remembered that those on the Spirit Plane have many times reported through mediums that our grief handicaps their progress on the Spirit Plane.

Chapter 3 mentioned judgement, or criticism of others, as a possible cause of disease because of the resentment or frustration that it brings to the one who judges. Being judgmental is also another manifestation of the drive for power with its resulting attempt or desire to control others. One way to deal with this is for the person to understand that what he sees in others is also inside himself, otherwise he would not recognize it. He is in fact projecting onto other people parts of his own psyche.

Sometimes the judgement or projection is accompanied by an intense emotional feeling; the one who is judging becoming very irate or upset, if it is a projection of a negative or undesirable facet. On the other hand one can project positive or desirable aspects from within, in which case the emotion may be one of excessive attachment to or adoration of the other person. This emotional charge is because the projector has that same characteristic, habit or quality within him and he is unaware of it; he has not allowed it into his conscious mind. The unconscious mind makes the projection in an attempt to reach the conscious mind by using the other person as a mirror or reflector, hoping that the individual will thus become aware of the projected content as his own.

Where there is no emotional charge involved the judgement or criticism may still be a projection. The one who judges is still forming an opinion of the other person based on his own experience of life and his own psychological make-up. He looks at them through his own filter, so to speak. Then too, he can only have a very limited knowledge of the psyche of the other person whose actions or mannerisms may be based on early childhood experiences or a later life that has been so different to that of the one who is judging that it would be incomprehensible to the latter. This may even involve unconscious influences brought over from a previous life of which the other person himself is unaware.

The psychological solution to this type of cause of disease is to ask the judgmental person to identify as clearly as possible those factors in others of which he is most critical, so that he knows what he has to deal with. Then he can re-own his projections, become fully conscious of them and take them back inside himself where they belong, saving the energy that is completely wasted in judging others and dealing with the subsequent frustration. This enables him to do something to change those things in himself that he does not like, if he chooses to do so. However, all of this is easier said than done.

A better way from the point of view of Spiritual Healing is to raise the whole problem to the higher level of unconditional love. Visually and mentally he should elevate the energy involved in the judging and frustration from the solar plexus center (the 3rd chakra) where it is concentrated, up to the heart center (the 4th chakra) transmuting it into unconditional love. (See chart on p. 264.) When one is able to love unconditionally there is no desire to judge, criticize or control the other person—they are loved just as they are, and the Divine, which is within each person as well as in the projector, is silently acknowledged.

Stress

If the cause of the illness is found to be excessive stress, then the sick person needs to examine every stressful situation that he faces, and decide which ones he can reduce or eliminate by making specific changes in his life. This may involve re-evaluating his needs, goals and attitudes, and establishing new priorities. If there are situations which he is quite unable to change, that is, he has no choice in the matter, he must learn to develop patience and equanimity, and to accept life as it comes to him without resisting or fighting it. In the words of the famous prayer:

God grant me
The serenity to accept the things I cannot change,
The courage to change the things I can, and
The wisdom to know the difference.

If someone we love has died we cannot alter that fact, but we can go through the grief process until we give up fighting God and accept the fact of the necessary separation. If possible we may realize that it is only temporary; that we will meet the loved one again on the Spirit plane after we too have parted from our physical body.

If we have lost a job, we can take all the necessary steps to find another, and then accept the time in between as a positive opportunity in which to re evaluate our goals, skills and desires, and to take a well earned rest. Again the secret is acceptance of the situation without fighting it mentally or emotionally, and without creating stress.

Physical relaxation, exercise, meditation and sharing of our feelings about the stressful situation, may also help us to deal with stress that cannot be eliminated. Developing, practicing or experiencing creative activities such as art, music and writing are other helpful ways of reducing stress, provided there is no striving for perfection and no self-judgement on the results of these ventures.

Some far-sighted employers are recognizing that excessive

stress in an individual employee's life, may justify time off with pay for stress release without waiting for illness to make sick leave necessary. This permission of time off in itself eliminates additional stress for some people who feel guilty by claiming to be sick when this is not literally true, according to the conventional interpretation of the word "sick".

Frequently the reaction to stress compounds the situation increasing the chance of disease or impeding the possibility of healing. For example, overeating, alcohol or drug abuse, smoking, retreat into isolation, depression, overwork, excessive sexual activity, or inability to sleep often result from excessive stress, usually as a conscious or unconscious attempt to escape from dealing with the stressful situation.

Parent-Child Conflict

What is the solution if it is discovered that the disease was caused by a negative emotion or stress which arose out of a parent-child conflict? If the parents have requested help from the healer, then the healer can make every effort to point out that the daughter, or son, is God's child and not theirs. They are stewards of the child, not owners. They have been given the great privilege of enabling a soul to come into this world so that it may continue its evolution, and of caring for and protecting that child during its early years, giving it physical, mental and spiritual guidance to the best of their ability, but they must gradually let go of the controls as the child matures.

If their child is already an adult, that child has his or her own life to live, lessons to learn, and spiritual path to follow, and they are entitled to be free of all controls, physical, mental, emotional or financial, which might hinder that growth and prevent them from realizing their full potential. It is best if only unconditional love remains as the connection between parents and adult children; in that type of relationship happiness and harmony will be realized for all.

This was very beautifully stated by The Prophet in the book by that name by Kahlil Gibran[2] when he said:

Your children are not your children.
They are the sons and daughters of Life's
longing for itself.
They come through you but not from you,
And though they are with you yet they
belong not to you.
You may give them your love but not
your thoughts,
For they have their own thoughts.
You may house their bodies but not their souls,
For their souls dwell in the house of tomorrow,
which you cannot visit, not even in your dreams.
You may strive to be like them, but seek not to
make them like you.
For life goes not backward nor tarries
with yesterday.

I do not believe that the son or daughter owes the parents anything. However, where independence, individuality and freedom are lovingly taught, and control is relinquished step by step as the child matures, the parents will usually receive unconditional love in return and the adult relationship will be one of joy and harmony.

Where such control is apparent, or even if a parent really believes that they are not controlling the son or daughter, but it appears to the healer that there may be an unconscious control that is creating problems for either the parent or the child, he can suggest to the parent (during the healing process) that they try to visualize their child and see if there are any connections between them. If they find that there are, (sometimes they see strings, or ropes or chains) then they are invited to visualize taking an imaginary instrument of their own choosing and cutting through all these bonds.

2. Reprinted from *The Prophet*, by Kahlil Gibran, by permission of Alfred A. Knopf, Inc. Copyright 1923 by Kahlil Gibran and renewed 1951 by Administrators C.T.A. of Kahlil Gibran Estate and Mary G. Gibran.

If the ties are very strong it may be necessary to repeat the process on another occasion. It is surprising that nearly everyone with whom I have used this technique has immediately been able to visualize such ties (which are of a wide variety), and mentally participate in the severance of them, sometimes with a great deal of emotion. It is incredible to witness the relief that this eventually brings to the parent, even though it may be painful at first. It also brings a sense of peace to the son or daughter; they are usually not consciously informed of this transaction and may be several thousand miles away, nevertheless they will subconsciously feel a release soon after the parent has released them by visualization and thought.

If it is the daughter or son who has come to the healer, and control by the parent is discovered to be the cause of the illness, then during the healing process the child can be encouraged to use the same visualization procedure, cutting the bonds and asserting their freedom. Then they should silently tell the parent that they are forgiven, and then radiate unconditional love to them so as to heal any wound caused by cutting the ties. We always have a choice in life, and they need to realize that they have chosen to remain under that domination, but that they can in fact obtain their freedom from that control by choosing to be free. This may be one of the main lessons that they have come to learn in this lifetime, and they can gain strength from the experience. Each of us is responsible for our own life and no one else's; that does not mean a selfish refusal to lend a helping hand to our fellow humans, but it does mean that we leave them free to run their lives, while we take full responsibility for running ours. Actually, while we accept the domination of another person we are hindering, not helping, their own soul's growth, as well as our own.

I have found that this technique of cutting the unhealthy bonds or connections by visualization can be further strengthened by the individual subsequently asking that a White Light be placed between themselves and the other person and at the same time visualizing that this is happening. Only unconditional love can penetrate that screen of light, and all other connections or attachments, whether they be those of control, those of being controlled, or those with sexual, emotional or mental origins, will usually remain severed. In other words, this additional step can be taken whether the visualization method is being used to eliminate (a) parent-child domination, (b) a continuing attachment to a former spouse or lover, (c) fear or some other negative emotion, (d) a connection to the idea of a specific disease, or (e) anything else that a person desires to eliminate from their life.

Conflict within a family is not always caused by one member trying to control another, although this is very common. There is also the situation where one or more members of a family project all of their problems onto one specific member, usually a child, and that member is unaware of what is happening and accepts the problems as his own. This causes the child much unhappiness and he may become completely lacking in self-confidence, neurotic, psychotic, or even autistic, in sheer self defense.

I recall one young woman who was born with cerebral palsy telling me that she grew up believing that she was the cause of all of the problems in her family, both those of her parents and those of her siblings, and she was absolutely miserable all through her childhood. Finally when she was 19 she moved out of her parents' house and struggled to live on her own, believing that she was relieving her family of all of their difficulties. Much to her surprise she noticed that the problems continued just the same for each member of the family. It gradually dawned on her that she had not been to blame, that she was gifted and attractive in her own right, and that she could lead a happy, independent life in spite of her physical limitations.

Modern family and marriage counsellors are well aware of this possibility and therefore will frequently insist on seeing the whole family, not just the one member who has come to them for help. There may be some situations therefore where a Spiritual Healer should recommend that the one in need of healing should seek professional family counselling as a means of determining the cause of the disease.

Guilt

Where the disease has been created by feelings of guilt the first step is to point out that these feelings do no harm to the other person (except in so far as they affect everybody because we are all interconnected). However, it is also clear that they are of absolutely no benefit to either party and they *do* harm the one who feels guilty. Therefore, there is every reason to try to resolve them, and no reason not to.

Secondly, if the offense is one that can be rectified, such as by returning stolen money or objects, then this should be done, preferably in person and with a request for forgiveness. If it is one that cannot be rectified, such as physical, mental or emotional pain, or irreparable damage caused to another, an attempt should be made to minimize the harm that has been done, to the extent that this is possible. Then a genuine personal apology and a request for forgiveness by the injured party should be attempted. This is not easy to do, but is essential if inner peace is to be restored.

> "If you are offering your gift at the altar, and there remember that your brother has something against you, leave your gift there before the altar and go; first be reconciled to your brother, and then come and offer your gift." (Matthew 5:23-24)

The Kahunas taught that one of the ways that one can make amends for harm done to another (where the harm itself cannot be undone) is to do good deeds for other people.

Another step which it is wise to take is to ask for the forgiveness of God, or the Universal Creator of All, since whenever we offend our brothers and sisters we offend God. The Bible makes it very clear that God is always ready and willing to forgive us, to the extent that we forgive others, but we have to ask first, and then we need to accept that forgiveness.

After all, if someone offers you a gift, it does not become yours until you accept it. To complete this process the offender then forgives himself, which is perhaps the hardest part of all. Failing to do so helps no one, and is implying that he knows better than God.

Sometimes the injured person's whereabouts may be unknown, or they may have died, and the offender will feel that it is therefore impossible to overcome the feeling of guilt. He should be assured that this is not the case; that restitution (where possible) should be made to the deceased's heirs or a suitable substitute. The absentee or deceased person can be visualized by the one who feels guilty; the latter can then silently express their sorrow for past actions and request forgiveness. After that, God's forgiveness may also be asked for and accepted. Thus it should be made clear to those suffering from guilt feelings that they do have a choice, and can either retain those feelings and suffer the consequences, or they can eliminate them in this way.

Confession of offenses against others or against God, which is such an important part of the religious practice of the Roman Catholic Church, has contributed much to maintaining the physical and mental health of the members of that denomination. Carl Jung said, in an interview, that it was not necessary to psychoanalyze Catholics because they had the confessional. The priests as confessors were not included as part of the procedures followed by the Protestant Churches after the Reformation, but were later replaced by psychologists and psychiatrists, and more recently by ministers trained as counsellors. Even with confession the cleansing is incomplete unless it is followed by repentance, restitution (where possible) and the asking and acceptance of forgiveness.

There is another factor that is inseparably involved in the matter of guilt and forgiveness, and that is the necessity also to forgive others for any offense we are holding against them. In the Lord's Prayer Jesus told us to pray, "Forgive us our debts as we also have forgiven our debtors," and then immediately after ending the prayer he added the warning, "For if you forgive men their trespasses, your heavenly Father will also forgive you; but if you do not forgive men their trespasses, neither will your Father forgive your trespasses." (Matthew 6:12-15) When Jesus wished to place extra importance on one of his teachings, he would repeat it immediately with slightly different wording, as he did in this case.

As recorded, this may sound as though Jesus was saying that God's love is conditional in this respect. Possibly the original meaning was that if we do not forgive others we will be unable to accept God's forgiveness, although it is always available if we ask.

So the one who is seeking to relieve himself of guilt feelings should also carefully examine his innermost thoughts to see if he is holding hostile, resentful or unforgiving thoughts against another, including the same person that he has offended. If these thoughts are discovered, they need to be replaced by thoughts of forgiveness, harmony and love, and where appropriate, expressed by word and action.

I recall the case of one young woman who had experienced repeated problems with her reproductive organs, in one form or another, over a period of nine years, and was now facing surgery to remove a cyst from one ovary and to correct an infection of her fallopian tubes which had failed to respond to drugs. The first healing session resulted in much relief from pain, but she knew that the healing was far from complete, and I felt that the cause had not been uncovered in our previous conversation.

Further discussion before the second healing session revealed that the problems started shortly after her step-father had started having sexual intercourse with her when she was only thirteen years old. She was a shy and innocent girl at the time and did not realize that this was wrong. Of course, he assured her that it was not, and that it was merely a way of showing his love for her. She did not, therefore, tell anyone, and it continued for some time until she discovered how wrong it was and refused his further advances. When she was sixteen she fell in love with and married a youth her own age. As she had experienced no sexual difficulties in her marriage she had no reason to suspect any connection between her current health problems and the earlier mistreatment by her step-father.

When I became aware of the timing of the events I asked if she was still carrying feelings of anger or resentment towards her step-father because of his behavior. She said there were some, but not a great amount. I also asked her if she felt guilty for her part in the activities; she said that she did not because she did not know that it was wrong until later. I suggested that in spite of this she might, at a subconscious level at any rate, be feeling guilty because she never told her mother or anyone else. As she thought about this, the pain, which had almost disappeared after the previous day's session, returned quite strongly, so we knew that there was a definite connection.

During the second healing session we did two things: (a) I asked her to visualize her step-father and then to see if there were any ties between them (and there were) and if so to visualize severing them and sending him on his way with unconditional love and forgiveness. This she was able to do.

(b) I asked her to turn her attention towards herself and to ask for God's forgiveness, assuring her that He did not condemn her and was always ready to forgive if asked to do so. She silently followed these directions and the response was an immediate, dramatic and intense vibration which coursed through my body and into her heart center (my hands were over that area) and through her whole body. This left no doubt in either of our minds that her prayer had been answered affirmatively, and all that she had to do was to accept the gift, and then to forgive herself. The healing then took place, no surgery was necessary, and when I spoke to her over a year later there had been no recurrence.

I have included much in this book on forgiving and asking for forgiveness because I have discovered that it is one of the most powerful spiritual instruments for healing known to humanity. In many other cases besides those mentioned, I have seen wonderful mental, emotional and physical healings follow when the sick person has sincerely forgiven and asked forgiveness. Judging by the comments of those who had been in therapy for many years it is unfortunately a method that is seldom used by therapists of any kind.

Negative Thinking

If the origin of the disease is discovered to be in the thought pattern of the sick person, then he needs to realize that he has complete control over his thoughts if he wants to, that he always has a choice, and, however difficult it may be for him, he needs to change the direction and content of his thoughts into the opposite of those which have caused him the trouble. It will probably take patience, practice, and will power, but again, the cure is within him; it does not come from outside.

Energy follows thought, whether it is positively or negatively charged. We have already noted that the human body consists of trillions of atoms each one containing many particles moving around in a specific pattern, at high speed. Yet this movement or vibration is slow enough for the body to appear to our physical senses to be solid. This pattern can be altered by negative thinking to form a disease or malfunction of the body. It can also be reformed into a healthy, harmonious pattern by positive thinking. God created the Universe and man by the power of thought, arranging the atoms into a beautiful, orderly, harmonious design, so it seems logical to assume that harmony of thought and attunement with Spirit will automatically rearrange the atoms of a diseased body into the original pattern, and that healing will result. Also since the particles of atoms are in constant motion, and themselves consist of energy, the healing can be instantaneous, if the attunement of thought is adequate.

One of the best ways to reverse the habit of negative

thinking is by the use of affirmations. This technique is described in some detail in Chapter 10 under the subheading *Changing the Contents of the Subconscious Mind.*

Conflict with Our Life Plan

It sometimes becomes apparent that the cause of a disease may be the fact that the diseased person is not following the plan for his life that was meant to be. The obvious cure in this case is for that person to make every effort to align himself with that plan which he intuitively and instinctively knows he should be pursuing. It may mean some drastic changes, possibly a reduction in income, but it will most likely bring health and harmony into his life.

In his interesting book, *You Can Fight for Your Life*[3] Dr. Lawrence LeShan reports on the case of a young lawyer who developed a massive brain tumor that had grown to the point where no surgery or treatment was possible, and he was given only a few months to live. Searching for some alternative, the sick man came for help to psychotherapist LeShan, who found that although the man had shown unusual musical ability as a child, he had been timid and withdrawn. He became a lawyer to satisfy his father, and married the girl his mother picked out for him. Believing that he could win the love of others only by doing what was expected of him, he sacrificed his own dreams. Learning from Dr. LeShan that he could fight for his life, he quit his legal career, became a professional musician with a symphony orchestra and divorced his wife. His tumor then gradually disappeared by itself.

Note that in this case there was probably also an element of unconscious inner conflict resulting from control by the parents which had been accepted too passively by the son.

Dr. Brugh Joy describes in his inspiring book, *Joy's Way*[1] his own drastic change from operating a highly successful orthodox medical practice to embarking on a personal search for transformation. Shortly after his 35th birthday he became aware that he was suffering from chronic, relapsing pancreatitis, involving frequent pain, and for which there was no known medical cure. There was also a strong chance that it could become fatal, and the incidents of pain were increasing in frequency. Five months later, during meditation he experienced a vortex of energy of great magnitude, and heard a loud voice telling him to leave the orthodox medical field and to "embark on a rededication of your Beingness to a deeper commitment and action."

He obeyed the voice at once, and started on a journey of discovery and teaching which makes fascinating reading. The point here is that his disease was healed the moment he accepted the guidance and followed the plan for his life that was made known to him. Five years later neither the pain nor any other symptom of the disease had reoccurred.

Another example is that of a college student who came to me because she could not stop crying and had no idea why. She was basically happy, and no sudden tragedy had befallen her. Our conversation revealed, however, that she was a natural artist, and never happier than when she was painting or drawing; when doing so she was completely absorbed and at peace. However, she realized that it was extremely difficult to earn a living that way and therefore she was majoring in a different field in order to give her another potential source of income. Because the course she had selected was a hard one she had no time for her art. I suggested that her creativity was thus completely blocked and that if she would "let it flow", at least sometimes, the tears would no longer need to flow instead. She followed this suggestion and the tears soon dried up.

Karma

As pointed out earlier, if the cause is Karmic, Spiritual Healing will have little effect until the lesson has been thoroughly learned. This does not mean that these situations are hopeless. We are told that it is possible for unconditional love by others to assist in reducing the burden of Karma and accelerating the assimilation of the lesson that it brings.

Another possibility for lessening the pain of Karma, but not eliminating it, is found in *The Aquarian Gospel*.[4] Jesus was talking about a man who had been born blind because in another life he had been a cruel man, and in a cruel way had destroyed the eyes of another man. Jesus went on to say:

> We cannot pay the debts of any man, but by the Word we may release a man from his afflictions and distress, and make him free that he may pay the debts he owes, by giving up his life in willing sacrifice for men or other living things.

In other words the healing of a disease and suffering that were created by Karma, may be possible if the sufferer is willing to sacrifice all aspects of his life in service to others.

There are three other possibilities of dealing with causes originating in a past life. The first is simply to become conscious of the past life event and its connection to this life, look carefully at the event as an observer, so that it is not necessary to experience the pain again, and then acknowledge that it was in the past life and not in this one, and therefore there is no need for it to affect this life. For example if an individual has migraine headaches in this life, past life regression may reveal that in a previous life they died from a shot or blow to the head, or their skull was fractured or crushed. Becoming aware of this, and letting go of it, may be all that is necessary to eliminate the headaches.

Awareness of this type of past life connection is also often most effective in releasing a phobia in this life such as claustrophobia, agoraphobia, fear of fire, water or heights and so forth. One young woman who came to me had a great fear of being in confined spaces. Past life regression showed that she had twice died of suffocation, once very slowly in a stone sarcophagous.

The second way of dealing with a situation discovered from a past life is to treat it as if it is in the present. There is no time or space in the spirit world, so forgiving someone or asking forgiveness of someone for an offense which occurred

2000 years ago can be just as effective as if it occurred yesterday. This was illustrated by the woman with the pain in her right arm described in Chapter 4. A combination of these first two methods is sometimes required to release the problem.

The third method is to recognize that it is possible to change the past, even past lives, since the past only exists in the individual's memory—subconsciously until the regression. Thus by creating in imagination and visualization a different ending to a life that ended in a situation which is causing a problem in the present, the cause can be eliminated. This may sound strange but, believe me, it works. Here is an example.

One man occasionally had an uncontrollable rage which seemed quite out of proportion to the event in this life which triggered it. Regressing him into three past lives he discovered that in each one he had died while feeling very angry. In one of the lives he was also angry with God for "allowing" the situation that upset him. I suggested that he create a different ending to each life so that his feelings at the time of that death would be peaceful. He did this and repeated the visualization daily for 21 days by the end of which his subconscious memory had been changed to one of peace and the excessive explosions of anger ceased.

Removal of Entities

If the cause of the individual's problem is suspected to be possession or attachment by one or more discarnate spirit entities, they can be removed in the following way.

1. If the search has revealed the possibility of possession by one or more specific known deceased individuals, such as a husband or grandmother, ascertain the names of these persons so that they can be addressed by name.

2. Ask the person who has come for help to take several, slow, deep breaths and then to relax as much as possible. (Hypnotism is not necessary.)

3. Ask them to picture a white light in the very center of their being. Then to watch it expand gradually throughout their body. When the body is filled they should watch it expand outwards in all directions to a depth of two or three feet until they are in a cocoon of white light. Simultaneously do the same thing for yourself.

4. If known entities are suspected ask them, one at a time by name, if they are present. If they reply "Yes" using the voice of the possessed person, carry on a dialogue with them asking why they are there, pointing out that they are spoiling the life of the individual they have possessed, and impeding their own spiritual progress and that they need and deserve to move on into the light where they will be much happier and can progress instead of being stuck as they are at present.

5. It is very important to obtain the cooperation of the individual and the entity. Therefore, ask the individual if they are willing to release the entity; if the answer is "Yes", which it nearly always is, proceed to the next question. If it is "No" for some reason, such as a mother not wanting to lose contact with a deceased child, then you must try to persuade the individual that it is in their own best interest, as well as that of the entity's, to release the entity. When this has been accomplished, ask the entity if it is willing to leave. Sometimes the answer will be "Yes" but sometimes it will be "No" because it is afraid of the unknown, afraid to leave the comfort of the known, or reluctant to give up the vicarious satisfaction of its cravings for alcohol, drugs, etc. In that case reassuring dialogue must be continued until it agrees to leave.

6. Then ask the entity to look up to the light. When they confirm that they can see it, even if it is only a tiny point, tell them to keep watching this until it expands, which it will. Then ask them to look for their Spirit Guides who will always be there waiting to help them move on. Then ask them to reach out their hands and grasp the hands of the Guides and go with them into the light.

7. After the entity has left, lead the individual into repeating the opening process of seeing the white light within and expanding.

If the process is completed successfully the individual will usually feel very different saying "I feel much lighter" or "A great weight has been lifted off me" or "I feel as though I am now the only one occupying my body" or "I feel in control of my life again."

I am indebted to Dr. William Baldwin, a past life therapist, for teaching me to be aware of the possibilities of possession or attachment, and how to recognize them and then remove them, as briefly described above. However, the removal of an entity has many facets, and each case is different, so it is recommended that further training be undertaken before the reader attempts to do this.

Hidden Benefits

If the search for the cause elicits an admission from the sick person that they are receiving some benefits from the disease, such as more attention, or avoidance of a situation they do not like, then they should be asked to take a good look at the cost in pain, suffering and inconvenience to themselves and others, as well as the actual financial expense. Once this has been assessed, ask them to compare the benefits with the cost and see if they are really worthwhile. Sometimes this is all that it takes to provide the motivation and will for a rapid recovery.

Willingness to Change

All of this assumes that the one in need is willing to change. I remember the case of a man who came to me in the advanced stages of a disease. He said that he was aware that the disease had been caused by his excessive smoking, drinking and working, all of which he had given up completely, and he was quite certain that he had learned the lesson that was meant for him in the experience. He was also sure that he would not resume any of these habits when he became well. However, his disease was progressively getting worse. Without wishing to be judgmental I received the impression during further conversation that these physical excesses were symptoms of a very self-centered man who found it extremely difficult to express love for others in the simplest of ways. I urged him to start sending unconditional love to everyone he knew, and to start expressing it in little acts of kindness wherever this was possible. Exploring this further on subsequent visits it became apparent that he was unwilling or unable to do this, and within a few weeks he died.

In another case, where the one in need was willing to change, the result was the opposite. He came to me three years after a colostomy. This is an operation necessitated by an infection of the colon and bowels requiring severance of the colon and installation of an external plastic bag to receive the waste products of the digestive tract. This must be replaced daily until the lower section of the colon has healed. The colon was not yet healed, and his doctor estimated that it would probably take another year before the colon could be rejoined and the bag dispensed with.

Discussing the possible causes he happened to mention that he took great pride in the care with which he selected the food that he ate so he was surprised at the infection. As he said the word "pride" he and I both sensed that maybe this could be a stumbling block to his growth, and therefore that this was the lesson that the disease had brought him. I pointed out that the opposite of pride is humility, and what could be more humiliating than having to carry around on your stomach a plastic bag which contained what should be in your rectum? He agreed that this was probably the answer, and he decided to change his attitude to one that was more humble. Six weeks later his doctor informed him that the infection had cleared up and the colon could be rejoined.

Realizing the importance of helping to determine the cause of an illness, many Spiritual Healers will take time before the actual prayer and laying on of hands or attunement, to listen to the problems of the one in need and whatever else he wishes to talk about that seems to be relevant. He listens without judgment and without telling the other person what to do, reflecting that person's feelings, and occasionally asking a question, if this seems to be appropriate. This preliminary "lending an ear" has three purposes:

(a) To help to put the sick person at ease, and to help him to feel more relaxed and receptive.

(b) To reveal some clues as to the cause of the disease, and thus help to guide the healer and the one in need. For example; often while he is telling his story the sick person will show anger or hostility towards certain individuals or situations or reveal judgemental or critical attitudes towards individuals or the world in general.

(c) To allow the healer to sense intuitively that which lies behind the symptoms of the sick person. This can happen only if the healer listens with an open non-judgmental mind.

Is a Psychotherapist Needed?

Having discovered the cause, which may have been buried deep in his subconscious mind, the sick person may need help in overcoming the problem and making the necessary changes in his psyche. It is a matter of choice whether at this time he employs the assistance of a professional psychotherapist, or continues to seek help through Spiritual Healing and his own prayers and meditation.

In helping to discover the cause, and pointing out the necessity for correcting the cause, the healer is involving the sick person in his own healing, which I feel is essential if he is to avoid a recurrence and to learn the lesson that the illness was meant to teach him. Orthodox, and some types of unorthodox medical practitioners such as acupuncturists, reflexologists, and, unfortunately, many spiritual healers, usually do not take the time to do this. The patient offers his body to the doctor, therapist or healer and asks to be healed; he is not really involved, except as the object of the healing application. If the healing is successful, the chances are he will resume his life as before (except for physical activity limitations placed upon him by the doctor), with the intended lesson not learned, and the strong possibility that the problem will return in some form or other.

Notes for Chapter 5

1. Brugh Joy, M.D. *Joy's Way.* J.P. Tarcher Inc. Los Angeles. 1978

2. Kahlil Gibran. *The Prophet.* Alfred A. Knopf Inc. 1923

3. Dr. Lawrence LeShan. *You Can Fight For Your Life.* p. 6 M. Evans and Company, Inc. New York. 1977

4. Levi. *The Aquarian Gospel of Jesus the Christ.* Ch:138 vs: 14-17. DeVorss & Co., Marina Del Rey, California. 1907

UNCONDITIONAL LOVE

OPENS THE DOOR

TO WHOLENESS

CHAPTER 6

WHY ISN'T EVERYONE
HEALED?

IT IS WELL known that not everyone who requests Spiritual
Healing from a well established spiritual healer experiences satisfactory results. Some are completely healed and
some realize partial relief, but for some there is no change
at all. Then, too, some are apparently healed but later on
the disorder returns. I have been able to find only a few
statistics on this. For example at Saint Stephens Episcopal
Church in Philadelphia, whose healing services are quite
famous, it is reported that the records show that approximately forty per cent of those attending the services who are
in need of healing are healed, the other sixty per cent are
not. The late Harry Edwards, whose healing clinic in England, and massive absent healing correspondence (10,000
letters per week) are world renowned, estimated that "over
eighty per cent of sufferers report perceptible easement and
improvement. Of this number over thirty per cent report
complete cures".[1]

My own experience confirms these findings. I keep a very
brief notation on each person who asks for help; although,
if they do not let me know the results, and many do not, I

have to exclude them from my data. I have learned from indirect feedback on a number of cases that some do not report the outcome because they do not experience an immediate healing and give up without any further effort. Others fail to keep me informed because they *are* healed and they feel that no further visit is necessary, and they do not see any need to write or phone since I seldom ask them to do so. (See "Non-Attachment to Results" at the end of this chapter). Excluding, therefore, those on whom I have no follow up information, approximately one-third were completely healed, one-third partially healed, and the remainder were not healed.

Thousands attended each of the famous healing services conducted by the late Kathryn Kuhlman, but only a hundred or so claimed to be healed at each service. Reporters who interviewed those who said they had been healed found that even many of these healings were imaginary or temporary, brought about by the tremendous collective faith generated by the emotional atmosphere of the service and its staging, and also by the people's great desire to believe that they had been healed. I have known personally of some who were healed permanently and others who attended many times without experiencing any relief.

At Lourdes in France, and at Fatima in Portugal, there are well known Roman Catholic healing shrines where many instantaneous, medically inexplicable healings have occurred. It is nevertheless a known fact that less than five per cent of those who visit the shrines are actually healed. The reason that this figure is much lower than the others is probably because no case is certified by the church as a healing without a thorough examination of the previous medical records and diagnoses, and a subsequent physical examination by a board of experts; whereas the other statistics are based almost entirely on the statements of the patients themselves. No doubt many other healings do occur during or after visits to these shrines, but they are not researched in this manner.

So, why isn't everyone healed?

We know that "With God all things are possible," (Matthew 19:26) and that this has been proved in individual cases of instantaneous healings of almost every type of disease known to man. It is also logical to assume that the same Intelligence that created our physical, mental and spiritual bodies, has infinite power with which to correct any malfunction of those bodies.

We also know that there is only one source of energy, and that is God, or the Divine Creative Intelligence. In fact God and Energy are synonymous, just as God and Love are one. You can become aware of the magnitude of that power by observing it in action in various ways. Have you ever stood by the seashore during a severe winter storm and watched the waves thundering against the rocks, and felt the power penetrating your very being? Have you watched the rise and fall of the tides, and sensed the tremendous energy it takes to move that enormous volume of water?

Perhaps you have watched moving pictures of an atomic bomb explosion, and gasped at the terrible force that is released by splitting a microscopic atom. If you should chance to observe a volcano that is erupting and spewing forth tons of molten rock from deep within the earth, think of the force that is contained beneath the crust of the earth which makes this explosion possible. It would be very difficult to plan the experience of an earthquake, but if one ever happens when you are within its range, you will never forget the awesome feeling of unlimited power shaking the very earth on which you stand.

These are all illustrations of that one energy, and it is the same energy that is available for healing, but in that case it is modified and controlled by the Spirit so that only the exact amount needed is transmitted to the right place. Yet, as we have seen, results are not always as effective as the sick one would like, or they are disappointing because there is no apparent change. There are many reasons for this.

Reasons Why Some Are Not Healed.

1. The fear and anxiety of the sick person may be stronger than their faith in the healing power of God. This is especially true when Spiritual Healing is requested at the last moment when the doctor has informed the patient and their loved ones that they are unlikely to live much longer. However, even in these cases there is frequently a reduction of pain and the arrival of a sense of peace; thus even if the patient dies in accordance with the doctor's forecast, the Spiritual Healing is not entirely ineffective.

2. The sick person may not be open to, and in fact may actually resist the inflow of the Divine power that is directed to him by the healer. God never imposes His will on us—we always have a choice. If we choose to reject His love and power, we are free to do so; we are also free to accept it with joy and gratitude.

Although the sick person's sincere belief in Spiritual Healing is not essential to success (as has been proved many times) it certainly helps. On the other hand if he is definitely opposed to the whole idea, he will probably make any attempt at healing completely ineffective.

As far as resistance is concerned, this is often the cause of pain—abandon the resistance and the pain disappears. You can prove this to yourself the next time you have a headache by trying the following experiment, preferably with the help of a friend.

(a) Take two or three minutes to relax your whole body as much as you can. Keep your eyes closed throughout the process.
(b) Now visualize the headache; try to picture it. In order to do this, request your friend to ask you the following questions:
What shape is it?
How wide is it?
How tall is it?
How deep is it?
What color is it?
After each question try to look at the headache and then answer the question as honestly as you can.

(c) Stay with the picture for a few moments, then your friend should repeat each question with the addition of the word "now" after the word "it". Again you answer them one at a time based on how the headache looks to you then.

(d). Repeat the whole process again as many times as is necessary until the picture disappears entirely, as it nearly always does. However, if the changes stop and the picture becomes static, your friend should ask you to create an imaginary opening in your body near the pain and to allow the remaining image of the pain to drain out through this opening.

If no friend is available you can ask the questions yourself, although this is not quite as effective. Alternatively you can put the questions on tape with suitable pauses in between each one.

What you will probably discover from this experiment is that the shape of the headache will change from a sharp, angular one to a smooth rounded one, or from a violent aggressive symbol (such as a hammer or a sword) to a more peaceful or harmless one. The size will gradually get smaller, and simultaneously the color will slowly change from black or brown, or a harsh intense color, to soft pastels or white. When the picture has completely disappeared you will find that the headache has also gone.

What has occurred is that in looking closely at the headache in this manner, all resistance to it is dissolved, and it no longer exists. This same technique will work on any pain, even if it has been bothering someone for a long time, at least to the extent that the pain is caused by resistance and tension. My wife recently tried the idea on someone who had had hiccups for several hours and it stopped that too!

3. Once a person becomes aware of the probable cause of his disease, e.g., hostility, anger, jealousy, criticism of others, etc., it is necessary for him to change the thinking, feeling, attitudes or life style that created and supports the cause; if he does not do this it is most likely that a cure will either be impossible or only temporary.

An example of this is a lady who had severe arthritis in both legs and both arms; walking and housework were very difficult for her. Searching for the cause she revealed that her husband had been unfaithful to her for many years without her knowing about it. When she discovered the truth she was very angry and immediately divorced him. The arthritis developed soon after that. Now, several years later, although she had not seen him in all of that time, she was still deeply resentful towards him.

After the healing session she was free of much pain and stiffness but it all returned within two days. This happened on three separate occasions, and it became apparent from our further discussions that she was completely unwilling to let go of the resentment and forgive her former husband. Consequently, she was also unable to release the arthritis and the relief from pain was purely temporary. At some level, she evidently felt that the "pleasure" she received from holding on to the resentment was worth more to her than the cost of the pain and suffering.

This lady, and others like her, want to be healed of the *symptoms* of the disease, the pain, the discomfort or the disfigurement but they are apparently unwilling to be healed of the *cause* because that would mean changing the way that they live or think. So their will is to stay "as is". Spiritual Healing, therefore, does not succeed for them because the law of Spirit is to honor the free will of the individual.

4. The one in need may refuse to search for the cause— probably because of fear as to what he might find. An example of this concerns a man who was faced with a progressive terminal disease. After all efforts (see Chapter 4.) to uncover the cause had failed we both felt that something really deep from childhood, or a previous life, must be involved; so I suggested that he have a reading from an excellent psychic. This he refused to do, saying he was not ready for it, although he had no doubts as to the psychic's abilities or authenticity. It is my belief that his real reason was a fear as to what might be revealed to him.

5. Unconsciously, the sick person may not really want to get well. Picture a woman who has devoted her life to raising her children and caring for her husband. She is now 45 years old and all of the children have left home and are involved with their own lives—they do not need her any more. Her husband has been given increased responsibilities in his job, and periodically he has to travel away from home; thus he too has less apparent need for her attention. She has never become interested in a career, volunteer work or a hobby; so there is no longer any meaning in her life. She is in the depths of despair. This stress and negative emotion induces cancer in her body, and she is told that she has about one year to live.

Suddenly her husband is greatly concerned, cuts down his travelling and office hours (even if this jeopardizes his future success), brings her flowers, helps with the household chores, and generally expresses his love and concern in tangible ways. The children start to telephone more frequently, come home for visits, or in other ways demonstrate their devotion to her. Previously they had assumed that she knew it and there was no need to express it.

Life now has meaning for her; she relishes the love and attention. She may, therefore, consciously or unconsciously, have no desire to recover her health and lose all of this again. Since we all have a free will, this desire may overrule any attempt at healing, even though she has asked for it.

6. If the sick person created the disease, consciously or subconsciously, to avoid or postpone a change, or to extricate himself from an unpleasant situation, then he probably will not want to get well and the healing will not succeed.

An example of this from my own experience was that of a woman who had been in a wheel chair for five years. She was brought to me for a healing session by a friend of hers, but with considerable doubt and hesitation on her part. I asked her what she would like to have help with and she said that she would like to be rid of the pain in her back and buttocks caused by constant sitting in a wheel chair. I then asked if she would like to walk again and to my amazement she said "No"! When I asked why, she replied, "If I could walk I would have to join the rat race again". I asked her what she meant by "rat race" and she said "Being a house-wife, caring for husband and children, keeping the house clean and all that sort of thing." Apparently she now avoided much of this as it was impossible for her to carry on these activities from a wheelchair. Instead she was attending col-lege with the help of volunteers for transportation and access to class rooms, and she was thoroughly enjoying it.

I explained that with Spiritual Healing there was no guar-antee as to results—she might lose the pain and still not be able to walk; she might be able to walk but still have some pain; she might be able to walk with no pain, or there might be no change whatsoever. It would depend on many factors (some of which are outlined in this chapter), but if it was going to work at all it was essential that she be completely willing to accept *any* result—neither she nor I could dictate to God what would happen. Finally she accepted one healing session and felt energy and some movement in her legs where there had been none for years, but she never pursued the matter any further. Eighteen months later I wrote to her to ask for permission to include this incident in my book. In an affirmative reply she changed nothing but did add an interesting further insight. She said "There are advantages to being in a wheelchair if one looks for them. People talk to me and listen to what I have to say now, whereas if I were 'able-bodied' I would be just another passing body! They seem to stop and listen because *they* think it is so wonderful that I am not a 'closet case' ".

If the person created the disease because of a sense of un-worthiness he will want to stay ill until some other difficulty or misfortune comes along to take the place of the disease and confirm his lack of belief in himself.

7. The sick person may be unable or unwilling to give up his own mental image of the disease and replace it with an image of his body without the disease. The image of the disease may be so strong that it prevents him from being open to the healing power being channelled to him by the healer. The healing power, or energy of life, is spiritual; a physical body is the result of the way that energy has been molded or formed by the mind of that individual. A person who has habitually used that energy with negative images, may therefore still do this with the life energy that he is receiving via the healer.

8. Even though the one in need has not received an apparent physical healing, he may in fact be healed in mind and/or in spirit, and this may be far more important for the growth of his soul. After all, what good is a healthy body if it is occupied by a bitter, self-centered mind, or a depressed, darkened spirit? The physical healing may follow much later. In fact it may never be realized in this lifetime, the handicap being necessary for that individual as a teacher of a lesson in patience, humility or other characteristic that was one of the special objectives of their incarnation in this life.

They might also be an example for other people of a great spirit enjoying life and blessing others in spite of their physical condition. I remember meeting a middle aged woman who had lost the use of both of her legs when she contracted polio at the age of two. The joy and love which radiated from her, notwithstanding her obvious handicap, was an inspiration to all who met her. Truly a service to humanity.

9. If it is believed that the cause is Karmic, then a healing is unlikely until the lesson it brings has been absorbed and indelibly learned, and the disease or pain is no longer needed.

10. The Hawaiian Kahunas had another explanation for healings that did not succeed. They believed that people

who have guilt feelings are unable to accept this type of healing, nor to get in touch with their own Higher Self. The individual may be conscious of these feelings, or they may be buried in his subconscious mind. They may be the result of his having actually done something which hurt another, or they may have been created by a strict religious training which imposed many man-made rules and regulations that the individual has been unable to follow completely. Consciously this has not bothered him, but unconsciously he feels guilty.

For a healing to be successful these feelings of guilt must first be cleansed or cleared away. Hurting others must be stopped, and old hurts must be recompensed. Guilt arising merely from early conditioning could be eliminated by rituals of fasting and prayer, or by doing something for someone else in need.

There is another factor that may be involved when it seems that guilt is the cause of a disease. Some people have chosen consciously, but more often unconsciously, the path of suffering as a means of atonement for their guilt. If this is so, and they continue to choose it, even after becoming aware of the choice, and the fact that there are alternatives, then Spiritual Healing is unlikely to be effective. They have a free will, and if this is their choice it will be honored.

11. Perhaps one of the most frequent reasons for failure to respond to Spiritual Healing is the unwillingness of some sick people to follow through. After one or maybe two visits to the healer without experiencing a complete healing, or at least a dramatic improvement, they abandon all hope of a healing and assume that Spiritual Healing does not work for them, and they do not return for further sessions. Maybe because Jesus always healed with only one treatment, and nearly always instantaneously, their expectations are for a similar experience, which is not always possible for the many reasons outlined here. It is more likely that if they persisted, and were willing to make the changes in their lives to eliminate

the cause they would be healed. Often some of the greatest lessons that we are meant to learn from an illness are patience and faith in the power of God, and by giving up so soon, the one in need is passing up the opportunity to learn these teachings.

Another reason why many people do not return to a healer for a second healing session is that they realize during their first visit that a change in their life will be necessary, problems will have to be faced, or a deeper search for the cause undertaken, but they are unwilling to make the effort.

12. There may be a combination of two or more of the above factors—the possibilities are infinite, and vary just as each individual differs from another in physical, emotional and mental characteristics.

13. Healers are sometimes asked to assist someone who has already entered the "flight pattern" for passing on to the next plane. Their time has come and they have accepted this, at least at a subconscious level, but consciously they, or those who love them, still cling to one last hope and seek a "miracle" which is not meant to be. In this case it is right for the sick one to pass on to the Spirit world at this time. Who are we to decide how long any one life on this earth should be? If the purpose of incarnation on the material plane is to have certain experiences, and to learn special lessons, in order to advance our soul growth and to move forward on the path to eventual fully conscious reunion with God, how do we know that 30 or 50 years on this earth are any less desirable than 80 years for any particular individual?

If someone's life work is done he will probably feel complete and ready and willing to terminate this physical existence, although he may find it difficult to leave those he loves. However, if he is afraid of death, or too attached to material things or his sensing body, he may hang on past the appropriate time and experience disease and pain resulting from the inner conflict.

If the Spirit world is the harmonious, joyous state of being that we are told it is, the tragedy inherent in an "early" death is not for the one who dies, but for those remaining behind who were attached to them and who miss them. Of course, if their love for the departed one were unconditional it would be free of attachment, and there would be no sadness on their part either. The probable negative reaction to this idea shows how hard it is to achieve that state of loving without any conditions.

There is a corollary to this however; if an old person experiences a disease it does not necessarily mean that it is the correct time for them to pass on. I always tell people in this situation that their body is giving them a message, just as it is for younger people with physical problems, and if they will seek for the cause, and learn the lesson that the message is bringing them, there is no reason why they cannot die at the right time while in good health.

I believe that we all can die peacefully without pain or discomfort—merely losing consciousness as our soul departs the body. There may be a gradual decline of physical strength and endurance over the years as these energies are transferred to the individual's mental and spiritual bodies, but the later years of a man's or woman's life can be, and in many cases are, their richest, most creative and fulfilling years. Eventually, of course, there comes a time when it is right for the body to cease to act as a vehicle for the soul, which then experiences a rebirth into the Spirit World; one more step in the ever changing pattern of its eternal life.

If we can reach a point of equilibrium between love of existence on this earth plane, and a desire for life on the Spirit plane, accepting life as one continuum, we no longer need to fear death, nor do we need to long for it. We become like a man in space who has arrived at a position where the gravitational pull of the earth is exactly balanced by the gravitational pull of the moon—he can just float without effort and with no conflicting forces to pull him in different directions; he is at peace.

At that place of perfect balance we can let life flow as it is planned by our Creator, in harmony with nature and our fellow humans, fulfilling our destiny for this particular incarnation on this earth, but always ready to move on to the Spirit world at the right time, with no fears and no unfinished business. It is reported that there are some Eastern mystics who have achieved this point of harmony to such an extent that they can go out of their physical body and into the Spirit World and back into the physical at will for hundreds of years.

It is interesting to note that nearly all of these blocks to healing are created by the *choice* of the sick person. Even those which appear to be beyond their conscious control may involve a choice by their Higher Self, either now or prior to this incarnation. I often point out to people that all through life, and in every situation, we always have a choice. Even if a disaster over which we apparently have no control hits us, we have a choice as to how we react to it; we can succumb to depression and despair and do nothing, or we can accept it as a lesson to be learned and make every effort, physically and mentally, to repair the damage or make the best of the new circumstances.

Temporary Healing

There are cases in which a complete or partial healing of the symptoms is experienced for a short time, and then the problem returns in full force with the same symptoms or different ones. I believe there are two reasons for this.

1. Sometimes the *cause* of the disease or dysfunction was never healed. As previously explained, discovering and correcting the cause of any disease is a very important part of any form of healing.

2. The reason may be a lack of positive input to replace the negativity which has been removed by the healing. A lot of energy was being consumed by the disease and by the inner conflict or repressed emotion which was causing the

disease. When this has all been eliminated, a healing occurs but it may leave a mental or spiritual vacuum within the one who is healed.

The energy which has now become available, because it is no longer being used for the disease or the conflict, needs direction. If the one who is healed fails to provide a positive direction the energy may take on some negative form and the disease may return, or some other physical, mental or emotional problem may become evident. Spiritual counselling by the healer or some other person may be necessary to avoid this.

Jesus warned of this danger when he said:

> When the unclean spirit has gone out of a man he passes through waterless places seeking rest, but he finds none. Then he says: 'I will return to my house from which I came.' And when he comes he finds it empty, swept and put in order. Then he goes and brings with him seven other spirits more evil than himself, and they enter and dwell there; and the last state of that man becomes worse than the first. (Matthew 12:43-45)

Importance of Soul Growth

I believe that the importance of Soul Growth underlies all of these explanations for different results from Spiritual Healing attempts. By this I mean that it is the variation in peoples' progress towards learning the lesson which the disease was meant to teach them for the evolution of their own soul that causes some people to be healed instantaneously, some after a series of sessions over several weeks, months or even years, and some to not respond at all.

Some people have already learned that lesson when they come to the healer and merely need a slight infusion of energy to change the pattern or habits of their body. The blockage to the normal flow of energies caused by their erroneous or repressed thinking, emotion or attitude has already been basically removed by their own growth and mental change prior to the healing session, or they are ready to make that change at once, and the healing that follows is instantaneous or almost so. In confirmation of this statement I have noticed that in most cases where an instantaneous healing takes place, it is followed by a radical change in the healed person's habits, attitudes or thoughts about life. In other words an instantaneous change occurs on other levels in addition to the physical.

Others are ready and willing to learn the lesson that is inherent in the problem, but it takes some time for them to make the required changes in their life. The healing power, which is Love, helps them to get in touch with their inner guidance and to make the change. Each case is, of course, different and the response is an individual one. It has been fascinating for me to observe the personality changes that take place in some people on a parallel course with their healing.

Still others are not yet ready to surrender whatever it is that caused their disease and so no healing occurs. The lesson may be a painful one, but, until it has been learned, the individuals cannot move onwards in their soul development. The disease may even result in the destruction of their physical body, but the lesson still has to be learned either on the spirit plane, or, more likely, in their next life on this earth. This is the spiritual law of progress and return to the awareness of one's union with God.

In view of all the possible reasons why a particular individual's disease is not healed after one or more sessions of Spiritual Healing it is apparent that this type of healing will never be one hundred per cent successful. Yet many people seize on the so-called failures as an excuse for denying that Spiritual Healing can ever be really effective. They say that it is all an illusion, thus throwing the baby out with the bath water. This is unfortunate but unavoidable since the choice is theirs.

The large variety of explanations for disappointing results in some cases, is also one reason why we must not judge another. Even if it was within our right to do so (which it is not) we could not possibly know all the facts of his present and previous lives upon which to base a fair judgement; only God and the person's own Higher Self (which is the Divine within him) knows the full story, and only God or his Higher Self may pass judgement on the way he has lived.

Non-Attachment to Results

It is very important that the healer should not be attached to results, because if he is it makes it difficult for his love to be unconditional. If he *wills* the sick one to be healed, then he may be interfering with that person's free will, which even God will not do. If he succeeds by sheer will power, then the other person will not have learned the lessons that the dysfunction was to teach him; nor will he have found his own inner guidance and strength. In this case there is every likelihood that the illness will return.

If the healer is attached to results then it is very possible that:

(a) If the healing is successful it will inflate his ego and he will start to believe that *he* accomplished the result, whereas it is only the power of God that can heal.

(b) If no healing is apparent then the healer will blame himself and consider his efforts a failure, which is a heavy load to bear especially if the person dies! Of course, this is no more the case than a successful healing is to his credit.

A spiritual healer, therefore, merely acts as a channel for the healing energy and unconditional love of God, sharing these with the one in need to use or reject in any way the sick person's Higher Self decides. Having done this the healer completely detaches himself, mentally and emotionally, from the other person and from any changes that may occur in his condition, while still continuing to love him unconditionally. Fortunately this necessary detachment is reinforced by the very fact that some are healed and some are not, because this is a constant reminder to the healer that he really has nothing to do with either the healing or the failure to heal. Nevertheless spiritual healers are seldom completely detached, however much they try to be, and most will rejoice when someone is healed instantly and dramatically, and are disappointed when nothing seems to happen and the sick one continues to suffer and even die. Complete detachment is not an easy state of consciousness to attain.

An integral part of this important non-attachment lesson is to leave the sick person completely free to choose whether to live or to die. Healers would not be able to be a channel for the healing power unless they had a great compassion for the sick and suffering. However, if this compassion is combined with their personal will that the sick one is healed regardless of the will of God in the matter, and regardless of what is best for the other person's own evolution and soul growth (which in reality is the same as God's will) then they are trying to impose their own desires without respect for the choice of the sick one himself. It may even be advisable to point out to the sick person that he has this choice, and that with pure unconditional love the healer will support whichever decision he makes.

This is true even for those who have been in a coma for days or weeks and are apparently unconscious of the human voice. If they are told in a clear normal tone of speech that they have the choice whether to leave their body and pass on to the spirit plane, or to return to the body and recover full consciousness, and that in kindness to their loved ones they should make a decision one way or the other, the message will usually penetrate their unconscious mind and reach their Higher Self. If it does, then this will be followed by their death or by their regaining consciousness, thus putting an end to the agony of indecision for all concerned.

Notes for Chapter 6

1. Harry Edwards. *The Healing Intelligence* p. 103. The Healer Publishing Co. Ltd., Guildford, England. 1965

THE SPIRITUAL POWER THAT HEALS

ALWAYS HAS BEEN AVAILABLE

IS NOW PRESENT

AND ALWAYS WILL BE

CHAPTER 7

ANGELS AND
SPIRIT DOCTORS

THE SUBJECT OF this chapter may seem a little strange to
orthodox Christians, or to those who have no belief in
an afterlife, but let us take an unprejudiced look at some
evidence that a spiritual healer does not work alone.

Angels

There are nearly three hundred references in the Bible to
the existence of angels. In the Old Testament there are
many records of angels appearing to men and women and
conveying messages from God to them, saving people from
disaster or danger, comforting them in times of hardship,
guiding them through difficult situations and revealing the
future to the prophets. The New Testament is also full of
references to the activity of angels in the lives of Jesus, his
family and his disciples. You will recall that at the time of
Jesus' birth, angels appeared to the shepherds, and they
appeared to Mary and Joseph on many occasions prior to,
and just after his birth. It was also an angel that told Joseph
to take the baby into Egypt to save his life, and later told him

155

it was safe to return. During his ministry Jesus often talked about angels as very real beings, and an angel appeared to his followers after his death.

Billy Graham, the famous evangelist, says that he is convinced that angels really do exist and help us in many ways. He has written a book entitled *Angels, God's Secret Agents.*[1]

The Christian Church continued to believe in angels for many centuries, as can be seen in religious paintings and frescoes. Gradually, however, their reality faded from popular belief and they became treated as figments of the imagination. There are those people in current times, nevertheless, who have seen or do see angelic beings and know that they are real, and that they exist to help us in many ways as part of their service to God. There are guardian angels to protect and to guide us, and healing angels to assist in channelling the Healing Power to those who ask for their help.

Geoffrey Hodson's book *The Kingdom of the Gods* is devoted to descriptions and colored illustrations of the various angels he has seen over the years. The title is deceptive because in the preface he makes it very clear that there is only one God; "an Absolute, Unknowable, Infinite and Unchanging Source and Foundation." He specifically refers to healing angels and says that "they carry out their mission largely, but not entirely, by the use of this power (a flood of corrective and vitalizing force) by restoration of the full function of the chakras concerned, and on occasion by the actual change of substances in the super-physical, etheric, and physical bodies. They also direct a powerful stream of cleansing, vitalizing and healing forces from their own auras and other natural reservoirs, through the physical, etheric and astral bodies especially, thereby setting up conditions under which the natural processes of elimination and of healing can restore the sufferer to health."[2]

Another testament to the reality of angels is given by Flower Newhouse in her book, *Rediscovering the Angels.* After describing many different kinds of angels, she says:

An interesting service is rendered by the Healing Angels. Theirs is the task of clearing the congested areas in our etheric bodies so that the flow of cosmic energies can affect the inner as well as the outer man. . . . There are at least three Healing Angels always about a hospital, but the prayers of individual patients or the devotions of anxious relatives often invite Beings who accept single cases. They first ascertain whether a patient is to be released from the body, or healed. If their investigation reveals that the person's span is not finished, they first arrest the illness and then work to enlighten the consciousness of the patient.[3]

In her book *The Soul and the Ethic* Ann Ree Colton, the well known spiritual teacher and author, says:

One should seek to become acquainted with his angels, so that they might teach him of the treasures of his soul—for the angels have guardianship over the treasures of the soul. When one begins to know his angels as familiar companions, the angels will pull aside the veil of the treasures of the soul; and he shall doubt not himself.[4]

Another who believed in angels was the late spiritual healer, Rev. Dorie D'Angelo. I asked her why she believed in them and she replied:

Because I have seen them, and because of the things I have seen happen as a result of their help. Everyone has a Guardian Angel and it is my great joy to introduce people to theirs if they want to meet them. I have seen my own Guardian Angel and he has been a great source of comfort and strength to me. I also see the Guardian Angels of those who come to me for help.

I asked Dorie how she saw them and what they looked like.

I only see them with my eyes closed. They look very much like people except that they are made of transparent light of different colors and shades. They are very beautiful and they have a great love for the person that they have been assigned to guard. There are also Healing Angels who come especially to help those who are sick if they have asked for healing.

I requested any special suggestions she might have on how to communicate with angels.

Oh yes! You must tell them what you want. You see they never were human beings, so they don't understand what people want unless they are told. The best way is to thank them sincerely for all the things in your life that you enjoy, such as love, joy, laughter, peace and so on. It is not the words you use so much as the attitude within you—it's a vibration. So if you are thankful and filled with gratitude it's like turning a switch on the radio, and you connect with the angels and they know what you want. You can also ask them to go ahead of you, and they will prepare the way, whether it's a journey, a business transaction, a new relationship or even a simple thing such as finding a parking place. It always works—I do it all the time—it makes life so much easier.

Spirit Doctors

Many spiritual healers readily acknowledge that they receive much help from discarnate spirits who were medical doctors when they lived on this earth, and who have continued in their desire to help ailing humans by ministering to them from the spirit plane. The knowledge and ability of these doctors have increased since they passed over from the earth plane and they too can act as channels for the healing power.

In some cases the healer goes into a trance and is possessed by the spirit doctor. One of the most dramatic examples of this situation is that of the English healer, George Chapman. He enters into a trance and a spirit doctor takes over his body and proceeds accurately to diagnose the problem and then to "operate" a few inches above the patient's body, frequently with excellent healing results. Also the doctor usually talks out loud using medical terms which are quite unknown to Mr. Chapman in his conscious state, since he was a fireman by trade and had had very little formal education. On several occasions a qualified doctor, still living on this earth plane, has been present and has carried on a technical discussion with the spirit doctor who uses Mr. Chapman's vocal chords as his instrument for communication.

The really unusual fact in this case is that the "Doctor" identified himself as William Lang, a famous eye surgeon who was born in 1852 and died in 1937. He had been the Ophthalmic Surgeon at Middlesex Hospital in London, and later at Moorfields Eye Hospital, also in London. All of these facts were later confirmed by the British Medical Society. Even more remarkable were the conversations between Dr. Lang, speaking through Mr. Chapman in trance, and several former patients and a former student of his, who were still alive and came to visit Mr. Chapman. Dr. Lang remembered them and discussed details of his previous experience with them as patients or student, which no one else could possibly have known. They not only confirmed the truth of his statements but recognized his speech and mannerisms. The full story can be found in J. Bernard Hutton's book, *Healing Hands.* [5]

Several months after I had written the above, a lady, whom I did not know previously, came to see me for some help with a physical problem. During the course of our conversation she happened to mention that on two previous occasions some years ago she had silently asked this same Dr. Lang to help her, and in both cases he had done so. On the second visit a clairvoyant had been present and saw Dr. Lang appear and "operate" on this lady. This occurred many thousands of miles away from England, where Dr. Lang usually "operates." The healing was successful, returning hearing to an ear that had been deaf for several years. We went on to talk about the possible cause of her present problems, and then proceeded with the healing session.

The next day she reported considerable relief from some of her symptoms, but no reduction in the size of a lump which appeared to be a swollen lymph gland. Six weeks later she returned for a second session stating that her doctor wished to perform a biopsy on the lump, but she was reluctant to permit this. This time my wife, who is also a healer, joined me in the healing but knew nothing about the lady's previous explanation to me about Dr. Lang. After several minutes of prayerful "laying on of hands" by both of us, I received guidance to tell the lady to silently ask Dr. Lang to come and assist us in the healing. She did so and reported later that he immediately appeared to her and proceeded to "operate" on the lump, and to remove material from inside it. My wife, who had never heard of Dr. Lang before, and did not know why I had asked the one in need to call upon him, reported later that she also became aware of a man standing beside her and "operating" on the lady.

Another well known "possession" by a deceased doctor was the case of Arigo, the famous unorthodox Brazilian healer. He was an uneducated peasant, yet he diagnosed the patients' problems without asking any questions and with incredible accuracy. This was proved by studying reports made by the patients' regular physicians prior to their visits to Arigo. He never saw these reports—they were examined by research workers. He would not have had time to read these first anyway since he treated an average of three hundred people a day. That is one every two minutes for ten hours! He also had a regular job to support his family, as he refused all payment or gifts for his service.

He also performed surgical operations, but unlike Mr. Chapman he actually operated on the physical body itself. He used any penknife or kitchen knife that was available, without sterilizing it, and yet never created an infection. Nor did he use anesthetics, but no patient ever complained of feeling any pain. He wrote complicated prescriptions (including unusual drugs from different parts of the world) at a fantastic speed and without any preliminary examination or discussion of medical history.

Arigo claimed that during the time he was operating or prescribing he was possessed by a deceased German physician named Dr. Fritz, and that it was he who made the quick diagnoses, and who operated and prescribed complex drugs. Those who watched Arigo work noted a change in personality during the hours in which he treated patients. He took on a brusque, almost arrogant air, his eyes changed and became radiantly piercing, and his Portuguese speech became affected by a harsh gutteral accent. All of this left immediately he stopped working with sick people, and he returned to his normal mannerisms and speech. So in his case it seems that the spirit doctor took over his body and mind, guided his hands, and told him what to prescribe.

In an interview between a Brazilian doctor and Dr. Fritz speaking through Arigo while in a trance, Dr. Fritz claimed that a group of other deceased doctors, each with their own specialty, worked with him to heal in the name of Christ. The full story can be found in John G. Fuller's book, *Arigo: Surgeon of the Rusty Knife.* [6] Unfortunately, Arigo died in an automobile accident a few years ago so further investigation of his remarkable, but controversial, healing abilities had to be terminated.

When I talked to Dorie D'Angelo about angels I also asked her about her spirit doctor. I had heard that this deceased, Scottish physician, Dr. Kirk, appeared to her ten years ago quite suddenly when her husband became very ill over the Christmas holidays, at which time no regular doctor was available. Dr. Kirk showed her how to save her husband's life. She told me that since then Dr. Kirk has always come when she asks him to help her with a healing. He does not take over her own body, as Dr. Lang does with George Chapman, nor does he give her instructions on what to do with a physical instrument, as Dr. Fritz used to do with Arigo. Instead Dr. Kirk goes to work on the etheric body of the one in need, and Dorie, with her eyes closed, sees what he is doing and describes his actions out loud.

After we had discussed this for some time I asked Dorie if she thought Dr. Kirk would join us and give me some more information on this subject. She said "I don't know; I've never done that before." Nevertheless she closed her eyes, and Dr. Kirk soon appeared to her and gave us some interesting information.

I had carefully recorded all of our discussions on a portable tape recorder; the angels' discussion on one side of the tape and the spirit doctors' on the other. However, when I attempted to transcribe the tape I found that the angel side was perfect but the doctor side was a complete blank. Also I could not remember anything that Dr. Kirk had said!

Believing, as I do, that there are no accidents in our lives and that every event has a purpose, I meditated on this situation and came to the conclusion that I was meant to repeat the discussion but this time to be prepared with specific questions to ask Dr. Kirk. So I wrote down some questions and Dorie very kindly agreed to give me some more time so that we could repeat the contact. In doing so it quickly became apparent to me that what transpired was far more comprehensive and valuable than the previous experience. It developed into a three way conversation with Dorie talking to Dr. Kirk and to me; I asked the questions of Dr. Kirk, who then talked to Dorie, and she would then repeat to me what he had said so that I would know and it would be recorded. (The tape recorded perfectly this time— did he erase it last time?) Here is the conversation almost word for word:

ALAN: Please ask Dr. Kirk to join us now.

DORIE: Thank you for coming Dr. Kirk. I know you have been here for quite a while today. We would like your help so that Alan may be able to inform other people about the work of spirit doctors. Anything you would like to say we would be happy to share with others.

ALAN: Dr. Kirk, I want to apologize for my error with the tape recorder last time. I also forgot everything that you said. Maybe this was to make me come back again and this time to ask specific questions. Could you please tell us how you do your healing work?

DR. K.: There is a vibrational energy of healing which I can flow through the patient. Sometimes it is very difficult because the vibrational energy of the patient is different— it is solid. I have to maneuver their energy to let the helpful energy run through. This is very difficult, and it cannot be done in one, two, or even three sessions. At other times the patient is already on that vibrational level and the healing can be instantaneous.

ALAN: Do you send that helpful, vibrational energy through the etheric body into the physical?

DR. K.: Yes.

ALAN: Does that then line up the atoms of the physical body with the perfect etheric body?

DR. K.: Yes, that is what I am trying to do. Sometimes I can do it in the etheric body and then it goes into the physical body; but again, sometimes thoughts of the patient may block it all and stop it happening. Sometimes it will continue to work until it does get in and affect the physical. It has to change the vibrational energy in the physical body.

ALAN: Are there other spirit doctors who work with you?

DR. K.: Yes.

ALAN: Are they specialists, so that you call them in to help you in special cases?

DR. K.: I call them very often for extra power and also for an extra pair of hands to help out in the situation.

DORIE: He is showing me four hands. Sometimes there are three Beings who work with him; they look very like tall, transparent figures, but each is one color of light. One is copper color.

ALAN: Are they angels?

DORIE: No. I don't know what they are; he calls them the Beings. They are probably a kind of angel. When he needs extra help he will call these Beings in and they stand at the feet of the patient, about two feet away. They stand there and Dr. Kirk will say, "This needs to be disintegrated; it needs to disappear; we don't need it." He then gives them something from the patient's body like a tumor, or rupture, or hernia, or something else like that, and the Beings put their hands on it and it disintegrates. They are a very powerful force to get rid of a condition which is very strong or very solid. I have heard about these Beings from other sources, that they come to help but they never speak, they just come and do their job.

ALAN: Dr. Kirk, are there any types of disease or abnormality that you cannot help?

DR. K.: If it is too fixed in the mind of the person so that the thought form is so solid that if you disintegrate it, it comes back again right away—that is very difficult to heal. Bones can be reformed into the right shape; bones can be rebuilt; even teeth can be fixed.

ALAN: In other words a great deal depends on the receptivity and the co-operation of the patient?

DORIE: Yes it does very much. When someone says to me, "Well, I have been everywhere and no one can help me," the "no one" includes Dr. Kirk too.

ALAN: One thing that puzzles me, Doctor, is that sometimes you appear to use a colored liquid, oil or powder, and sometimes you appear to use sharp instruments. Why are these things, which appear to be physical, necessary if we are dealing strictly with the spiritual healing power itself?

DR. K.: Everything in the physical world has an etheric or thought form counterpart; so, as you use material things on the material body, we can use its etheric counterpart on the etheric body. Something has to be used to change the vibration in the cells. When I show Dorie that I am using something which looks like a physical powder, liquid or instrument, and she describes this to the patient, this convinces the patient that something is being done which seems logical to their mind. Even though it is not there at all, it is impressed on their mind.

DORIE: People often say to me, "Dorie, what was that yellow powder Dr. Kirk put in my blood? Whatever it was it did me a lot of good and I wish he would do it again." But I do not know what he put in.

DR. K.: That is a good question, Alan, and it interests me. You see, the mental part of the patient that I am working with is a child and the child wants things, pictures. If you give the child something they think, "Oh! yes, I am better now—that cured me." In fact I call these things toys.

DORIE: I didn't know you were conning me with toys, Dr. Kirk!

ALAN: Do you ever get tired, Doctor?

DR. K.: No, we never get tired. There is no time in our world, so there is no reason to get tired; also there is no physical body to weigh us down. However, there is a sense of time in that things get done. In fact there is a timing now, that this kind of material should be disseminated as quickly as possible and as widely as possible. The vibrations and energies are right at this time, and also it is very necessary.

ALAN: Doctor, Dorie can see you and some of your patients can see you. How can I learn to see you and the spirit doctors who are working with me and whom others have seen?

DR. K.: In one way you are already seeing them with your feelings. If you *believe* that you can see them you will begin to be much more aware. When you close your eyes and squint them and say, "Let me see you," you will probably see flashes of light or color and gradually the spirits will be able to impress themselves on the seeing part of you.

ALAN: That ends my questions, Dr. Kirk. Is there anything else that you would like to add?

DR. K.: Yes. There are many spirit doctors and they want to help the people in the world; they are available when anyone asks for them; they are there. They will come to whomever they can communicate with. They work with many people who do not recognize that helpers are with them. If the person in need is desperately in need they are more likely to be aware of the spirit doctor.

Healers, or rather, channels for healing, should keep in very good physical condition—the power is then transmitted more easily. The healthier you are in every way, physically, mentally and spiritually, the more you will attract to you more powerful spirits and helpers. If you keep yourself in top condition you will have more connections with a greater power.

Jesus was a vibrantly healthy man who attracted people so strongly that they left their homes and their families to wander with him without shelter or food. He was so vibrant, and with him was a great crowd of spirits, angels and people. The more you can approach that magnetic vitality, the more you will attract to you the power you need on the material and spiritual level.

Also remember that the more you channel the power the stronger you yourself become in every kind of way.

ALAN AND DORIE: Thank you for coming, Doctor, and for sharing this with us.

DORIE TO ALAN: You know everybody thinks that I always see the doctor very plainly but it is not usually like that, although I did see him clearly today and he sat down in a chair beside you which I have never seen him do before. Normally I see his hands or some other part of him, but not all of him.

The other day I was very tired, so I sat down and asked him to please come and give me some energy, and because I was tired enough he came. Then it was so amazing because I saw this man of about sixty, the way he always looks, and all of a sudden it was as though that figure dissolved and behind it was this *beautiful* figure made of light, just radiant, radiant light. This light figure then took hold of my hand and lifted me up with him and showed me the world—it was very, very beautiful. Then we came back and I came into my body and he transformed into the normal figure that I have seen before. Then I realized that Dr. Kirk really is a light being, and he showed me that to let me know that all the power that is necessary is channelling through this figure of Dr. Kirk.

The majority of spiritual healers, including most of the "Psychic Surgeons" in the Philippines, if they are assisted by a spirit doctor, or several of them, are not possessed by a spirit, as Chapman and Arigo are. The healer is used as a catalyst, and the spirit works through the healer's etheric body. The healer may be able to see the spirit doctor and watch him work, as Dorie does, or he may only be able to sense his presence.

As previously mentioned, I once asked an excellent clairvoyant to observe what happened in the healing sanctuary while I was channelling healing power to someone else. In addition to many colorful energies and symbols throughout the process, he saw the hands and arms of an angelic being; he said they were "strong and white, with scintillating, silvery, moving dots or stars." He also saw the white hands of a being dressed in a purple tunic and hat like the green ones doctors wear in operating rooms. It was interesting that these hands only appeared when my hands were directly over the diseased part of the other person's body (although the clairvoyant had not been told what this was, and it was not apparent to the eye). The spirit beings evidently knew exactly where the power was needed. Since then others who are psychic have seen or become aware of the presence of other beings in some form or other. Some have felt hands touching them, opened their eyes and found my hands were over a different area of their body and not touching. One or two have been able to communicate with them.

Why is it that these spirit doctors appear to have so much more healing skills than they had when they were incarnated in a physical body? I believe there are two reasons for this. One is that after passing on to the Spirit World they have continued to grow and progress in intellect and knowledge. If this were not true life after death would have little meaning or purpose. The other is that in the Spirit World they have access to Master Teachers and Healers whom they were unable to reach while in a physical body, and whose knowledge and skills have now become available to them.

Some people may ask why these spirit doctors, healers and teachers are willing to serve humanity in this way instead of relaxing and enjoying a well earned peace and quiet where they are? I think it is because just as on earth we grow spiritually by serving our brothers and sisters of the human race, so do they on the Spirit plane grow spiritually by helping those in need on both planes.

To summarize, therefore, if we want the help of angels and/or spirit doctors, we must ask for their assistance. They recognize and respect the fact that God has given each one of us a free will, and they will not impose their own will or desires on us. On the other hand, they are eager to help us, not only because of their love for mankind, but also because it is through service to human beings that they grow spiritually and come ever closer to realizing their own unity with God. Apparently they seldom work directly with the one who is ill, but even in absent healing they usually need a human being who offers his physical body and mind as a channel for their use. This is analogous to the use of a human Medium for communication by a spirit entity to another human being. If we couple our request to them with a prayer that God's will be done, this leaves them free to work in accordance with that will, uninhibited by any desires of our own.

Notes for Chapter 7

1. Billy Graham. *Angels: God's Secret Agents.* Doubleday and Company, Inc, New York. 1975

2. Geoffrey Hodson. *The Kingdom of the Gods.* p. IX & 47. The Theosophical Publishing House, Adyar, Madras, India. 1952

3. Flower Newhouse. *Rediscovering The Angels.* p. 107. The Christward Ministry, Escondido, California. 1950

4. Ann Ree Colton. *The Soul and The Ethic* p. 81. ARC Publishing Company, P.O. Box 1138, Glendale, California. 1965

5. J. Bernard Hutton. *Healing Hands.* David McKay Company, Inc, New York. 1967

6. John G. Fuller. *Arigo: Surgeon of the Rusty Knife.* Thomas Y. Crowell Company, New York. 1974

THERE IS ONLY ONE

ENERGY

AND THAT IS

LOVE

EVERYTHING ELSE IS

AN ILLUSION

CHAPTER 8

YOU TOO CAN BE A HEALER

Prerequisites

MOST SPIRITUAL HEALERS seem to be in agreement that the ability to heal spiritually is not an exclusive gift for a few special people, but rather that it is possible for anyone to help others in this way, provided that four conditions are met by the would-be healer.

1. You must have a strong desire to heal the sick. Many people do not have such a desire, which is no reflection on them; there are many services to be performed for God's Kingdom—healing is only one of them. Those that feel led to serve in some other way should do so. However, you need to examine carefully the motives underlying your desire to heal others. If you find that these motives include a desire for money, power or fame, a wish to satisfy your own ego, or a need to fulfill other emotional requirements of your own, then you are unlikely to succeed as a channel for healing. You may, in fact, increase the problems of others, rather than reduce them. On the other hand, if your motivation arises only from a sincere love for God and your

fellow humans, and a desire to serve by becoming a channel for God's healing power, if this is God's will for you, then the first of the four requirements is satisfied.

2. You must have a real compassion for those that are sick or in pain. This does not refer to sympathetic, emotional feelings for them, but involves an unconditional love for all of God's creation, a deep caring for the other person as a perfect fellow child of God, regardless of age, race, religion, appearance or personality.

3. You must have faith in a Divine Creator with whom all things are possible, and believe with all your heart, mind and soul that there is no limit to the healings that are possible when the power of that Divine Force is channelled through you. Any limitations that you establish in your own thinking will tend to be reflected in your healing experience.

4. You must open yourself as a channel for the power of God, and pray that God will use you as a channel for that power, in accordance with His will. Another way of looking at this is in terms of consciousness. Humans are conscious beings, but their level of consciousness obviously varies tremendously. For some, life consists mainly in fulfilling the basic instincts for food, shelter, sex, survival, and participating in fairly routine work and recreation. Their awareness of other levels of consciousness, of their own and other people's feelings, and of spiritual truths is minimal. At the other extreme are those great spiritual teachers whose awareness of themselves, the total universe and the One Source is very high. They spend their lives in selfless service to others, not out of a sense of duty, but because of their love for God and all of His Creation.

Opening the Channel

I am often asked how I reached the point where I found that I could help people who were sick. This is not easy to verbalize, but I gladly share my own process in the hope that it will be of some value to others. I am not suggesting for a moment that this is the way for everyone—there are many paths to the same goal, this is only one of them.

I recognized that the first three conditions outlined above were existent within me; I had a great desire to be a channel for healing, and a real compassion for the suffering. I also had a strong faith that "with God all things are possible," (Matthew 19:26) and in Jesus' statement that "He that believes in me, the works that I do shall he do also." (John 14:12) The fourth requirement, opening the channel, was the hard one, and I am still working on it; I am sure I will always need to do so for the rest of my life. Following are the many avenues which I explored, many of them simultaneously, all of which I feel contributed in some manner to helping me to reach the point where I am—wherever that is!

1. *Prayer* I asked God to use me as a channel for healing, if this was His will, and to guide me in my search.

2. *Meditation* I tried many different ways, including initiation into Transcendental Meditation. No one way seems outstanding for me, and I continue to experiment. All teachers recommend a regular time each day, and for me 3 to 5 a.m. has proved to be the best. There is a particular magic in the silence and peaceful vibrations at that time, and I am certain of no interruptions.

3. *Contemplation* The silence and peace of contemplation is similar to meditation, but the mind is active instead of still. Some contemplate a flower or other physical object, but I have found that a word (e.g. Love; Light; God, etc.) or a short sentence is more meaningful, for example, "I am a child of God;" "_____ is a child of God;" "The Kingdom of God is within me;" "The truth will set me free."

4. *Self-Awareness* I made an honest effort to get to know myself. This included participating in groups organized for

this purpose (not "encounter groups" which seemed too violent and destructive to me). One of the earliest of these experiences was *est*, the intensive self-awareness, take-responsibility-for-your-own-life training organized by Werner Erhart. I actively participated in all the processes that are included in the two thirty hour weekends, and found most of them to be helpful, but did not experience any of the major revelations experienced by many people. To see two or three grown men faint simply because they had to stand up, along with fifty other people, and face the other two hundred members of the workshop in silence for about twenty minutes, was a big surprise to me.

The only part of the training that "got to me" was the foul language used throughout by the trainer when addressing the participants as a group or as individuals. However, when I signed up for the Graduate Review two years later, I was able to let that go, and it did not bother me. It finally sunk into my mind that when it was addressed to me I had a choice to ignore it or to let it annoy me, and that when it was addressed to others they had the same choice, and it was none of my business what reaction they chose.

Recording and interpreting dreams also became an important part of this search for inner awareness; I never realized until I started doing this ten years ago, how much I had been missing in information and guidance by ignoring my dreams. Now my dream journal is a valuable tool for growth. I also learned that it was important to watch my thoughts and to try to direct them on the right path, recalling that "as a man thinks in his heart, so is he."

Psychologists have learned that when someone becomes unusually emotionally charged by an action, statement or characteristic of another person, it is because the very thing which annoys or attracts him so much is within himself but has been repressed or never recognized. This attribute is noticed in the other and the energy contained within is "projected" onto them. Watching for my projections onto others, both positive and negative, revealed aspects of my inner being of which I was previously unaware. Claiming these as my own was not easy!

Listening to my "Inner Teacher" during meditation I sometimes receive helpful messages. One which was particularly concerned with this matter of self-awareness came to me like this.

Continue to search for the truth about yourself.
It seems to be elusive, but it is all within you and ready to come out. If you do not ask questions you will not receive the answers, regardless of the topic, and knowing yourself is no different. For example
What do you like most?
What do you dislike most?
What do you react strongly to in a positive way?
What do you react strongly to in a negative way?
What do you fear?
What do you love?
What are your desires?
What are your hopes?
What are your goals?
What could you do without?
What could you *not* do without?
What disappoints you?
What surprises you?
What are you critical of?
What do you approve?
What are you willing to give to others?
What do you want to receive from them?
What has life taught you?
What would you like to do over again differently?
What are your greatest faults?
What are your greatest strengths?
What makes you laugh?
What makes you cry?
What gives you a warm feeling inside?
What leaves you cold?
When you have answered all of these questions you will have a pretty good insight into yourself, and will know where you need to work, what you need to change, and where the conflicts are.

After I had answered these questions for myself, I analyzed the responses and found a definite pattern emerging as several of the questions revealed by their answers different aspects of the same characteristic. For example, life had taught me the importance of love from others; one of the things that I could not do without was love; and one of the things I feared was the loss of a loved one. By compiling all of the common or repetitive factors I was able to make a summary of a plan for action.

It has been said that it is more blessed to give than to receive. However, it is important that we are also willing to receive. Not only do we need the love and energy for our own growth, but unless we are willing to receive, how can others realize the blessedness of giving?

One of the major insights I experienced as I worked on opening the channel was my own lack of receptivity. When I was at Brugh Joy's ranch in Lucerne Valley he taught us how to sense the energy radiating from our own bodies and from the bodies of our fellow students. I became aware that I could not sense the energy from others nearly as well as most of them could sense the energy radiating from my hands. Meditating on this I came to the conclusion that I was not opening myself to receive the energy of others; I determined to do so in the future. Later on, while we were all lying on the floor listening to classical music played at high intensity, it suddenly dawned on me that maybe I had never really opened myself to receive the love of God. I, therefore, consciously tried to do just that and immedlately fell a wave of loving energy pour throughout my body, bringing tears of joy to my eyes. It was a beautiful lesson for me and an experience I shall never forget.

5. *Psychic Assistance* A private session with the noted psychic, Ann Armstrong, in which I specifically asked for revelation of psychological blocks to my spiritual growth, was a valuable step. Ann tunes in psychically to your strong and weak points and pulls no punches!

6. *Reading* I studied many good books on the subject of Spiritual Healing all of which were most helpful. This included the *New Testament,* which I consider to be the basic

text. Studying Carl Jung's psychology and information on dream interpretation, parapsychology and other religions was also very valuable.

7. *Seminars and Workshops* I attended a number of these that related to Spiritual Healing, including Dr. Lawrence LeShan's program described in his book *The Medium, the Mystic and the Physicist,* [1] several seminars offered by the University of California Extension at Santa Cruz, and the A.R.E. healing conference at Phoenix, Arizona. They all contributed valuable information and experience. However, the one that gave me the final breakthrough was the seventeen day Gathering For Higher Consciousness in the high desert, led by Dr. Brugh Joy, an outstanding young spiritual leader of the New Age. This was a truly valuable and unforgetable experience.

8. *England* I toured Spiritual Healing Centers in England, observing spiritual healers at work. In London I had the privilege of working for five hours with Peter Denton, who was in charge of the healing clinic at the Spiritualist Association of Great Britain at that time.

9. *Prayer Circle* Regular attendance at a weekly healing Prayer Circle led by Reverend Dorie D'Angelo was also a factor in opening the channel.

10. *Unconditional Love* Learning to love myself and others unconditionally was important. I learned from many sources that you cannot love others until you love yourself, but that isn't always easy—particularly as you get to know yourself better! The love for all (which actually is the healing power) must be unconditional, without attachment or possessiveness, and expecting nothing in return. I recognize that this is a goal, not an achievement, but it is worth striving for. Spiritual Healing is unity in love—unity with the other and with God—an at-one-ness in an atmosphere of unconditional love.

An interesting way of helping to develop the healing consciousness which was suggested by the late, famous medium, Arthur Ford, is to visualize yourself as being a spectator at one of the healings performed by Jesus. Pick out one that appeals to you, read about it several times until you are thoroughly familiar with it. Then sit in a quiet place with your eyes closed, relax completely, and breathe easily and rhythmically. Now in your imagination picture the scene where the healing took place—the buildings or countryside, the people, their clothes, and their curiosity as Jesus arrives. Picture in your mind the suffering and hope of the diseased person, their plea to be healed and their friends' support. Imagine the appearance of Jesus, his clothes, his hair, his face, and above all his eyes and the unconditional love that radiates from his whole being. Notice his gentle manner and voice as he grants the request for healing. Observe the initial disbelief of the sick person that the healing has actually taken place, and then the joy and excitement when they suddenly realize that they have been healed, followed by their gratitude and adoration. Feel the excitement and amazement of the crowd, of which you are a member. Imagine what went through your mind when the instant healing occurred. Did it change your life?

As a would-be spiritual healer, therefore, make every effort to raise your level of consciousness to include more and more from your own subconscious as well as the collective or universal unconscious, thus increasing your awareness, not only of your own complex being, but also of the Divine Creator and all of His Creation. The higher the level you achieve, the greater will be your success in opening yourself as a channel. However, I know of no quick way to self-realization; it has to be accomplished step by step, or layer by layer like peeling an onion, and there may be tears in the process too!

Let me add one note of caution to the search for higher consciousness and opening the channel. If you find a teacher who seems to be advanced spiritually, and has psychic abilities, which may or may not include the ability to channel the healing power, by all means attend his or her classes or study groups, *but do not give up your own power to the teacher.* A truly spiritual leader will never ask for this, and will reject it if you try to surrender your power to him. Especially be on guard against those who demand absolute allegiance to them rather than to God, and ask you to be unreservedly and irrevocably attached to their organization. Some will even ask you to give them all of your material possessions as proof of your non-attachment to materiality. The well known tragedy of Jonestown in Guyana, with its 900 plus suicides at the command of the leader has probably alerted many to this danger. The old saying "power corrupts and absolute power corrupts absolutely," has seldom had a better example.

It is therefore really as harmful to the teachers or leaders as it is to yourself when you give up your power to them. Actually when you do this you are feeding rich fertilizer to the drive for power that is one of the strong basic instincts which every man and woman must learn to control. You may recall that when Jesus was faced with the three major temptations in the desert, one of them was Satan offering him power over, and ownership of, all the world and its possessions if Jesus would worship him. Never give up your own power, except to your Creator.

Probably the most important and effective way of raising your consciousness to a higher, spiritual level, and thus becoming a clearer channel for the healing power of God, is frequently to contemplate or meditate on God and His many attributes. Some of these are: Love, Light, Joy, Perfection, Truth, Peace, Divinity, Unlimited Power, Infinite Intelligence, Justice and Harmony. If this is coupled with a sincere effort to purify your body, emotions, actions and thoughts, consciousness will gradually be raised to a higher level, and many former desires for physical and material pleasures will drop away of their own accord. The clearer your channel becomes, the purer and more effective will be the energy that is channelled.

Asking for Help

I believe that "Ask and you will receive" (John 16:24) is a spiritual law, and unless you ask for help and guidance, whether it is from God, Jesus, angels, or spirit guides, you are unlikely to receive it. If you did, such action on their part would interfere with your free will, which is one of God's greatest gifts to mankind. Therefore, ask for spiritual help, guidance and strength, and it will be received, but not necessarily instantaneously.

Patience

Whatever path you follow to open the channel will be your own and may be quite different from mine or anyone else's. It is safe to say, however, that it must include PATIENCE. Do not keep pulling up the plant to see how it is getting along—the stems, the leaves and then the blossoms will show one at a time when they are ready—the roots are also growing but never showing. God has placed this same miracle of life in all of His creation, in each plant, each animal and each human being. Now-a-days it seems that man is always in a hurry, but Nature is never in a hurry; it follows the flow of life which is eternal. Become a part of that flow and your channel will become clear at its own pace.

How Do You Begin?

You need have no concern about how you will commence to help people. Just as in the old adage, "When the student is ready the teacher will appear," so it is that "When the healer is ready the ones in need will arrive." You have asked for the help of God and His spirit guides in developing the ability to channel His power, and they will know when you are ready, and at the right time will direct those to you whom you can help.

It is also the experience of those who have been in this work for some time that there is usually what some might call "beginner's luck." That is, some rapid and dramatic healings will often occur at the start to encourage you and to enable you to persist with more difficult and slower moving situations later on. Otherwise you might be inclined to abandon the effort, feeling that you were not meant to be a channel. The early successful results will also increase your faith and confidence.

Naturally Gifted Healers

What about those famous healers who found that they had this ability when they were still children, or those who later in life discovered it by accident without making any effort to try to achieve the aptitude? Surely the same observation can be made of other greatly skilled individuals. Some seem to be born with them, like Mozart playing the piano brilliantly when he was only six, while others achieve the skill later in life by constant training and practice. I know of only one satisfactory explanation and that is the theory of Reincarnation; Mozart had probably been a skilled musician in a previous life and was born into this one with much of that learning stored in his subconscious mind. Likewise those spiritual healers who find that they have the ability without really trying, presumably had been spiritual healers in one or more previous life times.

Discovering What Is Right for You

As you grow in your ability to be a channel you will be guided into the method which seems right for you. It may be Absent Healing, Contact Healing, or some of both. In the use of your hands in Contact Healing you may be guided into one of the formats already described in Chapter 2, or you may develop some other procedure of your own.

Never Let It Become Routine

Once the practice of channelling spiritual power to others for healing has been started, it is important that it not become a mere routine or a burden. This is not likely to happen if the motivation for this form of service is one of unconditional love for God and all of His creation, including those who are sick. Nor is it likely to occur if you realize that acting as a channel for the healing power is a learning process, and that everyone who asks for help is also a teacher. No two situations are alike; the exact nature of the cause of the disease, the reaction of the other person to the healing process, the insights or visions they receive, the progress of the healing itself, and the spiritual growth or guidance that the healer gains from the experience, will nearly always be different with every case; it can be very stimulating and exciting.

One way to help to prevent any negative emotion being developed is for you to continue in the practice of prayer and meditation, and listening to your own inner voice.

The Power Is Not Your Own

It is also important always to remember and acknowledge to those seeking help, that the power is not your own, that you are only a channel for the Divine Forces, and that all glory and gratitude belongs to the Creator. If you believe that you are exerting your own power, or giving out your own energy, and that therefore the credit for healing belongs to you, you will most likely lose the ability to be of help to others and be lost in the tentacles of your ego.

Then, too, if you feel that you are transferring your own energy you will quickly become tired. Therefore, if at any time you feel drained and exhausted after working with someone, you need to recognize that you have probably remained closed to the Source, and allowed your own energy to be transferred. However, by opening yourself right away and visualizing the Universal Energy pouring into you through the top of your head (the crown chakra) you can renew your own supply and feel refreshed and energetic again.

Thus, if at all times you will consciously act as a channel, you will seldom feel tired since the Power is infinite and inexhaustible. In fact you may feel exhilarated as some of the energy remains within your own body as a residue.

This precaution is also closely related to the hazard of the healer taking on the disease, pain or other problem of the one that he is trying to help. If you believe that you are transferring your own energy, then the exchange is on a personal level and it is possible for the energy flow to work in the reverse direction, and for you to experience the discomfort or other symptoms being conveyed to your own body.

Physicists tell us that it is impossible for a lower energy field to transfer to a higher energy field—the flow is always the other way. So, if you are transferring your own energy, and it happens to be low (maybe because of helping several people in a day) and the energy field of the other is high (maybe because the disease itself has a high energy field like cancer, or because they are just naturally a high energy person) it leaves you open to absorbing the negative energy that you do not want. On the other hand, if you remain completely open to the Infinite Power, visualizing yourself as a channel, there is no personal interchange, and the power is so great that it is impossible for any reverse flow to occur, and you will remain immune to all of the other person's problems.

Some healers deliberately try to transfer the disease from the sick person to themselves by the use of their mind and will, and then heal themselves. This is a very dangerous technique (especially for a beginner) and one that I feel is entirely unnecessary; we are not asked to take upon ourselves another person's pain or Karma, only to help them work through it or to eliminate it, keeping ourselves free and clear on all levels.

Obtaining Permission

God has given every one of us a free will—we always have a choice; therefore it is unwise for anyone to attempt to heal someone else without their permission. If the other person is unconscious, or for some other reason is physically incapable of expressing his wishes, then permission may be granted by someone who is very close to him and who can honestly anticipate what his desire would be if he were conscious and able to communicate. This would also apply in the case of a baby or a child that is too young to understand what is involved. In these situations the permission of one or both of the parents may be obtained on behalf of the child.

In their eagerness to prevent pain and to preserve life, some healers will on their own initiative, or at the request of a friend or relative of the sick person, direct their healing efforts towards someone who has not requested this and has no idea what is being done. This is trespassing on the other person's freedom of choice, and even God will not do that. Of course, it makes it less likely that the attempt will be successful, but if it is, and the pain or disease is eliminated, or death postponed, this result may be directly contrary to the sick person's wishes. As we saw in Chapter 6, some people, for reasons of their own, do not want to get well, or may actually want to die. Also it may be that they will not learn the lesson that was meant for them, or that payment of their Karma is delayed only to be experienced later on.

Another possibility is that they are forced to live for a longer period in an unhappy environment instead of realizing the reward that they have earned, and passing on to the Spirit World where we are told the joy and peace far exceed anything on this earth plane.

Healing without permission may also prevent a possible increase in the understanding and faith of the sick person, which might have occurred if he had been aware in advance of the spiritual forces that were being brought in to assist in his healing. As pointed out in Chapter 2, it is even better if the one asking for help believes in the process of Spiritual Healing and the ability of the healer, and not only requests this type of assistance, but also wholeheartedly co-operates with the healer.

It is my feeling that healing without permission is really an ego or power trip—an effort to control the other person under the guise of doing good—and so should never be indulged in. Some organizations are encouraging their students to do this, telling them to go into meditation and to ask their Higher Self to ask permission of the Higher Self of the sick person; somehow the answer nearly always seems to be "Yes". I believe that only a very spiritually psychic individual is able to do this with the *certainty* that a clear answer has been received, and that it is not clouded or conditioned by their own desires. Therefore, in practice, this asking permission at a higher level is seldom a sufficient reason to risk trespassing on another person's free will. It also still leaves open the objection that the sick person's conscious mind is unaware of what has transpired and so he is less likely to gain in faith or understanding if the healing is successful.

Because healing without permission can be unconsciously motivated by one of the great, basic, instinctual drives of mankind, the desire for power, it has a dangerous appeal and the risk of this being expanded to controlling the minds and wills of other people is very real. With this power comes the danger of corruption which, carried to its logical conclusion, can produce a Jonestown mass suicide.

Even after permission has been obtained, be careful not to impose your will on the outcome. Even though it is natural for you to want the sick person to become well, (why else would you devote so many hours of your time to healing?), always accompany your efforts to be a channel for the healing power with the sincere thought "nevertheless, not my will but God's be done." In his book *The Autobiography of a Yogi*, Yogananda said that his Master Teacher completely surrendered himself to the Healing Power. This enabled it to flow freely through him and to perform many extraordinary healings, including giving sight to a man who had been blind from birth.

Actually, as previously explained, it may be right for the soul growth of the one in need that he should die at this time. Maybe he has learned all the lessons on earth which he came to experience in this life, and he can progress faster on the Spirit Plane. Sure, his friends and relatives will miss him, but maybe they also have lessons to learn from the temporary parting.

I have heard of several cases where the will power or self-centered desires of relatives, or even the doctor who looked upon death as a failure on his part, have kept someone alive for months, or even years, beyond their wish to remain on this earth. This happened even though the person indicated a desire to die very clearly by their words or actions. Once the relatives or doctor mentally and emotionally released them, they died peacefully within a matter of hours or days.

Some people are uneasy about the concept of "the will of God", feeling that this places them at the mercy of some unknown, maybe capricious Being. However, another way of interpreting that will is that it is the Law of the Universe. Thus to be subject to the will of God is to be in accord with the Law of the Universe and consequently become in harmony, or at one with, the Universe and with the Divine. Everything we do that supports life in any of its manifestations, and in its own way, contributes to our compliance with that Law of the Universe.

Some healers may not agree with me, but I believe that another area where our own will needs to be excluded from the whole process is in the mental direction of the healing power to a specific part of the other person's body. I feel that it is usually wise to avoid this. Preferably the power should be channelled to the total person, leaving that individual's own Higher Self and the Spirit Forces to decide how much healing energy is needed, and where in the body, mind, emotions or Spirit it is required. The truth of this precaution was brought home to me quite forcibly several years ago when my wife had been having considerable pain in her legs, mostly in the left one. She felt convinced that there was nothing organically wrong, and that it was merely a blockage of energy for some unknown reason. She asked for my help and I followed my usual procedure channelling energy over her whole body for three evenings in succession with a definite improvement each time.

She asked me to help once more, and this time to concentrate entirely on the left leg, which was the only area retaining the slightest particle of pain. I did this and the pain increased; she asked me to keep my hands over her leg until the pain had gone, which I did. Four hours later she woke me to say that she was in great pain and had not slept at all. What had apparently happened was that there was a blockage in energy flow above the thigh, and the excessive input of energy *below* that point had increased the problem, since it is resistance to the flow of energy that causes pain. By unblocking the area *above* the pain, it was quickly eliminated.

From then on I never tried to second guess where the power was needed. Later I received positive confirmation of the wisdom of being non-directive. This happened during the healing session referred to in Chapter 7, when a clairvoyant was present and observed the energy flow in terms of moving colors. At one point when my hands were over the other person's solar plexus, he saw "jagged, lightning-like bolts of vivid blue light" going down through my legs into the ground. As my hands moved away from that area, this light activity through my legs ceased. I interpreted this to mean that the energy was too much at that place in the body, and the spirit forces "grounded" the surplus without my being aware of the change.

Cooperation by the One in Need

The one in need can help to accelerate the healing process in several ways:

1. By his own prayers asking for Divine help in accordance

with God's will for him. Some people have become so out of tune with the Divine, and feel so alone and powerless, that they are not able to pray, even if at one time prayer was a regular part of their life. In these cases I offer to pray with them and audibly lead them in prayer, kneeling together if this is part of their tradition, but not if this makes them feel uncomfortable. One session together in this way is usually sufficient to open the prayer door for them and they can continue by themselves. It also makes a wonderful beginning for the healing phase itself.

2. By visualizing, several times a day, his body as perfect with no symptoms of the disease or other problem.

3. By mentally sending energy to the affected part of his body. Some people find it helpful to visualize each outgoing breath as moving to that place as energy. Others find it helpful to concentrate on mentally increasing the flow of blood to that part of their body, until they can feel it pulsating at that particular place, in the same way that the heart beat can be felt. This should also be done several times a day.

Energy follows thought so either method will increase the flow of energy to the affected part of the body. While this may seem somewhat in conflict with my previous suggestion that you should not try to direct the energy you are channelling, I feel that the situation is different. As a healer you are acting only as a channel and inviting the Infinite, Universal Power to flow through you; the amount and direction of that power needs to be free of your own will. This allows the sick person's Higher Self and/or the Spirit Forces to make these decisions. The sick person, on the other hand, using one of these suggestions, is inviting the energy into his *own* body and mentally directing it to a specific place where he knows it is needed; his own Higher Self is involved and will make certain that the energy is modulated and directed for his own highest good.

4. By changing his thoughts, attitudes, habits and actions in accordance with the insight he gains as to the cause of his illness.

5. By actively endeavouring to fill the vacuum created by the removal of negative energies with positive actions and affirmations.

If the sick person does not participate in his own healing in some manner he is unlikely to learn the lessons that the illness was meant to teach him.

Working with an Atheist

Sometimes you will discover that although someone has come for healing he does not believe in God by any definition, and certainly not in life after death. He has come because friends or acquaintances of his have been healed in this way, and he has reached the point of being willing to try anything. He has no real faith in Spiritual Healing, but if you can make him better anyway, that would be fine.

Although a sick person's faith in God and His healing power is very helpful to the healing process, a healing will sometimes occur in spite of its absence. If this does happen it will often result in the one who is healed being converted to a real faith. However, if the sick person is to grow from the experience, he usually needs to be involved before the healing occurs. You may feel that it is important for the one in need to pray for help, for healing, for strength, for joy, for forgiveness to overcome guilt that has created the disease, or just for guidance for his life. If you suggest this, the other person may say "I do not believe in God, so how can I pray to Him, or to any other Unseen Creative Force?" The suggestion here is to ask him to work on a theoretical hypothesis that God does exist, even though he does not believe it, just as research scientists often work to find out if a hypothesis has any validity. Thus he can be advised to pray: "I don't really believe that there is a God, or a Universal Power greater than Man, *but if there is,* then I now ask that "Something" to help me with my problem which is_____."

It is incredible how often this will result in an answer for an agnostic or even an atheist; sometimes it is dramatic enough to make him become a firm believer. This to me is further evidence of the incredible, Unconditional Love that God is and expresses.

Emotional Release

Periodically you will find (as do many other types of healers) that during a healing session the one in need will break out into uncontrollable sobbing and crying. Being of a compassionate loving nature your first reaction may be to place your arm or arms around the other person and attempt to comfort him with soothing words. Actually this is not a kind response as it tends to make him again repress the emotion which has started to find release as a result of the relaxing, yet vitalizing force of the spiritual power. If he is allowed to experience the emotion fully, and to release it through crying, however heart rending this may sound, the healing will commence and a great peace will follow. You may feel it wise to cease temporarily, the laying-on-of-hands or channelling of the power, and just to stand by and maybe hold the hand of the other person as a gesture of support while the trauma is being experienced. Then, when all is calm again, you could renew the healing process, if this seems right to you under the circumstances.

Releasing the One Who Has Asked for Help

It is very important to release the other person from any emotional or mental ties with yourself after a healing session. This enables him to accept and use the healing energies without any unconscious or conscious programming by you —he must be completely free. It also prevents you from being drained by a continuous tie and thought pattern. One well known American healer died at quite an early age a few years ago because he simply could not let go of concern and anxiety for those who came to him for help, even during his normal rest periods and vacations. He died of sheer mental, emotional and physical exhaustion.

Another way of saying this is, "Do not be attached to

results." If you are, then in addition to failure to release the other person, there are two other dangers:

1. If the healing is successful, you may start to think that it is your own power and skill that is involved, and your ego will become inflated.

2. If the healing is not successful, you may believe that you are a failure, and thus become discouraged and depressed.

I remember asking a Minister friend of mine why he did not introduce Spiritual Healing into his church and make it a definite part of his ministry, as Jesus did. His answer was, "But what if I failed?" This implied that he assumed that it would be his own power or ability that healed or did not heal, instead of recognizing that all the power and the glory belongs to God.

One of the hardest lessons I had to learn, was to refrain from checking up on those who came for help to see if they had been healed. Having become aware of their problems and having shared unconditional love with them, it seemed natural to show concern for their progress. However, the very fact of making a phone call to enquire as to their progress indicates a doubt as to their healing and an attachment to results. This thought arises more frequently than you might expect because the majority of people do not bother to notify a healer when they have been healed, assuming that this is not necessary; and they are right! Also many people do not come back for a second visit when they are not healed on the first one. They expect an instantaneous "miracle" and if this is not forthcoming they give up or go to another healer.

Therefore, as a general rule it seems best to avoid follow up calls to enquire as to the other's progress. A friendly indication of interest as they leave by saying "Let me know how you get on" is probably sufficient. However, where the other person seems to have a very low self-image, or leads a very lonely life, or is deeply distressed, it may be worthwhile to make a telephone call enquiring how they are getting along. One woman who had been in therapy for many years, individual and group, responded to such a call by saying

"You are the first one who seems to care." Needless to say I was glad I had made that call.

Confidentiality

It is an unwritten rule among all true spiritual healers that anything that the one in need tells the healer about their disease, their history and their feelings or other personal information is absolutely confidential, never to be discussed with others without their permission. In other words, the relationship between you and those who come to you for help, is exactly the same as that between an M.D. or psychiatrist and their patients.

Protection Is Important

Another very important precaution is to protect yourself against negative thoughts or energies that will inevitably be encountered in the course of everyday living, particularly in contacts with those who are sick. You open yourself as a channel for the healing forces, and therefore during the healing session and after it is terminated you will be open also to these negative forces unless you protect yourself both before and after. This can best be done by prayer and visualization.

For example; at the start of a healing session pray to the Father that both you and the other person will be cleared and cleansed and protected from all negative influences. Ask that both of you be filled and surrounded with a protective shield of Love and Light. After the healing, visualize your crown chakra as an open doorway in the top of your head being closed, and then visualize yourself as being totally enclosed in a transparent white light which will act as a protective shield around you without preventing the continuous receipt of good vibrations, spiritual guidance and healing energies. Again pray for protection for both of you.

Some take this one step further, surrounding the white

light with a green light for healing oneself and all those encountered, then surrounding that with a purple light or flame for transmutation to love of any negative forces that are contacted consciously or unconsciously.

Confirmation that this visualization really does create a protective light field around the visualizer was told to me by the clairvoyant referred to earlier in this chapter. When I had finished the healing process I sat down, and, with my eyes closed, followed the protective procedure outlined above. I had not told the clairvoyant that I would do this, so he had no idea what I was doing, except that he saw the shield of light being formed around me. In his own words: "The aura around you changed to a solid blue and decreased to about two inches thick, and it stopped pulsating." Why he saw blue when I was imagining white I do not know, but the important fact is that he saw a protective shield being formed.

Maintaining Energy Balance

If you become involved with this type of service for many hours each day, you will need to be on guard against becoming unbalanced in your own body. There is inevitably a concentration of energy at your heart center (the fourth chakra) through which the healing power of Unconditional Love is channelled to the other people. The Infinite Energy of the Divine is brought in through the crown center at the top of your head (the seventh chakra) but some is automatically drawn away from the lower centers during the healing process. These lower centers are in the feet, the knees, at the base of the spine (the first or root chakra), just below the navel (the second or sexual chakra) and at the solar plexus (the third or emotional chakra). Balance must be restored if you are to remain healthy in body, mind, emotions and spirit; this can be done by mentally sending energy to those points at least once a day. Physical exercise, such as walking or jogging, also helps to maintain equilibrium among your energy fields. (See chart on p. 264.)

Physical Manipulation of the Body

Some healers such as the late Phineas Quimby and Harry Edwards, recommended gently manipulating stiffened limbs or joints of a sick person after a healing session. This was not as a part of the healing process, but to show the other person, and to convince his mind, that he had been healed. They claimed that without this, the sick person may not believe that they have been healed; they may not really try to move their limbs and their mind would remain programmed in the belief that the limbs cannot be moved. Other healers feel that this is unnecessary, and leave the one who has been healed to experiment by himself with his new freedom of movement.

Cooperation with the Medical Profession

Nearly all successful spiritual healers co-operate willingly with the medical profession, for several reasons:

1. They recognize that doctors are also used by God for the benefit of humanity, and are not a force in opposition to healing.

2. Working together, the result is more likely to be favorable than if they oppose each other.

3. If the healing is above and beyond the doctor's expectations, it will be helpful to his understanding of the healing process for him to know that a spiritual healer has been involved. It will also add one more inch to the status of Spiritual Healing in the eyes of the Medical Profession.

4. If someone comes to a spiritual healer with a serious pain before seeing a doctor, the healer may succeed in eliminating the pain without eliminating the basic cause. If the one in need then goes to a doctor, the latter is handicapped in making a diagnosis because one of the chief clues he needs for that purpose, the location, type and extent of the pain, is not available to him.

5. If the one who has asked for help becomes worse, or

dies, after seeing a spiritual healer, but without seeing a doctor, the former might be held legally responsible, especially if he had assumed that the problem was not serious and had therefore not urged the other person to see a doctor immediately.

These last two reasons sound somewhat negative and lacking in faith, but, as pointed out in Chapter 6, even the finest of spiritual healers are unable to help 100% of those who come to them for the many reasons outlined in that chapter. Therefore, the wisest course is for you to advise the seeker to see a doctor first, to ask for a diagnosis and to tell the doctor that they plan to ask for the help of a spiritual healer as well, and would like to delay any recommended surgery or drug treatment for as long a time as the doctor will permit. When the patient returns to you and tells you of the diagnosis and recommended medical treatment, accept this without comment except to concur with any delay the doctor has approved. However, after one or two sessions of Spiritual Healing the one in need could be advised to ask his doctor to recheck his condition to see if it has changed and made the surgery or drug treatment unnecessary, or if the intake of drugs can be reduced. On many occasions in my experience, doctors have acknowledged a dramatic change and have cancelled scheduled surgery.

However, I recall one case where a woman came to me who was scheduled to have surgery in three weeks' time. After three weekly sessions of Spiritual Healing there was much improvement in all the symptoms and I pointed out to her that she now had three options:

1. To assume that she was healed and to cancel the operation, but I definitely advised against her making this choice.

2. To go back to her doctor and ask for a new biopsy to determine if surgery was still necessary.

3. To say nothing and to go ahead with the surgery as planned. She chose the third alternative which turned out to be most unfortunate because she nearly died, and the routine examination of the removed tissue showed that the need for

surgery had no longer existed. The operation had been quick and without complications, but the doctor had accidentally nicked an artery without being aware that he had done so. In the recovery room the artery burst, and only the alertness and fast action of the nurse on duty had saved her life.

In actual practice the need for you to advise people to see a doctor first will not often arise, as most people only seek Spiritual Healing after they have explored regular medical treatment and this has failed to cure them, or the doctor has informed them that their disease is incurable.

The difficulty with medical drugs is that they are all toxic, and they all affect the body adversely in one or more ways in addition to the desired effect. Thus as long as the patient is taking them he is absorbing negative energies in opposition to the positive healing energies, and reversing much of the benefits of the latter. Some people are taking as many as ten different prescription drugs at one time, and no one really knows what the effect of such a combination will be. If taken long enough the side effects of some drugs may be "permanent" in medical belief, although nothing is incurable in spiritual terms.

As stated above, never instruct other people to cease taking a drug prescribed by their doctor, or even to reduce the quantity or frequency of its consumption. You can, however, advise them to keep closely in touch with their doctor, to inform him of any physical or mental changes they experience, and to be monitored in other ways by the doctor. Where these signs indicate an improvement, they can then ask for permission to reduce the intake of drugs in some manner; if this is done it will increase the effectiveness of the healing energies. The doctor will probably give full credit to the drugs for any improvement, but that is unimportant as long as he agrees to a reduction in intake.

Unfortunately in most countries, including the U.S.A., co-operation by the physician with the healer is not so readily achieved; this is either because his medical training has convinced him that treatment of the body with drugs or surgery is the only way to approach healing, or because his ego or pocket book feels threatened by a mere layman being considered as having any power to assist in the matter.

I remember asking one pediatrician if he ever had cases where the child had an illness which he knew ordinary medical treatment could do nothing to cure, or which he was unable to diagnose even with the help of a specialist. "Oh yes," he said "sometimes I get a child who screams for 24 hours and I don't know what is the matter with them." So I asked him if he would consider suggesting to the parents that since he could not help the child they might wish to try a Spiritual Healer. "I believe in what you are doing," he said, "In fact we doctors know that we cannot heal anyone—it must be a higher power that heals—but I couldn't do that; you see there is an economic barrier between us." I was too shocked to pursue the matter any further!

How Long Should a Healing Take?

You will need to decide for yourself just how much time you feel that you want to devote to each person who comes to you. How frequently should you see that person? How many times will you see him? There can be no fixed rule; each case is different and you must be guided by your own intuition.

The late Ambrose Worrall, another well known spiritual healer, in his book *The Gift of Healing*[2] reported healings that took only minutes, or even seconds, and others that took years. One seven year old spastic boy, whose legs and arms had been permanently crossed and whose shoulders were severely twisted, came to Mr. Worrall every week for three years until he gradually became normal. A fourteen year old girl with an undeveloped left side of her body and serious brain damage was treated by him three times a week for the first year, twice a week for the second year, and once a week for the third year. Eventually the left side of her body matched the right side, and she worked in a regular office job, married and had healthy children of her own. Obviously this required great patience, persistence and trust on the part of the healer, the children and their parents.

I have also known the two extremes in my own experience. For example, a woman broke a metatarsal bone in her foot. At that time her doctor said no cast was necessary. A new X-ray taken five months later, because of increased pain, showed the bone to be completely separated, and the doctor said that under these circumstances a cast would be of no value. Two months later excruciating pain made walking very difficult; running and dancing, which she loved to do, were impossible. At this point she decided to ask for Spiritual Healing.

During the healing session the swelling and pain ceased immediately and she walked away with ease. During the following week she walked, ran and danced frequently without any pain or discomfort. A new X-ray at the end of that week showed that the bone had completely healed, with no longer any sign of separation.

On the other hand the following case of a middle aged woman is an example of a gradual healing, one step at a time. On her first visit she outlined these problems:

1. Very depressed. Tried to commit suicide three weeks before. Was saved by emergency treatment at the hospital.

2. Had headaches all of her life.

3. A motor accident eight months before had left her with damaged spinal discs in neck and lower back, causing much pain there and in her legs, and more headaches than before.

4. Varicose veins and blood clot in legs.

5. Taking Codeine for back, neck and leg pains, but it was making her feel very ill.

6. Taking sleeping pills for the same reason.

7. Had lost her job due to staff cut back.

8. Although she had always had a deep faith she found it impossible to pray.

After I prayed with her and led a healing session, she reported seeing a beautiful vision which duplicated both a dream she had had six years before, and a similar vision she experienced in her childhood; she saw Jesus clothed in a pastel pink robe standing against a background of pale blue sky. She found this to be very encouraging. She came for several more healing sessions with the following results.

7th day. Varicose veins and blood clot healed during this visit.

14th day. Feeling better; although sleeping was still difficult, headaches had ceased. A few days later she stopped taking codeine.

28th day. Pain in the legs disappeared during this visit and never returned.

34th day. Sleeping better. Now sensitive enough to feel the energy coming to her during the healing session.

43rd day. Legs still perfect. Back much better. Neck still needs a brace. Sleeping like a baby without any medication.

54th day. Very frightened. Doctor reported pre-cancerous cells in the uterus, stage 4, (stage 5 would be cancerous) and recommended an hysterectomy.

57th day. Doctor rechecked. Cells now at stage 3 which is less serious than stage 4.

64th day. Doctor rechecked. Cells now completely normal. Surgery cancelled. A current dream in which she saw her former supervisors smiling at her, forecast the return of her old job (which was the only one that she wanted), although from a realistic point of view this seemed to be most unlikely. During the healing session she heard the words "Everything will be better than you can possibly expect."

She did not feel it to be necessary for her to return for any further visits, but telephoned seven months later to say that she had been recalled to her old job.

One reason that a healing often takes weeks, months, or even years, is that it may take the sick person that long to change his style of living or thinking from that which caused the sickness in the first place. Only as these changes are made can the healing occur. Another reason is that in some cases the Higher Self of the sick person is aware of physical, emotional, mental or spiritual aspects of the person's total being, that have a greater need for healing than the specific dysfunction for which help has been requested. The healing power will therefore be directed to that greater need, and the physical healing originally requested may not transpire at that time.

It is apparent from all of this that one of the attributes needed by a spiritual healer is patience. If your *only* interest is in becoming an instantaneous healer, or a dramatic "platform" healer, then you are not likely to become a channel. If, however, you are willing to let the Spiritual Law and the sick person decide in each case how long a particular healing is to require, and are willing to give of your time as often as is necessary, then you will probably experience many instant healings as well as many time consuming ones.

Nevertheless, it is important to guard against anyone becoming dependent on you by frequent visits for real or imaginary illnesses. Lead these types of people to look within themselves for the guidance and healing energies that are there for everyone. Gently teach them to do their own work, so to speak, and not to rely constantly on others. We all need a helping hand from time to time, but not a permanent crutch.

You need also to be aware of the problem of transference, or projection on to you by the sick person of his unconscious problems or needs. This danger is well known in the medical and psychological professions, but it is also sometimes found in the field of Spiritual Healing. The one who is healed may look upon you as a father or mother, or a saviour; or because of the input of unconditional love-energy, misunderstand this for physical or emotional love and respond at that level. It can also take the form of rejection of, or hate for, the healer. Being aware of this possibility will enable you to enlighten the other person as to the truth, and to help them to take back the projections by becoming conscious of them.

The wide variation in results which every healer experiences will be a constant reminder to you that you have no control over the outcome—in fact, as has been said several times already, you really have nothing to do with it, except to open yourself as a channel to the best of your ability, and to surrender yourself and the other person to the will of God. It is God's power, His will, and the other person's receptivity, surrender and karma that decide, not you.

A Healing Sanctuary

If you are serious in your desire to serve in this way, you may wish to set aside a special room or small building as a healing sanctuary, which can be used exclusively for healing, prayer and meditation. The decoration and furnishing should be simple but reverent. Green is generally considered to be the healing color, and so can be used for the carpet, curtains or some other part of the decor, although some healers prefer blue.

If the technique to be used involves the other person lying down for your laying-on-of-hands, then you will want to build or purchase a table which is of a comfortable height for your use while standing. It is best if it is placed parallel to the North-South axis, with the head of the patient at the north end.

More important than any physical aspect however, is the mental and spiritual dedication of the room or building to the service of God and one's fellow beings. Prayerfully ask God and His ministering angels and spirits to fill the room with His Love, Energy, Power and Peace so that all who enter may experience these attributes and be healed in accordance with His will.

Sanitary Precautions

Perhaps it goes without saying that the healing sanctuary, and your body and clothes need to be clean and sanitary; that where someone has an infectious disease or skin problem and you use a laying-on-of-hands procedure, it is best to wash your hands immediately after working with that person. All creditable spiritual healers that I have observed or read about follow these simple sanitary precautions, however there was one who completely disregarded all of them, and that was Arigo, the Brazilian healer referred to in Chapter 7. He helped as many as three hundred patients a day, diagnosing and treating each one in a few minutes. He never washed his hands between patients, nor even sterilized the old knives that he used for actual physical operations, yet he never caused any infection. I am not suggesting for one minute that anyone else should try this; let us just say that Arigo was the exception that proves the rule. His case is further evidence of the power of spirit over matter.

Should You Charge for Your Services?

Some healers charge for their services or request a donation in a specific amount. Others accept voluntary donations of any amount, but never request anything specifically. Others charge nothing and refuse all donations.

Actually charging a specified fee would probably be illegal in most states, but donations are usually within the law. However, there is a division of opinion among spiritual healers as to requesting donations of specified amounts, accepting donations of unspecified amounts, or declining all donations.

Some of the arguments in favor of accepting donations are:

1. "Every laborer is worthy of his hire." (Luke 10:7)
2. Those who devote their full time to healing work and have no private income must accept donations if they are to live.

3. People have a need to express their gratitude, and feel unhappy if denied the opportunity to make a donation.

4. Donations can be passed on to some other worthy cause if the healer has no need of them.

5. In this materialistic age people have become conditioned to believe that there is no value in something that is free— "If it doesn't cost anything, it can't be worth much," is a common attitude. Actually in the United States the majority also believe that the higher the price the greater the value. Marketing executives often take advantage of this conviction and charge a price for an article that is much higher than the cost would justify and offset this by beautiful packaging and dramatic advertising.

6. Some people will hesitate to ask you for help if there is no charge, figuring that they ought not to bother you, but will not hold back if donations are accepted, assuming that since the service is offered at a price, they have a right to ask for help.

Some of the reasons suggested for declining all donations are:

1. Jesus never charged for healing.

2. The healing is a gift from God, and so should not be "sold."

3. Some people are too poor to pay, especially if the donation requested is a specified amount, and therefore they will not ask for help, although it should be available to them just as much as to those who can afford it.

4. Licensing authorities, medical associations, etc., are less likely to accuse you of practicing medicine without a license, and definitely cannot charge you with taking money under false pretences. Both of these claims have occasionally been initiated against healers by people who do not get healed, or by orthodox professionals who feel threatened by the fact that many are restored to health by Spiritual Healing.

5. The need of people to express their gratitude can be satisfied by suggesting that they make a donation to some worthy charity of their own choice.

6. If someone in need declines to ask for help because your services are free it indicates that his values are misplaced and he has little understanding of the healing gift of God, and that he probably has a lesson to learn in this area before he is healed. In other words this is his problem, not yours.

7. Not accepting any money leaves the healer completely free to suggest additional healing sessions without any conflict of interest on his part. Nor does it create any feeling by the one in need of help that the healer could be suggesting further sessions out of self-interest.

In my own case it seemed right for me not to charge fees or accept donations for myself, although where a donation was offered I usually suggested that it be made to a charity of the person's own choice, or one I named if they had none in mind. However, after following this practice for three years I started receiving occasional comments that some people were not happy with this procedure. I, therefore, made a small survey, asking people which of several alternatives would make them most comfortable and I discovered that the great majority would prefer to make a donation to me. Some even said that they had stayed away when they had needed help because they were not allowed to reciprocate.

It then occurred to me that there was another argument in favor of accepting donations which I had never thought of. By refusing to accept a fee or donation I was denying the other person the privilege and joy of responding in some way; I was preventing him from being a giver as well as a receiver. I had given my time (usually one and one-half to two hours per session) and enjoyed the pleasure of doing so, while they received. It was therefore selfish of me to refuse them the same enjoyment if they wanted this. Maybe at a subconscious level my ego and pride were also involved in refusing donations. I, therefore, changed my attitude and now accept donations from those that offer them, but at the same time making it clear that none is necessary if the person has very limited means or prefers some other system. I have been surprised at the relief this has brought to those that ask for help.

Of course, whether or not you accept donations, you will receive a far greater reward in the privilege of being of service to your brothers and sisters in this way, of seeing their joy when they realize that they are free of pain and disease, and of learning from each one who comes for help because no two personalities, disease causes, or resolutions are exactly alike; also of seeing the spiritual growth which often parallels the healing, and of sharing in the beautiful insights that some people experience during the healing process. I remember one young woman who felt sure she had been completely healed, but nevertheless came back for one last reassurance before leaving for home several hundred miles away. After this final session she slowly sat up with her eyes shining with rapture and amazement as she described the beautiful place she had been transported to, and the celestial music she had heard—an entirely unexpected and totally new experience for her. Others have marvelled at the angelic beings or spirit forms they have seen, or the helpful and meaningful guidance they received while the healing was in process.

Truly the non-material blessings received far exceed any material rewards that might be offered.

There is no one right way; you must decide for yourself what is correct for you under your particular circumstances, always remembering that the healing power is not your own to sell, only the time involved is yours for possible remuneration.

Notes for Chapter 8

1. Lawrence LeShan. *The Medium, The Mystic and The Physicist.* The Viking Press, New York. 1974

2. Ambrose Worrall. *The Gift of Healing.* Harper & Row, New York. 1965

GOD IS LOVE

therefore

LOVE IS GOD

GOD IS INFINITELY POWERFUL

therefore

LOVE IS INFINITELY POWERFUL

CHAPTER 9

ONE WAY OF CONDUCTING
A HEALING SESSION

THE PROCEDURE THAT I follow, which seems right for me
at this time, is outlined below.

1. My first objective is to make the person seeking help
feel at ease. After we have both been seated in comfortable
chairs in the quiet of the healing sanctuary, I ask them why
they have come. I encourage only a brief description of their
problem—not all the details which would merely reinforce
their mind and mine with the negative images. Have they
been to a doctor first and if so what is his diagnosis? Do they
believe in Spiritual Healing and/or a Divine Universal Power?
In addition to relaxing them, this helps me to tune into
where they are, and this makes the later channelling of
power more effective.

2. I then ask them if they can accept the idea that when
we have a pain, disease or malfunction, our body is giving
us a message that something in our lives needs to be changed.
That "something" may be physical, emotional, mental or
spiritual, but it is the cause that needs to be discovered—the
disease is only the result. Saying this is better than telling

them that they are responsible for the disease, which I have heard some modern healers (orthodox, unorthodox or spiritual) state to their patients. Saying that sounds more like a judgment or accusation, and puts the sick person on the defensive, or makes them feel guilty. I further point out that without discovering the cause, the healing of the symptoms will probably not take place, and that even if it does, it would only be temporary.

We then explore possible causes of their problem, using the various techniques outlined in Chapter 4 until we arrive at what seems to be the probable one for them. Usually when we hit on the right one, the person seeking help has an inner awareness that it is correct; sometimes their body signals this by a return of, or an increase in, the pain created by the disease. Sometimes the real cause is not uncovered during the first visit, in spite of a sincere effort to do so, but is found during subsequent visits.

3. I then explain to them briefly the procedure that I plan to follow so that they will not have any concern or anxiety about what is going to transpire. I assure them that I have no power of my own, but that I merely open myself to be a channel for the power of God to flow through me and for His will to be enacted. I also point out that with any type of healing no one can guarantee results, and that this is equally true of Spiritual Healing; also that when healings occur they may be instantaneous, fairly rapid, or take a considerable time—I have no way of knowing what is right for them.

4. After answering any questions they may have, I ask them to remove their shoes, eye glasses and all metal they may be wearing such as jewelry, watches, etc. The glasses tend to act as a screen or filter, and metal objects tend to impede the flow of the healing energy because they have energies of their own. There is, however, never any need to remove articles of clothing, other than a top coat or jacket which may be removed for comfort.

5. I then ask them to lie down face up on the waist-high

padded table, with their eyes closed, to relax completely, and to be as open and receptive as possible.

6. Then I center myself. This means that with my eyes closed, and in complete silence, I try to draw all my consciousness into my heart area, feeling unconditional love for God and for all of His creation, thus becoming attuned to the Spirit World.

7. I then audibly pray that I will be used as a channel for God's infinite love and healing energies, so that these can be used by the one who has asked for help, in any way that is right for him and in accordance with God's will. I also ask that we both be protected from any negative forces, and that we be surrounded completely with a transparent white light so that only that which is for our highest good may penetrate. At the same time I visualize the white light being formed around us.

8. If I feel in the need of additional guidance as to the location of the disease or the cause, I will then try to sense the energy emanating from each of the other person's major chakras. First I place myself into a receiving state of consciousness with my eyes open. Then I pass my left hand across each chakra, starting outside the field of energy radiating from the chakra, going through the field and then passing out of it. This enables me to sense which chakras (if any) are low or unusually high in energy. This may give a clue as to the area of the disease or the cause of the disease. Sometimes the variation may be due to previous surgery. For example, one person who had low energy in the throat chakra informed me afterwards that her thyroid had been removed.

9. Then closing my eyes, I place my two hands around the person's right foot, one hand beneath and the other above, both about two inches away. After two or three minutes I place my left hand over the top of the right foot and my right hand over the right knee, still without touching.

10. I continue placing my hands over each part of the body until I have covered the whole body in the sequence shown in the attached diagram. At all points I use both hands and

hold them about two or three inches away from the body. There are several reasons for this.

(a) By using both hands a greater flow of energy is possible because of the polarity between the negative pole of the left hand and the positive pole of the right hand.

(b) Psychics and mystics maintain that there is an etheric or vibratory body surrounding the physical body, but inseparably related to it. This body vibrates at the highest frequency that matter can contain. It holds a blueprint, or template of the perfect image created by God, and this is transmitted into identical form in the physical body when all is well. The etheric body itself can never be diseased or imperfect, but emotional or mental blocks can prevent its exact duplication in the physical. By keeping the hands in that etheric body a few inches away from the physical body, the love-energy radiates through the etheric body to the physical causing the latter to line up with that perfect image and thus be healed.

(c) Because I do not touch the ones seeking help, they are less likely to be distracted from remaining in an entirely meditative and receptive state in which to receive the love-energy, and to listen to their inner voice.

(d) When, as frequently happens, they feel a warmth or tingling, or even a coldness in some part of their body, they know that it is not a result of touching or mere body heat transference; they are therefore more likely to believe that something has really happened inside their own body.

After the whole body has been covered at a slight distance in this way I will often then gently touch either in the problem area or elsewhere. I do not believe that it makes any difference to the effectiveness of the healing power but in those cases where they are unable to feel the radiating power with my hands held at a distance (most people can) touching may increase their confidence that something is happening. Also there are those who have a great belief in the healing power of the touch of the hand. Maybe they recall that Jesus gently

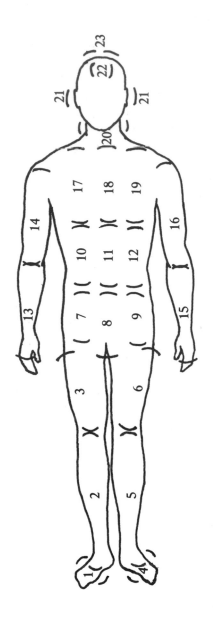

(= left hand   ) = right hand   Numbers = sequence

Palms down except for 21 and 23

For positions 20 to 23 inclusive stand behind the head

DIAGRAM OF HAND PLACEMENT FOR THE TRANSFERENCE

OF HEALING ENERGY

touched many of those he healed, or subconsciously they remember how their mother would soothe their childhood aches and pains with the soft touch of her hand. In other cases I sense that their life is void of all human touching, leaving an emptiness which can be very slightly filled in this way, possibly increasing their ability to receive the healing power. If there is no resistance to the energy flow I feel practically nothing in my own hands. However, if there is resistance to the energy, presumably due to some blockage, or negative energy such as cancer, in the other person's body, I feel a tingling in my hands, sometimes of such intensity that it could be called a pain. When this happens I keep my hands in that same place until the pain or tingling ceases.

All through this process, which takes about thirty minutes, I try to keep myself completely open to the flow of the healing power of God and His Infinite, Unconditional Love. I visualize it as flowing through me and out of my hands and heart chakra, into the other person to be used in whatever way accords with the will of God. I started visualizing the Unconditional Love energy as moving out of the heart center, or fourth chakra, because I had heard or read statements by various spiritual healers and teachers that this is what actually happens if it is truly unconditional. It was some time before I realized that this fitted perfectly with the statement by Jesus that, "He who believes in me, as the scripture has said, 'out of his heart shall flow rivers of living water.' " (John 7:38) While knowing that the energy being transferred is God's and not mine, I also hold to the thought that the one in need is my sister or brother, a fellow child of God, regardless of age, color or religion.

It is not easy to prevent unwanted, unrelated thoughts from entering one's mind during the half hour healing process, but when this occurs I bring my mind back to attunement with Spirit. For example, I may silently repeat the Lord's Prayer, or affirm to myself the attributes of God, the perfection of His creation, my surrender to His will for both the sick person and myself, my openness as a channel for His Infinite, Unconditional Love, the One-ness of God, Christ, the one in need and myself, or the fact that God is All There Is and we are both fragments of that totality.

11. About half way through the above silent procedure I audibly ask the one seeking help, to ask silently their Higher Self (or the God within them, or their Inner Teacher) what they need to know for their own guidance and healing, and then to be open to anything that may come to them by way of vision, pictures, thoughts, words or memories. If something comes to them in this way, they retain it for discussion at the end of the session if they wish.

12. After reaching the crown of the head I place my hands over their heart center (the fourth chakra) and if it seems appropriate, lead them through one or more of the visualization procedures previously described in this book. For example, letting go of fear or anger, forgiving someone for some hurt, asking forgiveness for something they feel guilty about, or severing unhealthy ties to a child or parent. There are no fixed rules for this; it is important to allow the visualizer as much freedom as possible to follow the leads of their own psyche.

Some people have difficulty in visualizing anything, but they may be able to get a sense of the presence of the other person by using in their imagination one or more of the other subtle senses of sound, touch, taste or smell. In most cases visualization is accomplished more easily with the eyes closed, but one artist found she could only visualize with her eyes open.

13. After the visualization has been completed (if it was used), I return to any place in the body where I know from the person's description of their problem, or from the resistance I have felt in my hands, that extra energy is needed, and I continue channelling energy to that place for several more minutes.

14. When I feel that my part in the work has been completed I pronounce an audible blessing which varies in form according to the circumstances. For example: "May the healing power of the love of God, and the guidance of His

Holy Spirit, be with you each moment of each day, in the name of Jesus Christ."

15. I then suggest to the person on the table that they take several more minutes before sitting up, as by that time they are usually in a very relaxed, almost partially unconscious state.

16. During these quiet minutes, mentally I completely release the other person from me, and visualize the contraction of the energy fields that have been expanded around them and myself during the healing process. I then reshield myself and them against all negative forces and influences of the outside world, in the same manner as step seven. This is very important because we have purposely made ourselves wide open to outside forces and it is most unwise to venture out into the world at large without protection.

17. When they sit up I offer them a pencil and paper and encourage them to write down any messages they received or visions they saw because, like a dream, these may quickly slide back into the unconscious if not recorded; also the sooner this is done the more detail is likely to be recalled. Recording the experience in this manner also creates a link between their conscious and unconscious mind, and between the left and right hemispheres of their brain, and thus contributes to their wholeness.

18. When the person feels ready to talk I encourage them to speak about any physical sensations they experienced during the process, and to share anything they received in words, or thoughts or pictures, either before or after asking their Higher Self the question in step 11, but only if they wish to do so. What they received is very personal and if they wish to keep it to themselves this is their privilege and I fully honor this.

I realize that this seems like a long procedure, and that many well known and successful spiritual healers accomplish dramatic results in much less time, and with much less movement of the hands; however, the above is what seems right for me at this time.

There are several reasons why a number of healers cover the whole body in this way:

(a) The healing power is transferred to each chakra, or body energy center (there are many more than the well known basic seven) and also through each of the hundreds of acupuncture points at which the skin is especially low in resistance to electro-magnetic energy.

(b) The sick person may not know exactly where their physical problem is located, because it is not necessarily where the pain is noticed, or they may be too embarrassed to tell the healer exactly what their problem is. In either case by covering the whole body these unknowns are automatically included by the healer.

(c) It may be necessary for the power to be directed to a different part of the body than to the one where the specific problem is located. For example: there are nerve endings in the feet which affect the eyes.

(d) Gradually as the transfer of energy proceeds, the other person becomes more and more relaxed, and thus becomes more open and receptive to the healing power, and much less likely to block it with their fears, anxiety or negativity. Some people become so relaxed that they actually go to sleep, which is an excellent reaction, because then there can be no mental resistance whatsoever from their conscious mind.

There may be another factor involved in this rather lengthy laying-on-of-hands. As explained in the chapter on Angels and Spirit Doctors, I definitely believe that there are a number of them working with me. Not only have several clairvoyants seen them, but a number of other people have spontaneously reported that they sensed or saw their presence. In some way, which I do not fully understand, the healer acts as a contact point or instrument for them, and this procedure would give them plenty of time and opportunity to apply their skills to any part of the body that is necessary. Of course, they, too, are only channels for the power of God, the One Source of all life and healing.

Whatever procedure you decide to use (many others are outlined in Chapter 2), always try to follow or develop one which helps the other person to discover and eliminate the *cause* of the disease, as well as to remove the pain or other symptoms (see Chapter 3).

One more suggestion is that you occasionally review Chapter 6 which describes the many reasons why some people do not get healed, even though they have asked for help. This may assist in preventing discouragement or disillusionment from setting in when you find that your efforts are not always successful. Also constantly remember that the power and the decision as to how it is used are not your own.

It may also be helpful to recall that sometimes when a person comes with a request for healing, others may have labored for many months or even years, to assist them in their personal growth, development and spiritual awareness, which was necessary before a healing could be accomplished. Now they are ready and you are privileged to assist in the final step, and a rapid healing is experienced. In other cases the journey towards wholeness is just beginning, and you are asked to help in the early stages—and no apparent healing results. The harvest comes later when you are not directly involved.

Finally, when someone approaches you for spiritual healing try not to see a physical body, regardless of whether it is old or young, ugly or beautiful, diseased or apparently healthy, *just see the God within them.* Before you is a child of God, made in His image, containing His Spirit, the Christ, and perfect in every detail. A particle of His substance; a cell of His body.

Difficult as this may be to achieve, know that the closer you come to this objective, the more likely you are to witness a complete healing.

I want to re-emphasize the heading of this Chapter. The above is *one* way of channelling healing, it is not the only way. For example, some people prefer to work from the head down to the feet. It is a good idea to experiment and find out which way works best for you.

SPIRITUAL HEALING

ONLY WORKS

IF IT IS MOTIVATED

BY LOVE

CHAPTER 10

AVOIDING DISEASE
AND HEALING YOURSELF

I HAVE FOUND that many people who ask for Spiritual
Healing have no idea that they are responsible for their
own lives and that which they experience in their own bodies.
It is an entirely new concept to them that they can contribute
to their rapid recovery, and in fact heal themselves. So, I try
to convince those people that this self responsibility and
power is something that they should seriously consider.
Every pain and disease that they have is a message from their
body that something in their lives needs to be changed, and
they need to search for guidance on this matter.

If the people merely want to eliminate the pain and inconvenience of their disease, so that they can go right on living
the way they were before their body brought them this message that a change is necessary, it really is not very helpful
for a healer to remove the symptoms. This would deprive
them of the opportunity to learn from the experience and to
grow spiritually.

If meditation and/or listening to their inner voice is something that they have never tried before, they may have difficulty in receiving any guidance when they ask for it during

the course of the healing session. A methodical, rational and common sense approach to the search for the "something" may therefore be necessary. Others ask how they can heal themselves, and others are interested in maintaining the good health that they already have. The following pages, therefore, include a "Design for Living" which can be used for all three of these purposes.

This outline is planned to encourage the one in need to participate in his own healing, and thus hopefully make it a transforming, growing event with a permanent restoration of health.

Body, mind, emotions and spirit are one, each dependent on the other, so the search for the cause of the disease, and the maintenance of health, must include all four.

The Body

Our body is a holy temple and needs to be treated as such. It is also the only one we have, so why be foolish and abuse it in any way?

Replacing Used Energy

Every day we expend enormous quantities of energy, not just in physical work, exercise and movement in general, but also in mental activity, and in the automatic, unending activities of life itself, such as heart beat, blood circulation, breathing and maintaining body temperature.* This energy must be constantly replaced, and there are four ways that this is accomplished:

1. By taking in food, itself a form of energy. Through assimilation the food is converted into the structure that your body requires. It stands to reason that the type of energy

*In the average person the heart pumps two thousand quarts of blood through the body every 24 hours, more than half the time in opposition to gravity.

we receive is directly related to the type of food (energy) that we ingest. A sensible diet is therefore an important factor in maintenance of health, and there are many good books on this topic. Some food must be cooked to make it digestible, but bear in mind that cooking destroys some of the energy as well as destroying or leaching out vitamins and minerals.

2. By drinking water. This contributes two benefits: it is a cleansing agent, thus will flush waste and harmful products from the body; in addition, it contains elements that are essential to life.

3. By exposing ourselves to sunshine. The sun is known to be the main source of energy for this planet. We absorb this energy by radiation and by digesting food that has absorbed it. We should plan our exposure with care because excessive exposure to direct radiation is known to be harmful, while complete avoidance of sunlight is also detrimental.

4. By breathing in fresh air, which is indispensable to life itself. Try holding your breath; after a minute or so it becomes agony and you must let go and breathe again. If your will is strong enough, you may even black out, but immediately you are unconscious your autonomic nervous system (which continues to operate throughout your life, whether you are awake or asleep, without any thought on your part) takes over; you breathe again and recover consciousness.

Air contains many elements that our bodies need, in addition to oxygen for purifying the blood stream. Some mystics contend that it contains *all* that we need, and that eventually we will learn to live without food. There are, in fact, a few well authenticated cases of individuals who have lived for years without food, (and others who have lived with almost none) relying on air, water and the power of God to keep them alive.

Here again the benefits we receive will be directly proportional to the quality of the energy (air) that we breathe. If the air is mixed with tobacco smoke or pollution of other kinds, we can hardly expect satisfactory results.

Harry Edwards, the former Dean of Spiritual Healers in Great Britain, who died in 1976, used to place great emphasis on what he called "Cosmic Breathing" for maintenance of health and vitality, and for healing of disease. By "Cosmic Breathing" he meant breathing in full inhalations, and while doing so, consciously holding in your mind the thought that you are breathing cosmic energy from the universe into your whole body. Then, while exhaling, visualize that all waste is being dispelled from your body. This is to be done several times, and repeated several times a day.

Buddha taught that the finest form of meditation is to be continually conscious of your breath coming in and going out.

Hatha Yoga, the branch of yoga which deals with the physical body places great emphasis on the importance of mentally breathing in and out through specific portions of the body to eliminate tension, pain and disease in those portions. If this is done between the exercises, or holding positions, that are recommended, then no stiffness nor pain is experienced the next day. Complete yoga breathing uses the abdomen and diaphragm, which is the natural way to breathe, though most of us breathe much less deeply than we might. The lungs are completely filled with each inhalation, and completely emptied with each exhalation. Yoga breathing also involves retaining the inhaled breath for several seconds to give the incoming oxygen full opportunity to purify the blood stream.

Common-Sense Precautions

Other common sense precautions to be taken in caring for your body are:

1. Exercising. This stimulates various bodily functions essential to health such as blood circulation, respiration and digestion. It has also recently been discovered that exercise stimulates the production of brain chemicals known as endorphins, which make you feel very good and eliminate depression.

2. Relaxing. This permits those life support systems to operate without restriction or obstruction caused by tension or exhaustion.

3. Avoiding well known hazards to life and health such as smoking, unreasonable intake of alcohol, caffeine or tranquilizers, consciousness altering drugs, and excessive intake of salt or sugar. (In 1976 the U.S. population consumed three and one half billion pounds of candy; that is 16.7 pounds for every man, woman and child. In the last fifty years the incidence of diabetes in the U.S. has tripled—maybe there is a connection?). We each have a free choice whether or not to expose our bodies to these dangers, but we must be prepared to accept the consequences if we do. If disease follows we must not blame someone else, or that fall guy, "fate."

4. Wearing proper clothing. Some authorities and sensitive people claim that polyester clothing can cause illness, especially asthma; therefore it is more healthy to wear clothing made of natural fibers such as cotton, wool or silk.

These then are the procedures that we need to take if we want to maintain our body in a harmonious and healthy condition. It is unfortunate that many people take better care of their automobile than they do of their body. Neglect of either results in the need for repair, and this may be very expensive or even fatal; the big difference being that if the automobile wears out you can always buy another.

If we deliberately fail to take reasonable care of our bodies we must not be surprised if healers, whether from the field of orthodox medicine or Spiritual Healing, or anywhere in between, are unable to help us. Maybe they can temporarily relieve the symptoms, but the problems will return as long as the causes remain. Until we appreciate, respect, and are grateful for, the magnificent physical vehicle each of us has been given, and care for it accordingly, we will be constantly reminded that we have not yet learned our lesson.

There is an interesting parallel in the Bible which tells us that when Jesus was alone in the desert the devil took him up to a high place and told him that the Scripture said that if he was the son of God, he could jump off and he would not be harmed. Jesus replied that the Scriptures also said, "You shall not tempt the Lord your God." (Matthew 4:3-7)

The Mind

Our mind controls our body whether we realize it or not.

The Conscious Mind

Contemporary writers have stated this in various ways: "You become what you think;" "You experience what you believe;" and "Thoughts are things." Edgar Cayce said "The mind is the builder, the body is the result." Thus it is clear that many people see the mind and the body as inseparably related. Consequently if anyone wishes to maintain a healthy body, and to eliminate dysfunction, he must monitor his thoughts, making sure that they are positive, uplifting and harmonious.

Negative thinking can be extremely destructive. Watch your thoughts and see if the negative ones outnumber the positive ones. Make a record of your statements, if you like, grouping them under the headings NEGATIVE and POSITIVE. This will give you a dramatic picture of your attitude towards life. Replace each negative thought with a positive affirmation about the same person, object or happening, as a means of training yourself into seeing the good in all of life.

For example, if you believe that because your mother or father died of cancer, therefore you will also, then you probably will; it will become a self-fulfilling prophecy. On the other hand you can constantly affirm that your body is unique, that it is your own, that its condition depends on the way that you treat it, physically and mentally, and that it has nothing to do with the way that your parent treated theirs. If you will constantly maintain this attitude, the chances are that you will remain healthy and free of cancer all of your life.

Other examples might be: (Negative) "John Smith's actions annoy me;" (Positive) "John Smith is free to act in any way that he wishes;" (Negative) "I cannot afford the high price of gasoline," (Positive) "God is my source of supply, I will always have enough for my needs;" (Negative) "Everyone has the flu, I suppose I will get it too;" (Positive) "I am healthy and free of disease and will remain that way."

Relaxation is just as important for the mind as it is for the body. Stress needs to be released before it creates a blockage in the flow of life forces within the body. One of the best ways to relieve the mind of stress is to meditate. There are many ways to do this and many excellent books on the subject (see bibliography). It is a good idea to try several different methods until you find the one that suits you best.

For some reason the word "meditation" horrifies a lot of devout Christians, who spend plenty of time in prayer. It seems that because the major emphasis on the teaching of meditation has come from the Eastern religions, it must be, in their opinion, heresy for Christians to meditate. This shows a lack of understanding about the meaning and purpose of the practice. Really all it involves is listening to God, or the wisdom of the Universe; whereas praying is talking to God.

If we do all of the talking and never listen, how are we going to hear the answers to our prayers, or whatever else God wants to tell us? It is said that God gave us two ears and only one mouth because we are supposed to listen twice as much as we talk. The Bible tells us that Jesus spent many hours in prayer, sometimes all night. Surely he did not take all that time talking to God, telling Him his problems, expressing gratitude for His blessings, and asking for His guidance? He must have spent just as much, if not more, time listening for the answers—that is, meditating.

An attitude of gratitude is also an important part of one's

armory. Regardless of our current situation, there are always many blessings to be grateful for, if we think about it. We may not be able to walk, but we can see and hear; we may be poor, but we can enjoy the love of, and our love for, our children. Be grateful to your body, even if it is not in one hundred per cent working order at the present time. Say thank you to your heart for consistently pumping your blood throughout your body, day and night for all the years of your life. Thank your lungs and chest for continually filling you with the breath of life, and your kidneys and liver for screening the poisons out of your system. Thank your bones, muscles and nerves for enabling you to walk, move, and control objects with your hands. Thank your five senses for the joy and protection they bring you; your brain for enabling you to think, reason and calculate. The list is almost endless.

If we take these blessings for granted and only complain about our problems, we contribute to our ill health of the body, mind, emotions and spirit. If we fill our hearts with gratitude to God for life itself, for His loving and forgiving heart, and for the many other great gifts we enjoy, we will contribute to the health and happiness of ourselves and those around us. Gratitude to the Universe and its Creator should also be expressed in action—by sharing our blessings with others; by lending a helping hand to those in need and by loving all those we contact in our daily lives.

The conscious mind can also be used as a positive healing tool, as we will see later on in this chapter under "Self-Healing." However, do not wait until you are ill to take advantage of the power of visualization. Whenever you think of your body, or any part of it, visualize it as perfect, with every blood vessel, nerve, organ, muscle and bone operating exactly as it should, and in perfect harmony with the rest of your body. If you see a picture, or hear a description of a diseased body, immediately dismiss it from your mind and replace it with a mental image of your own perfect body.

The Sub-conscious Mind

We have been talking about the conscious mind, but this is only the tip of the iceberg. Our sub-conscious mind contains far more information and experience than does our conscious mind, and therefore can have an even greater influence on the maintenance of our health. Everything that we experience, say or think remains in our sub-conscious mind long after our conscious mind has forgotten it, in fact it stays there for the rest of our life. This has been proved scientifically by applying electrodes to specific points of the brain which result in the prompt recall of events that took place many years before. Hypnotism has also enabled the mind to bring into consciousness information and events that had long since been "forgotten."

If you want to prove this to yourself you can try the following little experiment:

> Think of someone you knew many years ago—the greater the
> time gap, the more the experiment will convince you. You can
> recall their appearance and where you knew them and what the
> relationship was, but you cannot remember their name—you
> have not had any reason to use the name or to try to recall it, for
> years, and as hard as you try you are simply unable to think
> what it is. Now tell your sub-conscious mind that you want to
> remember that name. Repeat this command several times *and
> then forget the whole thing*. Resume whatever you were doing
> before and go on about your daily activities. A few hours later
> that name will probably pop into your head out of the blue.

This ability to store names, facts and figures indefinitely, may be very useful, but what we are primarily concerned with from the physical, emotional and mental health point of view is the fact that your sub-conscious mind also stores feelings and beliefs. These forgotten feelings and beliefs can have a drastic effect on your life, even controlling it without your realizing that this is taking place. They may also restrict the operation of your immune system.

There are several ways of tapping the sub-conscious for information which may reveal the cause of a disease, or the action needed to effect a cure or to maintain health. Some of these are dreams, dialogue with the sub-conscious (there are several ways of doing this) and hypnotism.

Dreams

Probably the recall, recording and interpretation of dreams is one of the easiest ways for an individual to tap his own sub-conscious without professional help. Your dreams can give you knowledge about yourself that you can learn in no other way. There are many good books on the market which can help you to interpret your own dreams. (see bibliography)

Many people will respond to this suggestion for studying dreams by saying "But I never dream" or "I know that I dream sometimes but I can never remember them." It has now been proven scientifically that everybody does dream several times each night; it is apparently a necessary release of tension while the mind continues to process the events, thoughts and emotions of the day, and the conflicts that are buried in the sub-conscious mind. In addition, dreams are intended to communicate to the dreamer information that is important to his own health, welfare and soul growth, if he will but listen to them.

For those who wish to remember their dreams, there are two simple rules which will nearly always result in dream recall if they are followed conscientiously:

1. Place a pencil and paper, or a tape recorder, by your bed when you retire. This is not only a practical preparation so that you do not lose track of the dream while hunting for recording materials during the night, but it also gives your sub-conscious mind a definite message of your intention.

2. Right before you go to sleep say to yourself, "I will remember my dreams, and I will write them down as soon as I wake up." Say this silently or out loud several times, and mean it.

If this does not work the first time try repeating the procedure for several consecutive nights.

In her interesting books *Dream Power* and *The Dream Game,* Ann Faraday[1] points out that dreams can be interpreted on three different levels, and not all the levels apply to each dream.

First level dreams are those which clarify recent waking experiences, calling attention to facts which the conscious mind of the dreamer had overlooked or dismissed as less important than other issues he was attending to at the time. So the first step in dream interpretation is to examine the dream to see if it contains any helpful information about external current events in the life of the dreamer. Dr. Faraday states that precognitive, or prophetic dreams also fall into this first level category. Therefore, the dreamer should examine all first level dreams for possible practical application, and determine what action, if any, he may wish to take in the light of the message brought by the dream.

If no first level interpretation seems to be applicable, Dr. Faraday suggests that one should then turn to the next level. Second level dreams deal more with the dreamer's *subjective feelings* about people and situations in the external world than with any objective truth about them. The first question to ask oneself is: Do the dream characters represent themselves (which is quite possible if the dreamer has been in recent contact with them), or do they symbolize someone or something with similar characteristics (which is more likely if there has been no recent contact with them in waking life)? Second level dreams enable the dreamer to examine the inner attitudes and prejudices which are affecting his actions and experiences in the outer world, and if necessary to change them.

If either first or second level dream interpretation (or both) explains the dream to the dreamer's satisfaction, it may not be necessary to explore the dream any further. However, if neither method results in understanding the message of the dream (or if it seems that there may be more to the dream), then the third level should be explored. This is the one that Carl Jung emphasized and wrote about extensively, namely to see if the dream contains information about the state of the unconscious mind of the dreamer, his own inner problems and his hidden resources of psychic energy.

In this level of interpretation one assumes that all people, objects and other symbols in the dream represent parts of the dreamer's own psyche, or total being, of which he is currently not aware. He may have repressed them, or never become aware of them, or has simply forgotten them. For example, a man who was raised with a very masculine outlook on life, being told "Big boys don't cry," and similar admonitions, may be entirely unaware that all men have a feminine side to their personality without which they could not be a whole person. A dream may then try to bring this to his attention with a feminine character or characters, which Jung called the "anima." Dreams of volcanoes or earthquakes may warn the dreamer that repressed anger or other emotion may result in an "explosion" or shaking of his apparently peaceful existence, if he does not do something about the repression.

Third level dreams also reach even deeper than the subconscious mind described above, and tap what Jung called "the collective unconscious." This includes instincts, drives, influences and knowledge from the rest of humanity, from the Universe, from current times, and from all of history, recorded and unrecorded. Dr. Faraday emphasizes, however, that such Universal images always have *personal* significance for the dreamer, and may be interpreted in different ways by different dreamers. The term "unconscious" used in the rest of this chapter includes both the subconscious and the collective unconscious.

I believe that there is also a fourth level of dreams in which information (often precognitive) is conveyed to the dreamer by a spirit guide or teacher, or maybe directly from the Source.

Dreams use symbolic language—they are very rarely literal in the message they give. Maybe this is because they are usually in pictures, although words when they are recalled are generally especially significant. It is important for the dreamer to explore the meaning of each symbol for himself, and not to rely on a so-called "Dream Dictionary." It is *his* dream, and it is *his* unconscious that has selected the symbols, and therefore his own interpretation is much more likely to be correct than are those of other people. For example, one woman dreamed that she was trying to get milk from a steer, and, of course, could not do so. She interpreted this as showing her that she was frustrated because she was trying to obtain needed nourishment from her husband but he was inherently unable to provide this. This gave her a new and helpful understanding of their relationship. Dream books usually state that a steer or bull is a sexual symbol, but for her this interpretation made no sense, whereas her own explanation fitted the facts and was helpful.

I have found that the dreams of a very sick person are an invaluable tool in the search for the cause of the disease, which is so important to discover if the healing is to be permanent. This is especially true of people with long term illnesses, or so-called "incurable" diseases. Their dreams have revealed hidden hostilities, angers, resentments and other repressed emotions concerning specific individuals or the world in general. Other dreams indicate the need for a change in diet, a reduction of food or beverage intake, and various types of guidance for the dreamer. Still others reveal what the dreamer is building with his waking thought patterns, which must sooner or later be manifested in the physical body.

Dialogue with the Unconscious

Another way of getting in touch with your unconscious and your own Higher Self is by means of a dialogue. There are several ways of accomplishing this; some people will find one way easier than another. If one method does not work for you, then experiment with the other suggestions.

1. Draw or paint a picture with complete abandon. Do

not try to copy anything, just let the pencil, pen or brush flow and express your inner feelings in any way that seems comfortable. No one else needs to look at your creation so it does not have to look artistic or sophisticated. The reason that the very act of painting or drawing whatever flows without conscious thought is in itself therapeutic, is because it is a transformation of energy. The energy that was formerly used to repress the contents of the unconscious, or to carry on a battle between two opposing desires or forces within the unconscious, is now permitted to transform itself into the act of painting or drawing and to express itself in symbols. Then too, by giving these inner thoughts or feelings a physical form they can no longer be denied reality and ignored; they are now in front of you to be observed and examined.

When you feel satisfied that nothing further wants to express itself in this manner at this time, select one part of the picture—an object, a symbol, a color, or whatever you feel particularly drawn to and start a conversation with it. Start by letting the object speak to you, describing itself. For example, it might say, "I am a tree, tall and strong, giving shelter to the weary, adding beauty to the world . . ." or it might say, "I am a tree, buffeted by the winds and reaching out for sunshine; my roots go deep into the ground . . ." (By letting the tree tell you about itself, you are projecting onto the picture your own inner feelings and thoughts). Then you answer back in any way that occurs to you and continue the dialogue from there. You may be very surprised that words come to you just as though the tree were talking to you. You may wish to record the dialogue in writing or on a tape recorder as it progresses.

2. After recalling and recording a dream, select a person or an object from the dream and dialogue with it in the same way. If this seems difficult to do, you may find it easier to use Fritz Perl's method, which is to place two chairs opposite to each other. Sit in one of them and imagine the dream character that you have selected to converse with is sitting in the other chair. Address that character with your opening

question. Then change places and sit in the other chair, become that dream personality and answer the question, pretending that *you* are still sitting in the opposite chair. Change places each time that you change roles. This adds a touch of reality to the dialogue and this helps it to unfold, and allows you to experience the feelings of that part of you which is represented by the dream character.

3. Since both the art and the dream are themselves expressions or messages from your unconscious, the dialogue in either of the above processes starts from contents of the unconscious which have already partially revealed themselves. This combination of dream or art with dialogue can therefore be very revealing and meaningful. However, you can take the process one step further, if you wish, and combine these two methods by painting or drawing a scene or a symbol from a dream and then dialoguing with that. This can be very powerful and instructive because it gives an outward form and reality to something that was brought to you from your unconscious in the dream.

4. A fourth way is to use what Jung called "Active Imagination." First relax your body as completely as you can, one portion at a time. Then imagine yourself in a very beautiful, peaceful place, such as a beach by the sea, a green meadow, a quiet forest, or a scenic mountain top. It can be a place that you are familiar with, or one that you create entirely with your own imagination. Picture yourself sitting down in a comfortable spot waiting for someone to appear—it is amazing how this usually happens. Then start a dialogue with that figure by saying "What have you come to tell me?" or "Is there something that you would like to tell me?" You may prefer to ask it a specific question that has been troubling you, or share with the figure your greatest desire. The resulting conversation may continue for many minutes.

5. Another slightly more difficult or sophisticated way is to dialogue directly with the unknown. First relax completely, and then, since you are going to open yourself to the Spirit World, ask for protection from all negative forces,

and mentally surround yourself completely with a white light. It is also important that your motives be pure, desiring only the good for yourself and others and asking to receive information to be used for service to humanity or for personal spiritual growth, never for one's own ego or power. Without these two precautions this method can lead to depression or serious difficulties as negative entities or thought forms take advantage of your opening.

Now enter into meditation in a way that is comfortable for you, emptying your mind of extraneous thoughts to the best of your ability, but without strain or tension. After ten or fifteen minutes of this, pick up a pencil or pen and write to your unconscious, to your Spirit Guides, to your Higher Self, or to your Guardian Angel, whichever fits in best with your beliefs, saying, "Do you have anything to tell me today?" Wait without stress for a word or words to come into your mind. When this happens write the words down however meaningless they seem; continue with whatever comes; you may be surprised to find that the words flow quite easily and quickly. Keep on until nothing else seems to come into your mind as part of the flow, and you sense that the guidance has finished for that time.

Do not try to understand or judge the words until the flow ceases, otherwise your rational mind (dominated by the left half of your brain) will get in the way of the irrational, intuitive right half of your brain which you are using in this process. When the words have come to an end, then go back and look at what you have written, and see what there is in it for you. This is known as guided writing and it can be very meaningful. I have received many messages in this way and some of those which relate to healing have been included in the next chapter.

Changing the Contents of the Sub-conscious Mind

Exploration of your sub-conscious mind by one or more of the above methods may reveal to you the cause of some illness or another problem that you are facing, so you need to know how to eliminate that source of conflict. Remember that the sub-conscious has no reasoning or logical power of its own; your conscious mind has to provide this and dictate to your sub-conscious mind what it wants.

Sometimes just becoming aware of the cause and really examining it closely, even mentally reliving it several times, will be sufficient to dissolve it, and to eliminate its unconscious influence on your life. In other cases positive affirmations may be needed to re-program your sub-conscious— that is, to create a new memory tape. There is no need to deny anything that is already in your sub-conscious. Feeding in the affirmative statements will gradually wipe out the old belief, just as it does when you record over a pre-recorded magnetic tape. Negative affirmations such as: "I will not get cancer." "I will not put on weight," tend to reinforce that which you do not want.

Suppose that you discover that your ulcers, or constant stomach cramps are caused by worry about losing your job or other financial security. Change this by constantly repeating to yourself several times a day (especially just before going to sleep), and out loud if possible, "I am serving my employer to the best of my ability and he needs me," "My material needs have always been met and always will be," "God is the source of all supply; I am His child and He will always supply my needs," or whatever positive statement is applicable and appeals to you. Gradually your sub-conscious will absorb this message and wipe out the old anxiety and your needs *will* be met and your stomach disorder will disappear.

Affirmations can be given additional power by writing them down several times each day. If they are spoken aloud and written down they involve multiple aspects of your being— your brain and memory, your voice, throat, mouth and ears, and your hand and eyes. Under these circumstances it is hard to imagine how your sub-conscious mind can fail to be impressed with the message that you desire to give it to hold and act upon.

Affirmations can be used to achieve anything that you

desire, and that is right for you, whether it is health, strength, peace of mind, joy, love, friends or material supply. They are made even more effective if accompanied by visualization of the desired result as being an accomplished fact.

A particularly helpful affirmation, which I often suggest should be written down and posted in a prominent place where it will be seen several times a day, consists of the words "I ALWAYS HAVE A CHOICE." This helps to counteract the tendency that so many people have, which is to blame the world, fate or other people for everything that goes wrong in their lives. By constantly reminding themselves that they do have a choice in every situation they learn to accept responsibility for their own lives.

If you *are* aware, or by one of the foregoing methods you *become* aware, that your life style, particularly your way of earning a living, is causing you much stress or unhappiness, remind yourself that there *are* alternatives and that you *do* have choices; then examine what these are in some detail and with free imagination, *before* you become sick. Do not wait for a disease to force you to make a change—don't kill yourself to live! Take charge of your life—accept full responsibility for how it is lived.

Feeding your Sub-conscious Mind

We have been talking about exploring the contents of your sub-conscious mind, and changing them when this seems to be desirable. Simultaneously you can be feeding new information into that repository which has so much control over your life. Fill it with positive thoughts of your own, and the wisdom of spiritually advanced men and women, either from the many fine books available, or from personal conversations. Fill your life as far as you possibly can with positive, uplifting, loving experiences, rejecting all negativity. For example, if you insist on reading about, and listening to, all the misfortune and evil which the newspapers, radio and television feature so prominently, this is what you are feeding into your sub-conscious mind and this is what you are liable to draw to you and to experience in your own life.

You are constantly building the power-house of your sub-conscious, whether you want to or not, so be sure that you are constructing the kind of influence on your life that you desire to have.

The Emotions

Expressing your emotions or feelings, and not suppressing them, is a very important part of holistic health maintenance and self-healing.

The fact that there is a direct correlation between repressed anger, anxiety or hostility and ulcers or heart disease is fairly well known. Less publicized is the fact that modern research shows a suspiciously strong relationship between repressed passion (whether it be anger, sexuality or creativity) and cancer.

So learn to express your feelings—act on them. If they are not compatible with your ideals or your spiritual nature, then try to transmute them into a higher level of feeling such as compassion or unconditional love. Maybe you will want to try the visualization technique for this described in Chapter 5.

Much emotional stress is caused by people trying to plan and control every detail of their lives (and often other people's lives too!), and then becoming upset because their lives don't work out exactly as they had planned. The secret to the peace and calm that most of us desire, is to let life flow at its own pace and unfold its own plan.

This does not mean apathy or lethargy on your part, but rather an attitude of allowing the good to come into your life; of knowing that there are no accidents, that every event we experience and every person that we meet occurs or arrives for a reason. It involves knowing that if we will seek to understand the lesson that each situation holds for us,

God's plan for our lives will gradually be revealed, we will be in harmony with it, and our emotions will be at peace.

Nor does this mean that we should not make any plans for orderly living as we feel guided to do so. However, these should be flexible and we should be willing to change them, or sometimes allow them to be changed by others, without annoyance or resentment, accepting this as part of the plan. Later on it may become very clear to us why the change occurred and we will be grateful for the unseen help or the lesson that was involved.

Impatience can create tremendous tensions in the body, and these impede the self-healing and immune mechanisms of the body and the flow of the various life support systems discussed in Chapter 2. This may also create disease. "Patience is a virtue," is an old adage with much truth in it.

Negative and destructive emotions can be controlled in intensity by proper breathing. If the rhythm of breathing is consciously slowed, the heart beat will also moderate in response, and the disturbing emotion, nervousness or tension will gradually decrease.

The Spirit

Since your body, mind, emotions and spirit are inseparable while you are living in a physical body, it is just as important to attend to your spiritual needs as it is to take care of the other three aspects, if you wish to be free from disease. If you are one of those people who firmly believe that there is no such Being or Force as God, Divine Intelligence, or Universal Power, then the foregoing statement may make you angry. If it does, take a good look at your anger, and try to identify the real cause; it may be quite different to that which it seems to be on the surface.

Spiritual Healing is a meaningless concept unless we acknowledge that there is some power or force or intelligence that is greater than ourselves. It is tough to operate entirely on our own, and eventually and inevitably it leads to disaster, but we are all free to choose that route if we wish to do so—

no one will stop us. However, once we admit to ourselves that there may be "something" that was involved in our creation and that it may still be interested in our continued existence, then Spiritual Healing becomes a possibility. If we then ask that "something" for help in maintaining our health, guiding our lives and healing our diseases, we have taken the first important step towards experiencing the reality of Spiritual Truth.

Suggested actions for the maintenance of Spiritual Health are described below:

Prayer

Whether or not you believe in a Supreme God, or merely in some impersonal Universal Power, it is important to express your feelings and wishes to whatever it is that created you and keeps you alive. Did you ever stop to wonder what it is that keeps your heart beating without ever stopping for maybe eighty years or more; and what keeps you breathing in and out, whether you are asleep or awake, conscious or unconscious? Be sure that your prayer includes praise and gratitude, and that requests include the needs of others as well as yourself.

Meditation

Meditation comes under the heading of spiritual activity, as well as mental, because it is by this means that we listen for the answers to our prayers, and for unsolicited guidance from our inner voice for our own growth and happiness. We all have an inner guide or teacher which is invaluable, if we but listen to it.

Radiation of Unconditional Love

Develop the practice of radiating unconditional love to all of God's creation. To the plants, flowers and trees; to the animals and birds; and to all human beings regardless of age, sex or physical appearance. Pure love is healing, life giving energy, and this habit will not only increase your own health and resistance to disease, but you will be channelling healing energies to others without realizing that you are doing so. Others will feel better just being within your vibrations, without knowing why.

Do Not Judge

One of the great commandments in the Bible is "Judge not, and you will not be judged." (Luke 6:37) Judgment of others turns out to be a real barrier to Spiritual Growth. Just how comprehensive this injunction is, was revealed to me in a psychic reading in which a Master Teacher explained it as follows:

> The world Karma bites at the edges of your aura when you allow it. When certain things happen out there and you think, "That's terrible," it isn't really, it is Karma, and it is their Karma; don't make it yours. It is neither good nor bad, it simply is. Let it go on by; don't stop it with feelings. It is as much a judgment to say, "Isn't it awful" or, "Isn't that too bad," if one were to see someone shot in the street, as it is to say, "That man is a fool." The admonition, "Judge not," covers every kind of judgment there is. Fear is not at the bottom of the troubles of the Earth—judgment is. Without judgment there would be no fear."

This, naturally, does not mean one would pass by on the other side of the street, and fail to render what assistance is possible. This would be ignoring another, equally important injunction given by Jesus, "Love one another, as I have loved you." (John 15:12) It does mean remaining sufficiently detached not to take on the other person's suffering which is not part of your own Karma.

Sometimes people do not realize that the admonition includes themselves as well as other people. This is why perfectionists often make themselves ill—they constantly condemn themselves as inadequate.

Surrender

Surrendering to the will of God, or letting go and permitting the Universal Good to operate in our lives, is essential for maintaining a harmonious disease free existence, and is often the key to a successful Spiritual Healing. I recall the case of a lady in California who was riddled with cancer and given only a few months to live. Her doctors had tried surgery, radiation, and chemo-therapy, all to no avail. She had a husband and three young children whom she loved, and she had prayed throughout her illness that she be permitted to live and raise her children and to continue to care for her husband.

Finally she called in some Elders from her church and asked for their prayers and laying-on-of-hands. During the course of these prayers she heard the phrase "May Thy will be done" and it made a deep impression on her. She realized that she had never said those words, nor anything like them, in her prayers. In fact, that was not her intention; she wanted to live. Right then she changed her attitude to one of complete surrender to the will of God, whether this meant that she die or live, and if the latter, whether the recovery was to be lengthy or quick; no longer did she demand a specific result. She also mentally placed her children and husband into God's care, knowing that His will for them could only be good.

From that moment on the cancer receded and she gradually made a complete recovery and lived to raise her children and be a loving companion to her husband.

Some people pray that they may be healed, "if it is the will of God;" however, this implies that God may not want them to be well. Since God is Love, and we are His children He must want us to be whole and perfect at all times. However, it may be right for our own spiritual growth and soul evolution for us not to experience an immediate healing and therefore, in God's wisdom, it may not occur. The right approach is therefore to pray "in accordance with the will of God" instead of "if it be God's will."

We humans jealously guard our own free will, and often are afraid to surrender to God's will, assuming that we know best what is good for us, which is far from true. Dr. Emmet Fox in his book *The Sermon on the Mount*[2] pointed out that people often assume that the will of God for them will not be pleasant, whereas it always means greater freedom, better health and prosperity and a more abundant life. If life is not going well for you, it means you are not expressing the will of God. It is the will of God that we should all be healthy and happy.

I recently experienced in my own life an interesting example of the need to surrender. For several weeks I had been making a conscious effort in my prayer and meditation time to surrender everything to God—my life, my ego and my will. Then quite suddenly I was tested as to the genuineness of my intention to be unattached to anything. First there was a dramatic change in the number of people requesting healing assistance. Practically no one came for several weeks, thus testing my attachment to being used as a channel. I found that this was not a problem for me. Secondly I drove 120 miles to conduct a two day workshop on Spiritual Healing. Usually 15 to 20 people attend these, and early indications from the organizer of this particular one led me to believe that it would be over-subscribed. Exactly two people showed up! I accepted this as God's will and the three of us had a fruitful two days.

I had finished this book and a friend of mine was doing an excellent job of editing it but suddenly had to postpone further work on it because of more pressing business. A friend whom I dearly loved moved away under circumstances which made future contact very unlikely, and there were several other events which required me to "let go." While none of these events was of drastic importance, each one was testing my sincerity in declaring my willingness to surrender everything and to allow God's will to work in my life without anger or frustration on my part. They were teaching me to be truly unattached to anything but God.

Meditating on this I discovered another reason for many of these events; I was being given time for further study. Without realizing it I had been on a plateau, and I needed to spend more time on my own inner growth.

Surrender to the will of God is indeed the secret, or the key, to rapid spiritual growth. The power is given to us only to the extent that God is certain that it will be used for His plan and purpose, and not our own. As we give up our own will, desire, and ego satisfaction, so we become aware of God's will, receiving the power, the intelligence and the knowledge of God.

If the phrase, "Surrender to the will of God," is a problem for you because of prior conditioning, try substituting the words "Allow the energy of Infinite Life to flow through and in you, without trying to force it into a pattern created by your own finite mind."

These two events, the surrender of personal will and the receipt of spiritual power, are always in harmony and balance. Therefore, as we grow spiritually, so will the power available to us grow, because we will never use it for anything that is not in accordance with the will of God.

Surely the ultimate goal for all of us is to realize that we are one with God; and therefore our real Self is Divine and God is All There Is. It seems that the best way to achieve this is to surrender our desires, our thoughts and our wills to God, so that His desires, thoughts and will become ours and we are truly One.

Just as a balloon ascends by casting off ballast or excess baggage one piece at a time, so we grow spiritually and rise to higher levels of consciousness and finer vibrations by casting off and surrendering to God all that blocks His will.

A special aspect of the act of surrender is to face up to the fact that one day you and every other human being will die; that is, you will leave the physical body behind and be reborn into the Spiritual World. Accepting the inevitability of this transition can be a very healing process for mind, emotions and spirit. Realize that it is only a part of the eternal life that you have been given; experience it in advance with your mind and imagination; give up attachment to, or possessiveness of your physical body, and you will no longer fear disease or death. Instead you will attain a glorious sense of freedom and trust in life.

There is an interesting exercise you can do by yourself which will help in really becoming aware of your physical mortality. First, imagine that you have just been told by your doctor that you only have one week to live, and that there will be no physical pain involved in your death. Then ask yourself, "How would I spend that one week? What would I do with those precious moments?" Write down your answer in full detail, and then later go back, examine this, and compare it with the way you are actually spending your time. You may be surprised to find that you are spending little, if any, time on those things which are really the most important to you, which would obviously receive top priority in that last week. As a result you may find that a rearrangement of your priorities in daily living is in order.

Practice the Presence of God

Develop the habit of reminding yourself frequently that you are living in the presence of God—not that He is spying on you and judging your every word and action, but that He is lovingly caring for you and willing your happiness—that He and His angelic ministers are eager and willing to help you *when asked to do so.* You are never alone.

There is much talk nowadays about raising your consciousness, or striving for higher consciousness. Since God is the highest form of consciousness, these are merely new ways of saying "Try to become aware of God," or, "Be attuned to Spirit." There are many ways of doing this; two of the best ways that I know of are:

> (a) Meditate on, or contemplate, the many attributes of God, such as Love, Light, Peace, Power, Truth, Beauty, Wisdom and Knowledge.

(b) Observe closely and appreciate the many beautiful manifestations of His thought in things such as trees, flowers, birds, animals and children. These have all been created by His thought, and therefore are projections of the beauty that is within God, or rather, *is* God.

These contemplations will help to develop an inner awareness of God that is completely free of all five physical senses.

How about Our Children?

If parents conform their lives to a healthy pattern for body, mind, emotion and spirit, they will do much to ensure the maintenance of good health, and the healing of disease in their children, especially the younger ones. The close tie between mother and child does not end with the cutting of the umbilical cord; in fact it is very important for the mental, emotional and spiritual development of the child that the bond be reinforced from the very moment of birth. You can find much wisdom on this in *The Magical Child* by Joseph Chilton Pearce.[³]

There is also an instinctive bond with the father which will be strengthed to the degree that the father devotes time and attention to the child. Because of these conscious and unconscious ties to both parents, the child is greatly affected by thoughts, emotions and beliefs of his mother and father. If these are positive, healthful and loving, the child will respond in the same way, even in the face of an accident or illness. If, however, the parent or parents are full of fears, anxieties and negative thinking, the child will absorb these, consciously or unconsciously, illness may occur, and healing will be difficult.

Many of the guidelines suggested in this chapter can be taught to children, who will readily accept the idea that health and healing are to be expected. In fact you may find to your surprise that your child is already in touch with, and can see, his or her Guardian Angel and/or spirit guides. Your child may not talk about them because either they assume that everyone else can see them, or they were laughed at, or told they were lying the first time they mentioned them to anyone.

Children can be taught to meditate, and most will quickly learn to enjoy the practice. It helps them to eliminate tension and to get in touch with their inner center which will be of value to them all through their lives. You will find many useful ideas for teaching children to meditate in *Meditation for Children* by Deborah Rozman.[4]

Children can also be encouraged to share their dreams and shown how to interpret them; this is much better than dismissing them with the statement that "they are only dreams." To a child dreams can be very real and a source of worry; to a parent they can be an invaluable assistance in understanding what is going on in the inner and outer life of their child. The Senoi Tribe in Malaysia makes a daily practice of dream discussion within each family, and the children are taught how to act on their dreams. It is interesting that within the Tribe there is no crime, no police force, no prison and no mental illness.

A discussion in which both parents and child freely express their feelings should also be encouraged and will eliminate much stress and source of disease. The spiritual training of a child has always been the responsibility of the parents; leaving them at Sunday School while the parents play golf or stay at home is no substitute; the child may even see it as a form of punishment. Certainly he gets the message as to what is most important to the parents, and will follow their example as soon as he possibly can.

Self-Healing

If you have a disease or malfunction that you would like to eliminate by your own efforts rather than by requesting the help of another, or if you wish to do all you can while being helped by others, start by reviewing the above guidelines for healthy living and then make such changes in your life as seem to be called for under the circumstances.

Study Chapter 3, Inner Causes of Disease, and carefully examine your own thoughts, emotions and stressful situations to see if you can ascertain the origin of your problem. If you are able to do this, then apply the logical remedies to correct what you have found. It is helpful if all of this is accompanied by prayer requesting guidance, strength and assistance.

Simultaneously with searching for and working to eliminate the cause, devote time to the symptoms, or what is normally called the disease. Several times a day find a place where you can relax in silence. Acknowledge the presence of a Power that is greater than yourself and ask it to come into your body. Visualize it doing just that, restoring to perfection any part of your body which is diseased or not functioning correctly, or that is causing you pain. Visualize your body as you know it should be. Give thanks for the healing that is taking place.

A variation of this technique is to visualize the healing power coming into your body, and then, by the power of your thought, direct it to the portion of your body that needs healing. If you find this difficult to do, then imagine the power coming in as you breathe in, and, as you breathe out, imagine that you are breathing the power into the affected part of your body. Energy follows thought; you may sense this happening.

Another way the conscious mind can be used as a positive healing tool is that which was developed by Dr. Carl Simonton who has become famous for his work with cancer patients. He uses a visualization technique. First he asks the patients to relax as much as possible, then to visualize the cancer in any way that they wish. After this has been accomplished he asks them to visualize their image of the cancer being dissolved or destroyed by some method of their own creation which is appropiate for the image they chose for the cancer. Maybe they will imagine a great increase in their white blood cells which promptly attack and destroy the cancerous cells; or they may picture some animal eating the cancer, which they have pictured as an octopus. This process must be repeated several times a day, and if done with sincerity will often contribute to healing.[5]

Still another way is to try to sense the pulsation of your blood (i.e. your heart beat) in any part of your body that you wish to heal. Energy follows thought, so there will be an increase in the supply of blood to that portion of your body. If you repeat this several times a day for weeks, or for months if necessary, healing will often result, because the increase in blood supply to that area brings with it a larger than normal amount of white blood cells.

After you have made an honest effort to follow through on all of the above points, if you find that there is no improvement, or much less progress than is desirable, then study Chapter 6, Why Isn't Everyone Healed, and see if you can discover which of the reasons for unsuccessful Spiritual Healing may apply in your case.

Maybe, long before you have taken all of these steps, you will decide it would be much simpler to take a pill or accept a minor operation! However, if you do, the cause will still be there so a reoccurrence of the disease or some other one is likely to be experienced; also you will not have learned the lesson that your body is trying to teach you. Eventually that lesson must be learned before you can move ahead on the spiritual path of soul development, so why not now?

In all of this do not give up too soon; keep on working at it—doing your part. History is full of scientific discoveries made or inventions created after years of patient attempts and failures; famous books published after rejections by numerous publishers; people finally succeeding far beyond the average in some occupation after failing ignominiously at many others. You may have many lessons to learn from your illness, but rest assured that once you have learned them the need for the disease will cease, and the healing will probably occur.

A friend of mine, who is a psychiatrist, experienced a beautiful example of self-healing. I feel that it is particularly impressive because being an M.D. he completely understood the seriousness of the medical diagnosis of his illness and the possibility of it becoming fatal. In other words he had more negative thinking to overcome than a layman would. Fortunately, although his education had taught him to believe in orthodox medicine, he had also learned in subsequent years that there were alternative methods of healing. Here is his story in his own words which he has kindly permitted me to include in this book.

In January 1978 I was hospitalized with Infectious Hepatitis. I improved and was released in five days and told to rest for at least two weeks. I rested for four days and then feeling quite good I resumed a slightly less heavy schedule. Three weeks later I was rehospitalized with Bilirubin 9.5 (normal is zero) and liver enzymes over 1000 (normal is 0 to 10), which is very bad. I lay in the hospital getting sicker every day. Within two weeks my Bilirubin was 13.5 and enzymes over 2000. My M.D. (a hepatologist) said I had less than a 50 per cent chance of living. I reviewed my life and reasons for living, knowing it was now my decision. It came to me that I was given the disease as an opportunity for a personal demonstration of self-healing.

I immediately began intensive meditation and visual imagery to heal myself. In five days my Bilirubin was 5.8 and enzymes less than 1000. One week later I left the hospital and three weeks later my blood tests showed no evidence that I had ever had liver disease. I took a planned trip to the Middle East and ate and drank freely. Upon my return my blood tests continued to be perfect. Recent follow ups, one year later, continue to show perfect liver functioning.

Live in the Present

One other factor which is becoming increasingly recognized as important in the maintenance of good health and the activation of self-healing is to live in the present, to live in the NOW. Living in the past is a terrible waste of time and energy and can contribute much to depression and disease in the present. Living in the future is equally pointless and damaging since it causes us to miss the experience and the opportunities of the present, and to create worries and concerns about events which may never happen.

Living in the present frees us to respond in the way that is right for us at that time, and to realize the maximum potential from each moment. The best way to ensure a satisfactory future is to do our best to make today all that it can be.

In summary, therefore, if you follow these guidelines for your good health you will be performing your part in keeping it that way, in experiencing healing by your own efforts or in co-operating with a spiritual healer in freeing you of any disease which might arise in spite of these precautions.

Notes for Chapter 10

1. Ann Faraday. *Dream Power.* Coward, McCann and Geoghegan Inc. New York. 1972. *The Dream Game.* Harper and Row, New York. 1974

2. Emmet Fox. *The Sermon on The Mount.* Harper and Row, New York. 1934

3. Joseph Chilton Pearce. *The Magical Child.* E.P. Dutton, New York. 1977

4. Deborah Rozman. *Meditation for Children.* Celestial Arts, Millbrae, California. 1976

5. Carl Simonton, and others. *Getting Well Again.* J.P. Tarcher Inc, Los Angeles, California. 1978

LOVE ALL OF GOD'S CREATION

UNCONDITIONALLY, EXPECTING

NOTHING IN RETURN.

ALLOW GOD TO DIRECT YOUR LIFE.

CONSTANTLY REMIND YOURSELF

THAT WE ARE ALL ONE.

CHAPTER 11

GUIDED WRITING

THIS CHAPTER CONTAINS two sections. The first consists of teachings from the Master Osiris who spoke through a Medium while I was working with her for her own healing of a serious disease. I have permission of both to include his words which seem to have universal significance and value.

The second section includes guidance which came to me during meditation over a period of four years, as I developed the ability to be a channel for the healing power, and then used it to help others. I do not know who or what guided my thoughts as the words on each topic flowed from my pencil without ceasing.

I hope readers will judge the words in this chapter for themselves without prejudging the source, which is really not important if the words have value. I believe they do.

There is a special way in which this receipt of guided writing has proved to be helpful in my healing work. I sometimes present to my spirit guide, during early morning meditation, the names of those who will be coming for healing that day, and then ask for special guidance for each one. I have found that often I will receive information on these people which is helpful in their visits, especially in uncovering the causes of their illnesses.

I realize that many writers on spiritual matters warn against the dangers of opening oneself to guided writing as they fear negative entities may take the opportunity to convey false or misleading messages. My feeling is that if you protect yourself in the same way as is recommended before opening yourself as a channel for the healing power (see Chapter 8) there is no danger in listening for such inner guidance. Of course if the guidance is negative, inflationary or evil in any way, you can quickly turn it off and refuse to accept it. Always remain in control to that extent.

SECTION 1

MESSAGES FROM OSIRIS

Planning Your Future

Planning an uncertain future is against all the rules of health and wholeness at all levels. You are not to plan your future to the extent that you do; you are pushing your own laws through. It is much easier to obey the ones that already exist, which cannot be improved upon anyway.

Surely you know that illness or sickness is a defense against the truth; in your making your own rules a fragment of truth has pierced your own construction and brought chaos. Truth always brings chaos to untruth and the body responds with illness. All you have to do is to open yourself to the truth of your being, which is always as God created it—sinless.

You mortals are always trying to do it yourselves, never understanding that we long to help you, and stand ready to help at the smallest dilemma. What is the dilemma? There seem to be many dilemmas, but they are all one dilemma— one problem. All problems that seem to be there are but one; and that problem has a solution—the solution is opening yourself to the truth that you are. It is a matter of becoming what you already are, instead of worrying and struggling to make something of lesser value because of a misunderstanding in early years that "God helps those who help themselves;" so throw that on the heap of other valueless things, words, sayings, proverbs and axioms. Replace it with "God helps those who allow Him to help them," and all you have to do is to rest in that. It is so much easier than you make it.

Karma

Your own Karma is one thing that you do have charge of. To an extent, the Lords of Karma spin it out for you as fast as you can take it, or as fast as you want it. Man was not born to weep, nor to suffer, nor even to be uncomfortable. Man was created in the image and after the likeness of God, which is Joy. There is great ease in Joy—it is so easy. How can you not see how easy it is to be free wherever you are and whomever you are with. Do not shackle yourself with things or people. Do not shackle other people with your thoughts or your speech.

Guidance will come—has come—will come again. Doors will open. "Behold, I stand at the door and knock;" who will open the door? Must I knock *and* open the door? Do you see how easy it is to be free? Open the heart and the mind—they must be open at the same time—and allow the peace that passes all understanding to move into the very center of you. Then watch the need for decisions and decision making drop away like dust off an old garment.

Surrender

God's will for each person is an unfolding process and will be given when it can be understood and dealt with. While some may disagree, no more is ever given than can be borne. God's will for each and every one is that you be a perfect expression of His love; that is what is meant by, "Be ye therefor perfect as your Father in heaven is perfect," simply surrendering as an instrument for the expression of God.

You cannot do it; you cannot change; by yourselves you can do nothing. Pray for nothing, expect nothing; truly turn it over to the will of God, and "All things shall be added unto you." There is too much misunderstanding; everyone who is trying is trying in vain, trying too hard. Try less and trust more. Rest—relax—let go—let God; that is your only responsibility. That is all faith is; letting go and letting God work His wonders through you.

Many people pray for healing, pray to God for healing, which is praying amiss. God does not make you unwell, therefore He does not make you well. It is a matter of remembering, recollecting and moving yourself into the knowing that there is but one power; but that is not a power *over* anything; there is no power *over*—that cannot be—there is only one Power, and that Power is Perfection.

Have you lost your way? Turn it over to the Power. You cannot direct your lives; not from the beginning has any man been able to direct his life successfully; he is too feeble; it has never been expected of him; it is error. Time and again it was said, "Seek ye first the Kingdom of Heaven and all these things shall be added unto you." All that people hear is "and all these things shall be added unto." Seek you first the Kingdom of Heaven—a state of consciousness where perfection is supreme and nothing else prevails.

Do not think that you do not work, but when you are on the path, not deviating left or right, and seeing with clear eyes, and hearing with the inner ear, the work becomes joy. The Father within doeth the work.

If you are ill the most important step for you to take is to surrender all you are and all you ever hope to be, unto the Father and let His grace be your sufficiency in all things—in everything. There is no space, no place, where God is not. If you deny Him, He is still there but you have missed the opportunity. How many times does it come? Like forgiveness, seventy times seven; but like the grain of sand in the oyster, each time it is turned away a little veil of resistance grows around it until that shining grain of sand is completely obscured by dalliance and procrastination, excuses, justifications, rationalizations, and all of the ego's bag of tricks.

If you have not wisdom, ask God for wisdom. If you have not love, ask God for love. If you have not Truth, ask God for Truth and an understanding heart.

Death Has No Reality

It has been said that death is the last enemy to conquer. *Fear* is the last enemy to conquer because Fear is the cause of death. Fear has no reality except what you give it; as death has no reality except what you give it. Healing has no reality except what you give it because sickness has no reality.

From where we are in the Spirit World the difference between life and death in many respects is nil—there is none. It is not the great change that you think of it, even when you are thinking of it with as much clarity as you can command or know. So many of the followers of the Seers and Sages would say, "Don't leave us," when it came time for the latter to go on, but they could not really leave anybody because there is no place to go.

It is just all a matter of vibration and particle molecular structure—remember that. Reaching out you cannot touch it; it can move through you, and you can move through it, but it is not another place. You do not seem to be aware that you live on many planes at the same time, all the time, not just in your sleep but in your waking too. This is very hard for you to understand or recall, but the more developed you become the more aware you become of it.

It is amazing how you people hang on to this earth plane; when once it has done with you, and you have done with it, life on this plane only becomes painful. As long as you are functioning and productive and serving, life goes along rather smoothly, although there are always ups and downs; but when you have run your course and completed your commitment it can get very tenuous and feel very uncomfortable; this is to help you see that the decision to live or die is not important. The world, as you call the earth, is not that comfortable.

Dying is the one impossibility in the Universe. Then too you humans get to thinking that the Universe is involved with your living and dying, but it isn't. The Universe does not care whether you are what you call alive or dead; you have to crawl out of that and get up there where everything is interested in you.

SECTION 2

MESSAGES TO THE AUTHOR

Healing

Healing is an art; healing is prayer; it is loving; it is surrender to God's will, by the healer and the patient.

It is opening to truth, to All There Is; becoming aware of God in every pore of one's being; concentrating on God's perfection and the perfection of all His creation; shutting out at least temporarily all outward thoughts; concentrating one's whole being on the Divine and channelling God's energy and love to the other, however unloveable they may appear to be.

Healing is a wonderous experience for both as it brings one closer to reality—to God and to His will for the lives involved; nothing but good can be experienced this way, but it may not be the good that one plans or desires or expects. You must not determine in advance what the results shall be; there may be lessons to learn or Karma to work out, and the one who desires to help would be unkind and harmful to interfere or disrupt this working out. By being completely open to God's will, to the results, whatever they might be, but filling one's heart with love and trust and faith, one can guard against such interference.

> Here we are Lord. We love you and we know you love us. Please show us the way, light our paths and give us the strength to follow your directions.

Study and absorb this; it will become meaningful and helpful.

God may want the patient to change his diet, give up some habit, change his way of living or thinking, or learn some lesson in living. This is not for the healer to say, but if both are sincerely seeking God's direction it will come from within the patient—he will know instantly or gradually what he should do; if he then follows that direction to the best of his ability the healing will follow. It may take a short time or a long time—it depends on many factors—but faith, trust and patience are essential. Hold constantly to the thought that, "With God all things are possible." They are not miracles, they are just a conscious realization of the Good, the Perfection, the Reality that *is* God's creation.

Holistic Healing

Healing encompasses the whole man—Mind, Body, Spirit and Emotions. Grasp this thought; hold onto it; it will help you in the concept and practice of spiritual healing.

The whole man is holy because he is like God, made in His image, and, being whole, lacks nothing—masculine and feminine, positive and negative, a circle complete in itself, meeting itself where it started because there is no beginning nor ending of a circle, like the cycle of life in eternity.

Imagination plays a large part in sickness and health, so be careful what you imagine—what you let your mind create. Let it flow, but guide it; like a river it needs banks to control it, to prevent it from flooding over everywhere. When the flood happens it is not only destructive, but it also loses its forward momentum.

Like your thoughts right now; if they scatter in all directions they lose momentum. So, relax and flow, but gently prod your mind when it gets out of control, out of bounds.

The reward for this will be greater understanding and peace—greater communication with your other side, with your inner being.

Afflictions

Afflictions come to all in some form or another to awaken you to the necessity of turning inwards away from the pressures and distractions of the material world to find the God within. They may be accompanied by mental, emotional and/or physical pain but this is part of the awakening process. A smooth, peaceful, painless existence lulls you to sleep and then no growth occurs.

When faced with affliction each of you has a choice. You can work with it and learn from it, treating it as a messenger sent to guide you inwards to face reality, or you can complain, rail against God and fail to accept any responsibility for it. It takes courage to admit that you may have had something to do with the cause, that there may be a very good reason for the affliction, and that there is something you can do about it. It takes courage to seek the healing necessary to dissolve the affliction, but if this is done the reward will be great.

Always the main objective must be to seek God's will in the situation. What is life trying to tell you, what are you being told to do, what must you change in your attitudes, thoughts and beliefs if the affliction is to be overcome?

Sometimes an affliction will be sent to a family, a group of people, or even a whole nation, in order to waken them to the necessity for a change. Again the choice is there for the group or nation to make the change or to ignore it and continue to flounder. History is full of examples of both choices, and the results are there for all to know. Some nations who made the choice to ignore the warning no longer exist as a unit or in some cases as a physical entity—they disappeared beneath the ocean!

So if affliction comes to you, do not complain, but rather seek to understand the cause and learn the lesson there is in it for you. As in any form of education, some lessons take longer to learn than others so do not get impatient if it seems to be a lengthy one.

Remorse and Guilt

Remorse and guilt are useless feelings. Remorse to the extent that it means repentance, is O.K., because correction of your feelings or actions by redirection onto the right path is necessary if you are to grow and eliminate negative thoughts and activities. First you must feel sorry for the error, then feel the desire to make amends, to correct it in any way you can, then you must *do* something about it.

God is always ready and willing to forgive you when you ask Him to—that is part of the action you must take on your own initiative.

But remorse, to the extent that it means morosely moping over your mistakes, reviewing them in your mind over and over, merely impresses them in your consciousness and does nothing to correct the error or help anyone who has been injured or abused by you.

Guilt is also useless—a heavy burden placed on man by man. All it does is depress and destroy the misguided individual. It does not help you to grow, it does not help the one you hurt, nor is it required of you by God, as so many have erroneously taught.

So rejoice in the fact that God is always willing to let you try again, to learn from your experience, and to change your thinking or actions. Once you have done that consciously and intentionally, without reservations, then you have learned that lesson once and for all, for this life and all future lives. You have profited by the experience and grown another inch, ready to move on to the next experience. Remorse and guilt merely hold you back.

Another thing you will find is that remorse and guilt are often at the root of illness or disease. They gnaw at your vitals and block the flow of life-giving and life-supporting energies just as effectively as if you had turned off a valve.

Ask for God's forgiveness and take some action to correct your error, and you will open that valve and the energies will flow again.

Power

God is power—infinite power; power to create the Universe, the galaxies, many galaxies; so much power that it is impossible for you with finite minds to grasp the meaning of more than a fraction of it. Yet that power is within each one of you because God is within you. So you must learn how to tap that power so that you can use it for good—for His Kingdom.

The marvelous thing is you do not have to do anything, it is already there waiting to be used; you just have to get yourselves and your egos, out of the way and let it be, let it flow through you like "rivers of living water," as St. John said.

As the power flows, so it will automatically clean up all discord and disease in its path; lining up bodies, minds and lives in accordance with the harmony and beauty of God's plan for His creation.

The only thing that can stop the flow and effectiveness of that power is you, not because you are more powerful, but because God has given you a free will; and if you choose to oppose the power, and try to prevent its flow, God will not force it, He will withhold it so that you can experience the folly of your own choice, and eventually return to His way when you find that your way does not work. That is the kind of lesson that really sinks in; after that, you do not follow God's way because you should, or because you are told to, but because you *know* in every fiber of your being that it is the correct way for you, the one that will lead to success and harmony for your life.

Power can be expressed or experienced in many different ways. It may be felt within; it may be realized in events without. It may be an experience where you find yourself powerless to prevent something from happening, and afterwards you realize that it was for the best; or it may be one where you are able to alter the course of events by prayer or power of thought.

Energy

Energy flow is so important; it clears the channels and conducts the life force—in fact it is the life force—and flows to needed portions of the body giving them life, perfect life, so that no disease is possible.

You will become more conscious of this energy; you will feel it flow through you and will see it, or the absence of it in others. You will become sensitive to it, so that you will know where problems lie.

The ability to demonstrate the flow of energy will gradually appear and with it the ability to heal, to unblock the patient's own natural healing flow of energy which is abundant, in fact unlimited, since this is the power of God, the essence of life.

Imagine yourself as a tube through which the energy flows; the faster and freer it flows, the more it can cleanse your own body and that of the patient. Relaxation is essential, otherwise the tube is constricted, and that obstructs or slows down the flow.

But "Don't push the river," still applies; you can't push the energy through the tube, that would be like pushing one end of a long piece of string; it would merely bunch up and the other end wouldn't go anywhere.

Healing Vibrations

Vibrations are involved in healing by the Spirit. The rate of vibration used by the spirit doctors, or by the Philippine psychic healers, is very high, and it can only operate through a healer who is tuned to a higher rate than that normally used or experienced by the average human.

This high rate comes closer to, or matches the vibrations of the atoms that make up the physical body, and thus is able to rearrange these atoms into the natural perfect form created by the thought of God; and healing results. The human brain has a higher rate of vibration than the rest of the body, and therefore is more difficult to heal.

"Becoming open" to the power is therefore the same thing as "raising your level of vibration" and can be achieved only by meditation, prayer and living a life that expresses love and purity—purity of action and thought. This is really the purpose of the experience of life on this physical earth. Every day presents opportunities, in different ways to different people, for experiencing and learning these lessons.

But it does take time, effort and will power similar to that given to their chosen task by an Olympic star or concert pianist. *It isn't easy*—but it is so worthwhile!

Unconditional Love

Resources are plentiful, in fact unlimited, so never feel that you are dependent on your own supply; this would soon be exhausted and you would feel depleted as you shared what you have. Rather just be a channel for these unlimited resources and energies, and then you will merely feel cleansed and refreshed.

Do not feel or accept responsibility for the manner in which, or the extent to which, the other person uses these energies or resources that you channel in their direction. That is entirely their choice and responsibility, and not yours. They have a free will, just as you do, and only by exercising it as they choose can they grow in strength and understanding.

When you start to feel responsibility for their reaction, and disappointed or discouraged because they do not appear to have benefited from the love-energy that you have attempted to channel in their direction, then you are not sending that love *unconditionally*—you are mentally or emotionally attaching a response condition and taking responsibility which is not yours to take.

Keep free of all conditions and attachments to results; just *love* without strings or expectations. We know this is not easy; the ego gets in the way; past conditioning interferes; and genuine concern and compassion for the other become confused with the need to set the other free—to let them just be themselves.

So center into your own inner being and just *be* love, and don't look back. Live in the now.

Unsuccessful Healings

It is just as wrong to blame yourself for a "failure" in Spiritual Healing as it is to take credit for a "success." In both cases you were merely a channel for God's power; if it succeeded and a healing took place, the glory is God's, and the patient's gratitude should be directed to God, as should yours.

Likewise if no healing, or only a partial healing, takes place you must always remember that God will never impose His will on the patient. The healing cannot take place if they are not open to receive His love and infinite healing power, or are not willing to make the changes in their lives and thoughts that inside themselves they know must take place if they are to be in tune with God's purpose and His creation.

In either case, therefore, you are just a bystander, willingly being an open conduit for that power but having nothing to do with its source or its effectiveness, except in so far as you may block the flow by your thinking that you are the source, or entitled to praise when the results are satisfactory.

You should be grateful for the healings that take place, and awed at being used by God or His ministers as a tool to carry out His purpose in each individual case. In fact, the more your own heart is full of gratitude and praise for the marvel of it all, the more open you will be to this power, and the less inclined to burden yourself with responsibility for "failures."

There is so much involved in the health and harmony of an individual that it is impossible for you to know why disease or disharmony occur. There is the Karma carried over from a previous life, or earlier years in this life ("As you sow, so will you reap"). Then there is the mental attitude of the individual right now which has so much to do with the operation of their physical body; mind and body are one and cannot be separated. In addition, the individual's thoughts each day and every day are so much more powerful than anyone ever realizes ("As a man thinketh in his heart, so is he.")

His thoughts literally create the universe around him, and the physical body he inhabits. Every cell of that body is constantly being renewed, and his thoughts to a large extent decide the perfection or imperfection of each cell.

So, stand back, rejoice at the privilege of being used by God, but take no credit and no blame for what occurs within those who come to you for help.

Clearing the Channel

In order to be a clear channel for healing you must get out of the way *completely*—surrendering the other person and yourself to God's will—merging both with the Divine Source of all—recognizing the one-ness that *is;* and in that consciousness the healing can take place instantly.

Hang on to that; meditate on it; let it sink in so that it becomes an indivisible part of your conscious and subconscious mind. The glory of God can shine forth in all its wonder when you step aside and allow it to be. Of course, you cannot stop it or dim it in reality, but you can block it from your consciousness, and so can those who wish to be healed. By your words, thoughts and actions, therefore, you can help to disperse the clouds that seem to be between you and reality, and to destroy the illusion that most humans believe is reality. Wake up to the TRUTH—the perfection of God's creation.

Obviously if you really believe that you are acting only as a channel, with no power of your own, then all this makes sense. The more you can silence your own desires and will, the more likely it is that a healing can occur, and instantly at that, *if it is meant to be,* if it is the right result for the soul growth and evolution of that particular person, and therefore in accordance with the will of God.

As you grow yourself, so you will become more conscious or aware in a subtle sense what that will is in each case. Every situation is governed by God's will and no healing takes place through you or any one else unless He so wills it. We, too, are powerless to help unless this is the case. Jesus himself will never intercede unless he knows it is the will of God.

Self-Healing

Cause and effect—this is evident throughout the world, whether you are talking about disease or any other discord, or about health and harmony.

God is Love, and Love caused the creation, and thus the effect is beautiful and loving. Man, with his free will lets other thinking creep in, and this cause results in undesirable effects.

If you want to stop a pot of water from boiling, you do not do anything to the boiling water, you turn off the heat, which is the cause, and then the boiling water or the effect will change.

So the secret of permanent healing is to get at the cause, and this is why self-healing is possible. If the sick one will honestly examine his thoughts, emotions and actions, and compare them with the teachings of Jesus, he will usually become aware of some point that is not in line with those teachings. If he will then work to correct that discrepancy, healing will follow.

If, in spite of his honest self-examination, he is unable to see where he is in error, then he should pray for guidance on the matter; pray that his eyes be opened to the cause and that he will have the strength to eliminate it.

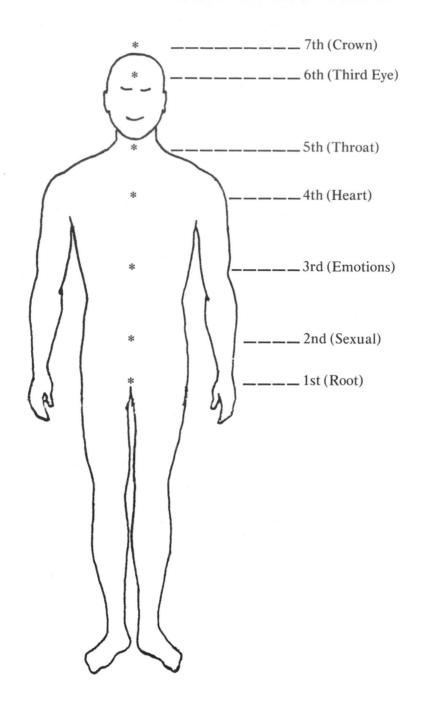

* —————————— 7th (Crown)

* —————————— 6th (Third Eye)

* —————————— 5th (Throat)

* —————————— 4th (Heart)

* —————————— 3rd (Emotions)

* —————————— 2nd (Sexual)

* —————————— 1st (Root)

BIBLIOGRAPHY

Angels

Colton, Ann Ree. *The Soul and the Ethic*. ARC Publishing Company, Glendale, California. 1965.

Davidson, Gustav. *Dictionary of Angels*. Collier-Macmillan Canada Ltd., Toronto, Ontario, Canada. 1967.

Graham, Billy. *Angels: God's Secret Agents*. Doubleday and Company, Inc., Garden City, New York. 1975.

Hodson, Geoffrey. *The Kingdom of the Gods*. The Theosophical Publishing House, Adyar, Madras, India. 1952.

Mould, Pochin. *Angels and God*. Devin Adair Company, Old Greenwich, Connecticut. 1963.

Newhouse, Flower. *Rediscovering the Angels*. The Christward Ministry, Escondido, California. 1950.

Dreams

Faraday, Ann. *Dream Power*. Coward, McCann & Geoghegan, Inc. New York. 1972.

Faraday, Ann. *Dream Game*. Harper & Row, New York. 1974.

Garfield, Patricia. *Creative Dreaming*. Simon & Schuster, New York. 1974.

Hall, Calvin. *The Meaning of Dreams.* Harper & Row, New York. 1953.

Sanford, John. *Dreams, God's Forgotten Language.* J.P. Lippincott Co., Philadelphia and New York. 1968.

Stewart, Kilton. *How to Educate Your Dreams to Work for You.* The Stewart Foundation for Creative Psychology, 144 E. 36th St. New York.

Healing

Bach, Edward. *Heal Thyself.* The C.W. Daniel Company, Ltd., London, England. 1931.

Bailey, Alice A. *Esoteric Healing.* Lucis Publishing Company, New York. 1953.

Boyd, Doug. *Rolling Thunder.* Random House, New York. 1974.

Cooke, Ivan. *Healing by the Spirit.* The White Eagle Publishing Trust, Liss, Hampshire, England. 1955. Revised 1976.

Edwards, Harry. *A Guide to the Understanding and Practice of Spiritual Healing.* The Healer Publishing Co. Ltd., Burrows Lea, Shere, Guildford, Surrey, England. 1974.

Edwards, Harry. *The Healing Intelligence.* The Healer Publishing Co. Ltd., Burrows Lea, England. 1965.

Fuller, John G. *Arigo: Surgeon of the Rusty Knife.* Thomas Y. Crowell Company, New York. 1974.

Goldsmith, Joel S. *The Art of Spiritual Healing.* Harper & Row. 1959.

Goldsmith, Joel S. *Realization of Oneness.* The Citadel Press, New Jersey. 1967.

Hutton, J. Bernard. *Healing Hands.* David McKay Company, Inc. New York. 1967.

Joy, W. Brugh. *Joy's Way.* J.P. Tarcher, Inc., Los Angeles, California. 1978.

Kuhlman, Kathryn. *I Believe in Miracles.* Prentice Hall, Inc., Englewood Cliffs, New Jersey. 1962.

LeShan, Lawrence. *The Medium, the Mystic and the Physicist.* The Viking Press, New York. 1974.

LeShan, Lawrence. *You Can Fight for Your Life.* M. Evans and Company, Inc., New York. 1977.

Leuret, Dr. F. *Modern Miraculous Cures.* Farrar Straus and Cudahay, New York. 1957.

McKelvey, Gertrude D. *Finding God's Healing Power.* J.B. Lippincott Company, New York. 1961.

Pelletier, Kenneth R. *Mind As Healer, Mind As Slayer.* Dell Publishing Company, New York. 1977.

Ponder, Catherine. *The Healing Secrets of the Ages.* Prentice-Hall, Inc. Englewood Cliffs, New Jersey. 1967.

Sanford, Agnes. *The Healing Light.* Macalester Park Publishing Company, Plainfield, New Jersey. 1947.

Sherman, Harold. *Your Power to Heal.* Harper & Row, New York. 1972.

Sherman, Harold. *Wonder Healers of the Philippines.* DeVorss and Co., Marina Del Rey, California. 1967.

Simonton, O. Carl and Others. *Getting Well Again.* J.P. Tarcher, Inc., Los Angeles, California. 1978.

Spraggett, Allen. *Kathryn Kuhlmann, The Woman Who Believes in Miracles.* The World Publishing Company, New York. 1970.

Worrall, Ambrose A. with Worrall, Olga N. *The Gift of Healing.* Harper & Row, New York. 1965.

Meditation

Dass, Ram. *Journey of Awakening, A Meditation Guidebook.* Bantam Books, Inc., New York. 1978.

Goldsmith, Joel S. *The Art of Meditation.* Harper & Row, New York. 1956.

LeShan, Lawrence. *How to Meditate.* Little, Brown and Company, Boston-Toronto. 1974.

Puryear, Herbert B. and Thurston, Mark A. *Meditation and the Mind of Man.* A.R.E. Press, Virginia Beach, Virginia. 1975.

Rozman, Deborah. *Meditation for Children.* Celestial Arts, Millbrae, California. 1976.

Reincarnation

Fiore, Dr. Edith. *You Have Been Here Before.* Coward McCann & Geoghegan, Inc., New York. 1977.

Hall, Manly P. *Reincarnation, The Cycle of Necessity.* The Philosophical Research Society Inc., Los Angeles, California. 1971.

Head, Joseph and Cranston S.L. *Reincarnation, The Phoenix Fire Mystery.* Julian Press/Crown Publishers Inc., New York. 1977.

MacGregor, Geddes. *Reincarnation in Christianity.* The Theosophical Publishing House, Wheaton, Illinois. 1978.

Moore, Marcia and Douglas, Mark. *Reincarnation—Key to Immortality.* Arcane Publications, New York. 1968.

Moore, Marcia. *Hypersentience.* Crown Publishers Inc., New York. 1976.

Stevenson, Ian. *Twenty Cases Suggestive of Reincarnation.* American Society for Psychical Research, New York. 1966.

Sutphen, Richard. *Self-Help Update.* A catalogue of past life regression tapes. Valley of the Sun Publishing, Box 2010, Malibu, California, 90265.

Wambach, Helen. *Reliving Past Lives.* Harper & Row, New York. 1978.

Spiritual Growth

Fox, Emmet. *The Sermon on the Mount.* Harper & Row, New York. 1934.

Levi. *The Aquarian Gospel of Jesus the Christ.* DeVorss & Co., Marina Del Rey, California. 1907.

Murphy, Joseph. *The Power of Your Subconscious Mind.* Prentice-Hall, Englewood Cliffs, New Jersey. 1963.

Parker, William and St. Johns, Elaine. *Prayer Can Change Your Life.* Prentice-Hall, Englewood Cliffs, New Jersey. 1957.

Trine, Ralph Waldo. *In Tune with the Infinite.* The Bobbs Merrill Company, Inc., New York. 1908.

Yogananda, Paramahansa. *Autobiography of a Yogi.* Self-Realization Fellowship, Los Angeles, California. 1946.

Miscellaneous

Chaplin, Annabel. *The Bright Light of Death.* DeVorss & Co., Marina Del Rey, California. 1977. (Depossession)

Pearce, Joseph Chilton. *The Magical Child.* E.P. Dutton, New York. 1977.

Friday, Nancy. *My Mother My Self.* Delacorte Press, New York. 1977.

Harding, M. Esther. *The Way of All Women.* G.P. Putnam's Sons, New York. 1970.

Verny, Thomas, M.D. with Kelly, John. *The Secret Life of the Unborn Child.* Dell Publishing Co. Inc., New York. 1981.

Wickland, Carl, M.D. *30 Years among the Dead.* Newcastle Publishing Co Inc., Van Nuys, California. 1974. (Depossession)